Embodied Care

Embodied Care

Jane Addams, Maurice Merleau-Ponty,
and Feminist Ethics

MAURICE HAMINGTON

University of Illinois Press
URBANA AND CHICAGO

∞ This book is printed on acid-free paper.

Library of Congress Cataloging-in-Publication Data
Hamington, Maurice.
Embodied care : Jane Addams, Maurice Merleau-Ponty, and feminist
ethics / Maurice Hamington.
p.   cm.
Includes bibliographical references and index.
ISBN 0-252-02928-3 (alk. paper)
1. Caring. 2. Body, Human (Philosophy) 3. Addams, Jane, 1860–1935.
4. Merleau-Ponty, Maurice, 1908–1961. 5. Feminist ethics. I. Title.
BJ1475.H3   2004
177'.7—dc22   2003023515

For Stephanie, Rosemary,
Helen, Armand, Marilyn, and Peter

Contents

Acknowledgments

I would like to thank everyone who assisted me in writing and researching this project. The myth of academic scholarship portrays it as accomplished by individuals when in fact it is a collaborative endeavor. I owe a debt of gratitude to Nancy Tuana; she not only taught me a great deal about feminist philosophy but has been an inspirational mentor and friend who was instrumental in shaping this book. I would also like to thank Scott Pratt for introducing me to American pragmatism and kindling my interest in Jane Addams.

Anne McGrail, Dorothy Miller, and Barbara Pope were kind enough to review the entire manuscript carefully and give me many helpful suggestions. Numerous others who have read portions of this project in various forms and given me thoughtful feedback include David Abram, Will Davie, Margaret Bayless, Will Cowling, Greg Johnson, Mark Johnson, Terrance MacMullan, Cheyney Ryan, Shannon Sullivan, and Gail Weiss. Those who participated in sessions where I presented elements of this book at the annual meetings of the Merleau-Ponty Circle, National Women's Studies Association, and Society for the Advancement of American Philosophy provided me with a great deal of provocative feedback. The anonymous readers provided by the University of Illinois Press offered me numerous suggestions that improved the analysis in this book. I would also like to acknowledge the support of Joan Catapano at the University of Illinois Press in shepherding this project into existence. Finally, I will join the readers in thanking Bruce Bethell, associate editor at UIP, who made a significant contribution to the clarity of this text.

My partner, Stephanie, and our daughter, Rosemary, have been very supportive and patient during the time-consuming process of writing this book. Our dogs, Snoopy and Woodstock, provided many embodied experiences but were not in the least bit patient . . . they never are.

Embodied Care

Introduction:
Care—an Evolving Definition

The history of care shows that, at one level, care is a
precondition for the whole of moral life.
—Warren T. Reich, *Encyclopedia of Bioethics*

Breathing differs somewhat from most other involuntary body functions. The
process continues without conscious control, as do all such functions, yet we
can consciously and intentionally regulate it. We can attend to and control
our breathing or completely ignore its ongoing rhythm in our lives. In fact,
despite its involuntary nature, it figures as a focal point for relaxation and
wellness techniques that involve efforts at deep, slow breathing. Care, too, is
so basic to human functioning that we can easily overlook it as a significant
element in moral decision making. When we choose to do so, however, we
can attend to care, cultivate the habits of care, and thematize care. Still, care
is such an integral part of our daily activity that it remains ignored and unthematized.

The many uses of the word *care* demonstrate this term's centrality to popular discourse on relational considerations.[1] It is difficult to imagine negoti-
ating our day-to-day existence without drawing extensively on notions of care
or relying on the subtle habits of care that govern our social interactions (e.g.,
touch, eye contact, posture, inflection). Until recently, perhaps because care
is so basic to human existence, Western philosophical discourse has largely
ignored its significance in human morality.[2]

Although many mainstream philosophers may not have fully accepted care
ethics, certain pockets of thinkers are giving it a great deal of attention. The
Encyclopedia of Bioethics devotes twenty-five pages to care, discussing the
history of the notion, its application to health care, and the contemporary
understanding of an ethics of care. Despite this lengthy treatment, a clear
definition of care never emerges: "The history [of care] reveals, not a unified idea of care, but a family of notions of care."[3] In this book I will attempt

to contribute to the evolving understanding of care by attending to its embodied aspects. Specifically, I will address how physicality—our embodied nature—contributes to care. Furthermore, I will explore how such embodied care advances social morality.

Before going too far into the arguments, I should clarify some terminology. First, I distinguish "care" from "care ethics." I view care ethics as an expression of a moral theory derived from the work of feminist theorists such as Carol Gilligan and Nel Noddings. The term *care ethics* implies a self-contained theory of ethics that can be compared and contrasted to other theories. Aside from chapter 1, where I consider various care theorists to assess the state of the discourse, this book addresses care rather than care ethics. This distinction rests on my understanding of care as more than just another ethical theory. Care is an approach to morality that is basic to human existence—so basic, I will argue, that our bodies are built for care—and therefore can be woven into traditional theories. Care is a way of being in the world that the habits and behaviors of our body facilitate. Care consists of practices that can be developed or allowed to atrophy. Indeed, although I will theorize about care, care is not a moral theory in the traditional sense.

So what is care? There is a great deal of confusion surrounding its definition. As Nel Noddings explains, "Most people agree that the world would be a better place if we all cared more for one another, but despite that initial agreement we find it hard to say exactly what we mean by *caring*."[4] Part of the confusion may be due to the contextual nature of care. Because care does not rely on the universal principles or formulas that other ethical approaches employ, it cannot be completely articulated apart from the particular agents and situations involved. Another aspect of the confusion surrounding care may be due to the embodied and affective knowledge that informs care, a point for which I will argue later. Such knowledge does not easily translate into well-defined terms.

Even the theorists who write about care ethics struggle to define care. Carol Gilligan never really delineates exactly what constitutes care, and Nel Noddings's definition of caring as receiving others on their own terms has been described as "less than rigorous" by at least one critic.[5] Nevertheless, several attempts have been made to compile a definition of care. Grace Clement offers the following characteristics of care ethics: it (1) takes a contextual approach to morality, (2) assumes human connectedness, and (3) takes the maintenance of relationships to be a priority.[6] Daryl Koehn places relationality at the core of her definition of care ethics: "For the care ethicist, ethical acts are caring ones of a certain sort. They are those acts in which the caregiver actively concerns herself with attending to the individually expressed needs, feelings and interests of the cared-for and strives to create a shared self with people who are similarly committed to a secure world in which beings are nurtured and given an opportunity to realize fully their individuality."[7]

Joan Tronto and Bernice Fisher offer a broad definition of care that emphasizes action, community, and interrelatedness but is still very general: "We suggest that caring be viewed as *a species activity that includes everything that we do to maintain, continue, and repair our 'world' so that we can live in it as well as possible.* That world includes our bodies, our selves, and our environment, all of which we seek to interweave in a complex, life-sustaining web."[8] In subsequent work Tronto identifies four elements of care as attentiveness, responsibility, competence, and responsiveness.[9] Attentiveness refers to the capacity to become aware and understand individual others prior to any care. To take responsibility, according to Tronto, is to offer care out of willingness rather than duty or principle. One must be competent to offer care, which makes it more than an intention. Finally, in recognition of asymmetrical power relationships, Tronto suggests that the caregiver must be responsive to the position and needs of the object of the care.

Peta Bowden goes so far as to embrace the ambiguity in the definition of care. For Bowden, to define care fully and precisely is to lose something of its open-ended and complex nature. In the conclusion of *Caring: Gender Sensitive Ethics,* Bowden writes, "My point has not been to produce a consensus, or to catch the essence of care, nor yet to unearth some hidden truth that shows that there has been implicit agreement all along about the meaning of caring. For it is my claim that it is precisely these kinds of aims that tend to lead understanding astray, and to cause us to overlook the complexity and diversity of the ethical possibilities of care."[10] Bowden has captured the notion that care is a concept of great depth and cannot easily be dispensed with as a philosophical tangent. In the spirit of Bowden's approach, I am not offering a definitive understanding of care; rather, I am attempting to bring to the fore embodied and social aspects of care that have been previously overlooked.

The account of care used in this book is compatible with the preceding definitions, although it differs in its emphasis on the body. I offer the following as my operating definition: *care denotes an approach to personal and social morality that shifts ethical considerations to context, relationships, and affective knowledge in a manner that can be fully understood only if care's embodied dimension is recognized. Care is committed to the flourishing and growth of individuals yet acknowledges our interconnectedness and interdependence.*

Essentially the rest of this book is devoted to explicating this understanding. I aim to contribute at least two points to existing definitions of care. First, care cannot be fully understood without attending to its embodied dimension; second, care can be a viable component of social ethics, but only if its corporeal aspect is addressed. Because I will argue that the workings of the body are central to a care-based approach to ethics, I have adopted the term *embodied care* to describe what this book proposes.

Given the complexity and pervasiveness of embodied care, I will distinguish three of its interrelated aspects: *caring knowledge, caring imagination, and caring habits.* These three aspects are so intertwined that the definition of any one of them involves its relation to the other two.

The notion of caring knowledge attempts to expand traditional understandings of knowledge to include that which is known to the body. For example, the body has the ability to capture the subtleties of emotions communicated outside explicit language. For an analogy, consider how eating a good meal elicits a joy that does not translate well into words. The body "knows" many things, including how to care, through its transactions with its environment. Like any knowledge, caring knowledge can be developed and attended to, or it can be neglected and lost. The body acquires habits that are an expression of its knowledge. These habits have epistemological significance. Not a mere repetition of movement, habits are physical practices of knowledge held in the body. Habits can be of many different types, one of which is caring. Caring habits are practices of the body's caring knowledge.

Like caring knowledge, caring habits occur through the body. That is, caring habits are the practices of embodied beings that contribute to the growth and well-being of self and others. Because we exist in a physical world, caring habits are an outgrowth of the kinds of bodies we inhabit. The habitual nature of care is the body's capturing and acquiring of physical movement. Some habits are simple, with relatively little invested meaning. Other habits are complex and may require the orchestration of a number of simple habits. For example, basic activities of the body such as the manner in which it perceives the world and focuses attention are simple habits necessary for care, whereas the social habits of care will reflect the coalescence of many simpler habits. Nevertheless, simple and complex habits should be viewed as continuous with one another because they both emanate from the same body.

Although caring habits can be inculcated through practice, they are still open-ended and thus transact with new situations in the environment. The caring imagination refers to our ability to transcend our physical limitations and extrapolate our caring knowledge to others, even relatively unknown others. The caring imagination melds traditional rational approaches to morality with an appreciation for what the body knows.

This book can be viewed as a progression from current understandings of care ethics to what I will describe as embodied care. Chapter 1 unpacks my definition of embodied care by reviewing current schools of thought on care. The ethics of care has been variously described as feminine ethics, virtue ethics, an ethical theory that competes with justice-based approaches to morality (deontological or teleological), and an approach to morality that is something other than a theory of ethics altogether. I review the theorists who support these various positions both to draw from them and to distinguish my definition from theirs. Ultimately I conclude that care does more than underpin yet another ethical theory: it is the very foundation of morality rooted in our body and our bodily practices.

Tracing a theoretical arc, the next three chapters explore caring habits, caring knowledge, and caring imagination and their complex interactions. In chapter 2 I argue that care is a corporeal potential realized through habits. The capacity to care is an aspect of embodiment. Cultural differences will result in varying manifestations of caring, but the bodies that human beings inhabit give everyone the possibility of care. The work of the Continental philosopher Maurice Merleau-Ponty will be used to develop a notion of embodied care through a phenomenological analysis of the body's habits. As a corporeal potential, care can be cultivated or diminished through habits and practices. I will also suggest that caring habits are not just instinctual but integrate the epistemic (caring knowledge) and the ethical. Knowledge of the other creates the potential to care. The more we know about someone, the greater the potential for caring. Much of our understanding of others is rooted in our bodies and therefore not always available to our consciousness.

Chapter 3 explores the cognitive dimension of caring habits in the caring imagination. Contrary to common usage of the term *habit* as rote acts, caring habits open up imaginative possibilities that would otherwise remain closed. For example, all the embodied experiences and habits of care that went into being a parent opened for me a caring imagination into what the experiences of other parents might be like. In ethics the imagination, like care, is largely overlooked. I suggest that care involves a complex weaving of imaginative processes with embodied practices.

I address three of those processes. One is the imaginative ability to empathize with unknown or little-known others. The corporeal dimension of care clearly establishes the link between direct experience and care, but a caring imagination is a necessary element for understanding how we care for those outside our sphere of experience. The second imaginative process is a caring imagination as a mode of critical thinking. As I will suggest in chapter 1, care is more basic to human existence than is any ethical theory. Therefore, the application of rules or consequences is not necessarily antithetical to care. The caring imagination will provide the opportunity for reflection—it will consider rules and consequences—but will not grant them universal or absolute status. The third imaginative process is the ability to consider one's subject position in its psychosocial context. A healthy, caring imagination should be able to understand caring activities and habits in their environment and avoid exerting undue power over those for whom we care or allowing us to get lost in the caring for others.

If my claims about caring habits and knowledge are taken seriously, then social cohesion depends partly on developing habits of the body that strengthen our caring imaginations. Chapter 4 returns to a discussion of habits to address the sociopolitical aspects of care. The American pragmatist Jane Addams provides a philosophy of democracy and citizenship that involves embodied practices to stimulate a caring imagination. For example, Addams valorizes the caring habit of active listening, a practice not usually associated with morality. The reciprocal, relational, and responsive aspects of care require the caregiver to listen. Such listening may be broadly defined as attending to verbal and nonverbal communication in interpersonal relations as well as listening to indirect forms of communication, such as the news media, to "hear" the plights of distant others. Listening is a habit of engaging and activating care. For Addams, caring habits such as active listening are not just positive options but indeed part of our moral responsibility to experience one another richly so as to produce the internal resources necessary to act on one another's behalf.

Chapter 5 applies embodied care to the currently contentious issue of same-sex marriage in the United States. Given my development of the body's role in morality, how do the practices and habits of care inform a divisive social issue such as the legalization of gay marriage? This chapter will highlight the aspects of the issue that would be addressed if embodied care were at the forefront of moral consideration. Adopting care as a new way of thinking about morality would move the dispute away from a search for who is right and who is wrong in this issue, although I will take a position on the matter. More relevant is the way our embodied practices inform our caring imaginations to develop the possibilities of human flourishing in this instance.

Ultimately my aims are both modest and radical. In a certain sense embodied care is a modest proposal because it does not generate a new theory for adjudicating moral dilemmas. The claims surrounding embodied care are modest, too, because they can never be absolute or universal. Terms such as *potential, possible,* and *tends toward* permeate this book because our corporeal existence and affective relationships encompass ambiguities that preclude the certainty we often crave in our moral theories. Nevertheless, embodied care is also a radical proposition because it calls for a fundamental shift in our thinking about morality, a move toward an aspect of epistemology and ethics that has been largely ignored in philosophy: the body. References to "embodied" and "affective" knowledge also permeate this book as it pursues a radical reorientation of what counts as moral understanding. The embodied dimension of care will lead to the demanding moral mandate that we experience one another, particularly those who are unfamiliar to us, which is itself a radical imperative.

1. The Landscape of Current Care Discourse

A chapter in American history about something that appears to be a quint-essentially noncaring struggle for power reveals the pervasive significance of care. In the 1840s Frederick Douglass (1818–95) became a powerful force for the abolitionist movement through his brilliant oratory and captivating writing. Douglass addressed social justice in his speaking tours, but he knew that his message had to bridge the tremendous gap between his experiences and those of white audiences in New England and the Midwest. His dark skin elicited objectification: "I was generally introduced as a 'chattel'—a 'thing'—a piece of southern 'property'—the chairman assuring the audience that 'it' could speak."[1] Douglass had been a slave and knew the violence of living as a powerless member of society. In his autobiography he identifies the turning point of his life as a moment when he physically stood up to his owner, Covey. His righteous retaliation was transformative, and Douglass universalized the experience: "A man, without force is without the essential dignity of humanity."[2]

Though it may appear odd to begin a chapter on care with a historical figure who is associated with the use of rights, power, and politics, I contend that Douglass's writings and speeches also employ care, particularly given the entire sweep of his message.[3] Douglass did not merely articulate an abstract treatise on political philosophy meant to sway the moral calculations of the audience. He used personal examples with which his audience could identify, at least partially, thus creating the context for connection and empathy. One indication of Douglass's attempt to make a personal connection is his decision to write three autobiographies rather than one. His evolving thoughts on abolition led to new interpretations of his life, but each biography is grounded in his experiences. Douglass shares his personal story to connect with his readers while making his political plea. For example, early in *The Narrative* Douglass recounts the whipping his beloved Aunt Hester received:

> Before he commenced whipping Aunt Hester, he took her into the kitchen, and stripped her from neck to waist, leaving her neck, shoulders, and back, entirely naked. He then told her to cross her hands, calling her at the same time a d—d b—h. After crossing her hands, he tied them with a strong rope, and led her to a stool under a large hook in the joist, put in for the purpose. He made her get upon the stool and tied her hands to the hook. She now stood fair for his infernal purpose. Her arms were stretched up at their full length, so that she stood upon the ends of her toes. He then said to her, "Now, you d—d b—h, I'll learn you how to disobey my orders!" and after rolling up his sleeves, he commenced to lay on the heavy cowskin, and soon the warm, red blood (amid heart-rendering shrieks from her, and horrid oaths from him) came dripping to the floor. I was so terrified and horror-stricken at the sight, that I hid myself in a closet, and dared not venture out till long after the bloody transaction was over.[4]

In Douglass's wrenching witness, the reader is drawn into the lurid details of Hester's pain and her young nephew's fear. It is unlikely that many who read this account or hear it spoken have experienced a whipping of this magnitude, but everyone has experiences of fear and pain that can provide the substance for a visceral reaction. It is this visceral response that provides a physical (embodied) bridge to the compassion and sympathy that Douglass hoped to elicit in his audience. Indeed, to hear this account and not wince with disgust might spur an accusation of noncompassion. Douglass wanted to garner a sympathetic response to make the kind of compassionate connection that would invigorate action on behalf of his cry of injustice.

Philip S. Foner attests to the effectiveness of Douglass's rhetoric in *The Life and Writings of Frederick Douglas,* which collects a number of firsthand accounts of Douglass's speaking skills.[5] These accounts indicate that Douglass was capable of eliciting laughter, suspense, and tears from his audience as he interjected his personal stories with abolitionist rhetoric. Eric Sundquist argues that it was his ability to mix a moral message with personal narrative that made Douglass a successful orator and writer: "Douglass's blending of his campaign for black freedom and black rights with a telling of his own representative story constitutes the key to his own rise to self-possession and historical greatness. When he transfigured the text of his scarred slave's body into the *Narrative,* Douglass changed 'property in man' into property in himself, as it were, and created a public 'American' self."[6] Sundquist finds the "language of revolutionary liberation and the language of sentiment" virtually synonymous.[7] A personal investment that comes through caring is a necessary element in the kind of deep social change that the abolitionist movement sought. Social movements are virtually always accompanied by passions that are fueled by personal connections and experiences. As Joan Tronto argues, "Care is a way of framing political issues that makes their impact, and concern with human lives, direct and immediate. Within the care framework, political issues can make sense and connect to each other. Under these conditions, political involvement increases dramatically."[8] Douglass's tales of physical pain, hunger, shame, and anger went beyond the direct experiences of most who heard them, yet as human beings, all had experienced analogous feelings on which their moral imaginations could draw to sympathize with this one man's plight. Furthermore, in delivering his speeches, Douglass's physical presence added to the sentiment of the message by forcing the audience to confront the face and body of their abstract stereotype of the Negro slave. The body standing in front of them, despite its differences from their own, gave the audience a context for commonality because it had a face, arms, legs, facial expressions, and hand gestures and spoke of recognizable emotions such as fear, pain, and joy.

In William Garrison's commentary on Douglass's first abolitionist speech, the physical presence of the speaker is given equal status with the message: "I shall never forget his first speech at the convention—the extraordinary emotion it excited in my own mind—the powerful impression it created upon a crowded auditory, completely taken by surprise—the applause which followed from the beginning to the end of his felicitous remarks. . . . There stood one, in physical proportion and stature commanding and exact—in intellect richly endowed—in natural eloquence a prodigy."[9] Certainly Garrison was an accomplished orator and could have delivered an equally spirited speech, but the abolitionists recognized the significance of having the audience hear from, and therefore make a connection with, a freed slave. The connection was not always consciously made, but it could be felt and understood in the bodies of those listening. The messenger as well as the message contributed to the connection. When Douglass spoke of his childhood as a slave, the audience could share in the embodied understanding of youthful experiences. It is unlikely that the attendees would be compelled to care simply because of some abstract moral injunction, but the physical presence and personal narrative created a possibility for a human connection: a significant participant in caring relations that could not take place in any other way. Hearing Douglass speak provided more understanding than could a mere collection of facts about a freed slave. There was an affective connection with the audience. The lives of those in attendance were disrupted to an extent that propositional knowledge could never match.

Michael Meyer, who edited a selection of Douglass's works, acknowledges the significance of the physical connection with the former slave: "His mostly white audiences were confronted with an articulate, intelligent, handsome man who gave the lie to the shuffling, dark stereotypes propagated by pro-slavery advocates."[10] This confrontation combined with Douglass's personal stories to create an opportunity for the audience to care in ways that they could not always recognize consciously. Douglass did not make a direct plea for caring. He spoke of justice and moral indignation. *In the midst of arguments about justice and rights, however, care is present as a subtext.* Caring knowledge and caring imagination would help animate both empathy and the subsequent possibility of action on the part of Douglass's audiences. The moral potential of human connection through physical and metaphorical presence should not be underestimated.[11]

* * *

The rest of this chapter will fulfill three important functions. First, it will clarify the definition of care that will be elaborated throughout this book by contrasting my project with existing discourse that focuses largely on creating a theory of morality, or "care ethics." Recall my definition of care: an approach to individual and social morality that shifts ethical emphasis and consideration to context, relationships, and affective knowledge in a manner that can be fully understood only if its embodied dimension is recognized. Care is a complex intertwining of *caring habits* (embodied practices of interaction), *caring knowledge* (the embodied understandings instantiated through habits), and *caring imagination* (extrapolations from embodied knowledge to understand situations beyond our immediate experience and to imagine caring courses of action). Although I also draw from each of these approaches, I will differentiate my views from some of the current schools of thought on care ethics. Because they lack a connection to the body, the categories, metaphors, and vocabulary of existing moral theories cannot fully explicate care. Care has the potential to challenge what constitutes the traditional moral domain in large part because of its affective epistemology (caring knowledge). Following Kant's dictum that "reason's proper function is to produce a good will," much of Western tradition views morality as a rational outcome of the mind.[12] I suggest instead that the human capacity to care rests largely on a kind of embodied knowledge that defies easy reduction to detached theories of ethics and epistemology. Care is more than the basis for an ethical theory; it is a basic aspect of human behavior integral to our interrelationships. Care is facilitated by our corporeal existence, yet it can be developed or retarded by the practices we adopt. In this respect, care is linked to the habits our bodies develop.[13] Care requires activities of the mind and body in a way that traditional categories of moral philosophy are ill equipped to conceive.

This chapter's second function will be to survey the current, predominantly feminist literature on care ethics by organizing various perspectives into clusters or constellations of thought. In the short time that care has been a part of moral philosophy's vocabulary, it has generated a great deal of discussion, both favorable and unfavorable. Despite some superficial analyses that lump them all together, theorists amenable to care have adopted divergent perspectives.[14] For example, Carol Gilligan and Nel Noddings are often cited as the founding mothers of the current wave of care discussions, and indeed their initial publications on care were written within a few years of each other, but they have different academic backgrounds that lead their versions of care in divergent directions. Rather than simply review each author's position, I have clustered the schools of thought on care around important themes that are more prevalent in some writers' works than in those of others.

As an outgrowth of clarifying my definition of care, the third function of this chapter will be to elucidate the normative dimension of care. Critics often dismiss care ethics as ambiguous. When facing the question, "What ought I to do?" the deontologist and the teleologist have concrete responses, whereas the care ethicist equivocates. This equivocation should not be mistaken for relativism. Care ethics illuminates the aspects of moral dilemmas to which we should attend (e.g., the relational or emotive aspects) but has no formulaic response at the abstract or theoretical level. Because they present a limited number of variables, artificial cases make for an awkward application of care ethics. The care response is much clearer, however, when the individual is part of a lived context. As we move through this book, the normativity of care will become more defined, but not in a prescribed way. In the following section I will identify what normativity exists among feminist care ethicists and augment that in the next chapter by exploring what embodiment adds to the normative thrust of care. I begin this clarification by offering a brief background to care ethics.

Feminist Origins of Modern Care Discourse

Although a groundswell of work was leading to the realization that care should be given greater attention, the 1982 publication of Carol Gilligan's *In a Different Voice: Psychological Theory and Women's Development* may be seen as the landmark and perhaps mythologized event that provided the catalyst for focusing attention on care.

As is often recounted, Gilligan made a significant discovery about an alternative moral voice while working as an assistant to the acclaimed Harvard psychologist Lawrence Kohlberg (1927–87). Kohlberg had devised a widely recognized structure for measuring moral development along a six-stage hierarchy.[15] Kohlberg drew heavily on Jean Piaget's two-stage theory of moral development, Kantian deontological ethics, Rawlsian social contract theory, and utilitarianism for his understanding of ethics. In Kohlberg's hierarchical theory stage 1, "obedience and punishment," and stage 2, "instrumental purpose and exchange," are referred to as *preconventional*. Self-interest and deference to authority motivate actions in these stages. Stages 3, "mutual interpersonal expectations, relationships, and conformity," and 4, "social systems and conscience," are called *conventional* and are marked by attempts to conform to society's rules and obligations. Stages 5, "social contract or utility and individual rights," and 6, "universal ethical principles," are the *postconventional* levels where morality is associated with universal principles exhibited by impartial, autonomous judgments. Kant's deontological ethics of rational principles provides the basis for Kohlberg's highest level of morality.

Kohlberg's original work was developed exclusively with male subjects; when the moral arguments of women were analyzed using Kohlberg's theories, they seldom demonstrated moral behavior beyond the conventional level. In particular, the research analysis showed many women's moral deliberations to operate at stage 3, with its emphasis on relationality. Rather than see a flaw in women's moral decision making, Gilligan saw a fundamental error in the approach taken; a dimension of morality was being overlooked: "[The] different construction of the moral problem by women may be seen as the critical reason for their failure to develop within the constraints of Kohlberg's system."[16] To distinguish this different moral voice from the capacities Kohlberg was measuring, Gilligan identified two categories: justice and care. "Justice ethics" represents the approach traditionally favored in philosophy and religion: morality is based on universal principles and abstract moral concepts. Here Gilligan is primarily characterizing justice as deontological, although to the extent that teleological ethics impose abstract notions such as the measure of utility, justice can be identified with outcome-based ethics, too. Gilligan's "care ethics" is a relational approach to morality that avoids generalization in favor of particularity and connection.

The major distinctions between Kohlberg's and Gilligan's approaches to morality center on concepts of connection, particularity, and emotion.[17] For Kohlberg, morality is absorbed in what constitutes right action and principle. For Gilligan, morality concerns the connections between people and the relationships established. Whereas Kohlberg (through Kant) assumes that individual moral agents are autonomous and thus freely enter relationships that elicit duties, Gilligan views individuals as entangled in a web of dynamic relationships, not all of which are freely chosen. For Gilligan, humans are interconnected, and ethics is an expression of sustaining these connections, which are concrete and therefore particular. Whereas Kohlberg stresses universal principles, Gilligan believes moral action requires knowledge of particular others and their circumstances, not a universalized case. She claims that, although care cannot provide the "right" action for all people at all times, it will indicate the appropriate action given the circumstances. Connection also implies more than the autonomous rational agents making detached moral decisions valorized by Kohlberg's work.[18] Whereas Kant avoids the emotive, Gilligan's approach embraces feelings as a moral capacity that facilitates an ethical response. For Gilligan, emotion has a significant role in creating connection and motivating action.

The differences between Gilligan's and Kohlberg's approaches are exemplified in their treatments of the "Heinz dilemma" between property and life:

> In Europe, a woman was near death from cancer. One drug might save her, a rare form of radium that a druggist in the same town had discovered. The druggist was charging $2,000, ten times what the drug cost him to make. The sick woman's husband, Heinz, went to everyone he knew to borrow the money, but he could only get together about half of what it cost. He told the druggist that his wife was dying, and asked him to sell it cheaper or let him pay later. But the druggist said, "No." The husband got desperate and broke into the man's store to steal the drug for his wife. Should the husband have done that? Why?[19]

Kohlberg argues for abstraction from the particulars of the case. "It would be right to steal for a stranger because the right to life should be accorded universally to all men whose lives can be saved regardless of personal ties."[20] Kohlberg uses the language of rights and develops a principle for moral action that transcends this case. Gilligan, in posing the Heinz dilemma to an eleven-year-old girl, Amy, finds an alternative moral voice of caring reflecting a connected and particular response. Amy seeks a creative solution that goes beyond stealing or not stealing, such as an agreement to pay the druggist back over time: "If Heinz and the druggist had talked it out long enough, they could reach something besides stealing."[21] Gilligan describes Amy as framing the solution in "a network of connection, a web of relationships that is sustained by a process of communication."[22] Kohlberg's response to the Heinz dilemma seeks a clear solution—a rights-based trump card—for all similar cases with little regard for the power of interpersonal negotiation. Gilligan, in considering Amy's response, offers a more tenuous solution contingent on human interaction.

In a Different Voice appears to be an unassuming, relatively short psychological study of the ways men and women respond to moral dilemmas, yet this understated book sparked a tidal wave of responses, commentary, and criticism. Virtually every feminist ethicist would subsequently have something to say about care. Not all the commentaries have been favorable.[23] Nevertheless, Gilligan performed the crucial function of naming the previously anonymous role of care in morality. Her original work raised more questions than it answered, perhaps an indication of the magnitude of her discoveries. In attempting to clarify a definition of care ethics, many theorists have staked out different positions.

Constellations of Care

To provide a road map through the proliferating understandings of care ethics, I have organized the different perspectives into four clusters of thought that identify care as (1) a feminine value, (2) a virtue, (3) an alternative to justice, or (4) something more than an ethical theory. These should be considered constellations of thought rather than mutually exclusive and stagnant schools because many key figures cross categories as they continue to develop their ideas. For example, Gilligan's perspective on care evolved over time. Although much of her later work is ignored in philosophical commentaries, Gilligan moved from viewing care as an alternative to justice to arguing that the approaches based on these two phenomena are intimately bound up with each other. Each of these categories has important theoretical considerations that bear addressing. For example, is care ethics tied to a woman's nature? Does care ethics supersede a justice approach?

Care as a Feminine Value

As I develop the claim that there is an embodied dimension to the affective knowledge that informs care, it is important that gender not be a barrier to an empathetic response. Otherwise, embodied care becomes a concern for women alone. Indeed, even some scholarly works (particularly by those that do not read Gilligan or Noddings carefully) express a rather widespread belief that care ethics is gendered female: care belongs to a woman's ethics, while its complement, justice, belongs to a man's ethics. As I will discuss later, this gendered dichotomy is particularly problematic for care ethics because it limits the application and significance of care. In fact, a careful review of the literature reveals that, although the language of essentialism sometimes slips into their arguments or a superficial reading of their work may give the impression that essentialism is being advocated, few feminist ethicists strongly support the idea of care as an exclusively feminine value. Gilligan's work, however, particularly her earliest writings, exemplifies some of this confusion. Gilligan identified care through gender differences, and she applied a feminist analysis to her observations of the moral decision making of men and women. She made several ambiguous statements that have led many to believe that she was offering a type of ethical gender essentialism (care = female; justice = male).[24]

The far too common interpretation of Gilligan as an essentialist is not fair to the full corpus of writing and research she has offered since the publication of *In a Different Voice*. The essentialist characterization of her work ghettoizes Gilligan's analysis and masks the revolutionary potential of care. Gilligan has come to understand justice and care as inexorably intertwined: "Themes within the basic melody of the care voice may be enriched by adding themes of the justice voice, in counterpoint."[25] Unfortunately, many theorists, feminist and nonfeminist, treat Gilligan's research as if it ended with *In a Different Voice* rather than started there. Cressida J. Heyes, although critical of Gilligan for not emphasizing power relations, debunks the idea that Gilligan is essentialist by examining her later writings. Heyes believes the misreading of Gilligan is in part due to the misunderstandings between second- and third-wave feminism, "Our third wave revisions of the political work of second wave feminists need to avoid an epistemological critique that persistently fragments categories without exploring their empirical adequacy or political importance. . . . Gilligan, far from being 'an essentialist,' has moved toward a politically informed anti-essentialist method."[26]

Perhaps an even more ambiguous position appears in the early writing of Nel Noddings and other theorists who place mothering relationships at the center of care ethics. Noddings's first book on care, *Caring,* appeared only two years after Gilligan's *In a Different Voice* but has little crossover in methodology or sources. Noddings avoids strict essentialism yet unapologetically views an ethics of care as a woman's domain: "An ethic built on caring is, I think, characteristically and essentially feminine—which is not to say, of course, that it cannot be shared by men, any more than we should care to say that traditional moral systems cannot be embraced by women. But an ethic of care arises, I believe, out of our experience as women, just as the traditional logical approach to ethical problems arises more obviously from masculine experience."[27] Noddings grounds care in women's experience rather than in biology. For example, Noddings argues that women prefer to begin the analysis of a moral dilemma not from abstract principles but from concretized circumstances.[28] A specific application can be found in the biblical story of Abraham's willingness to sacrifice his son to demonstrate his faith (Genesis 22:1–19). Noddings finds this story morally abhorrent from a woman's standpoint. This myth is traditionally employed in the Judeo-Christian tradition to demonstrate Abraham's great faith in God. Noddings, however, focuses on the relational aspect of the tale.[29] She declares the sacrificial impulse found in this story to be anathema to women.[30]

Noddings's gender-based dichotomy further manifests itself in the distinction between "natural" and "moral" caring. Natural caring provides humans with the faculties for moral caring. Natural caring is akin to (but not the same as) an instinct that humans share with many other animals. For Noddings, the paradigmatic example of natural caring is the mother-child relationship. "For many women, motherhood is the single greatest source of strength for the maintenance of the ethical ideal."[31] Since little decision making takes place in such natural caring, Noddings uses the term *ethical caring* for the more numerous circumstances where one must choose to care. She admits that the difference between the two is not always clear. Noddings's emphasis on the central role of women's experience makes her work ripe for claims of essentialism, but a careful reading reveals that she is arguing for a socially constructed standpoint rather than an essential nature.

One complexity in the analysis of care as a particularly feminine value stems from references to "mothering" or the "maternal." Many who write about care view the maternal relationship as paradigmatic for a caring relationship. For example, Noddings observes that "girls often quite naturally learn these [caring] skills by close and continuous apprenticeship to their mothers."[32] Nevertheless, these theorists are often quick to qualify mothering as a role that can be assumed by men or women and that has little to do with gender beyond its historical association with women. In *Maternal Thinking* Sara Ruddick makes a number of moral and epistemological claims for the mothering relationship. For example, drawing on the writing of Jane Addams and Olive Schreiner, Ruddick argues that many women are more morally indignant over the prospects of war than are their male counterparts, a difference she attributes to the experience of motherhood.[33] Nevertheless, she does not view this moral perspective as an exclusively female position. "I did not—and still do not—acknowledge sexual differences in parental work. Men can participate in every aspect of mothering except lactation; both women and men can perform paternal functions."[34] Maternal practices, although historically associated with women, are separated from strict gender attachments. In the end Ruddick is not an essentialist.

Although her view of men's involvement differs from that of Noddings or Ruddick, Diemut Elisabet Bubeck also puts forth a claim for the gendered nature of care. She argues that care is feminine value in four ways: (1) Care characterizes that which is called feminine and marks that which is not masculine. (2) The prevalent division of labor assigns care to the woman's portion. Women are typically given the job of maintaining relationships and caring for others. (3) Care matches women's psychology. Female identity is tied to notions of connection rather than autonomy. This view is consistent with Gilligan's research. (4) Women endorse the ethics of care more often than men do. Although women are capable of employing a justice-based approach, there are no expectations that they do so.[35] Bubeck adamantly views care as a feminine value, but she stops short of advocating biological gender essentialism. She argues that the absence of historical cases of matriarchal societies with the power structures that patriarchies manifest does not establish care as a genetic characteristic of women. Bubeck favors the view that care ethics is gendered female because of social constructions. Even when men have acted with care, Bubeck believes, they have done so as a result of rules derived from a role (e.g., father and husband) and not as an authentic expression of care from the male persona: "The care is thus not given on the basis of their 'male nature,' but more significantly on the basis of their social and/or emotional relation to the cared for."[36] Bubeck's critique of male efforts to care contrasts interestingly with Noddings's notion of natural caring. For Noddings, the proximal relations created out of parenting animate natural caring, which, although a good, is morally ambiguous because of its reflexivity: natural caring as a habitual response involves less ethical effort than does moral caring. In examining the same parental relationship for a man, Bubeck views the resulting acts of care as animated by duty or role requirements.

The superficial perception that care is a woman's value is misleading and not supported by the literature. Few if any theorists are willing to make exclusively gender-based claims concerning care. There is little argument in opposition to the idea that care has historically been the purview of women and women's labor, but a historical association cannot establish a normative claim about care. The issue of the gender connection to care can be seen as a background-foreground concern. Care has been in the background of male-dominated approaches to ethics, but it has been in the foreground of women's moral identity. It is time to rectify the imbalance.[37] Focusing on care is a robust approach to morality, albeit a paradigm shift that requires new ways of thinking about morality.

That care is richly possible for embodied beings no matter their gender is important to my development of the body's role in care in the next chapter. A woman who has had a child is in a better position to empathize with a woman who is pregnant because of their embodied knowledge, but that does not preclude a man from caring and using embodied resources to inform that care. Despite rhetoric to the contrary, and not to dismiss profound socially constructed differences, ultimately men's and women's bodies are much more alike than they are dissimilar.

Care as a Virtue

In recent years the popularity of associating care with virtue ethics has grown. Virtue ethics emphasizes personal character rather than good outcomes or moral duty. Because care ethics questions the use of a moral calculus and does not offer clear moral mandates, many theorists have characterized care as a type of virtue. This characterization is supported by the fact that virtue ethics focuses on the agent rather than moral principles governing discrete actions.[38] The modern renaissance of virtue ethics is credited to Alasdair MacIntyre, whose seminal work *After Virtue* provides a preliminary definition of virtue as "an acquired human quality the possession and exercise of which tends to enable us to achieve those goods which are internal to practices and the lack of which effectively prevents us from achieving any such goods."[39] MacIntyre describes "internal goods" as activities that are beneficial to the entire community that engages in them. There is a prerequisite that certain features of the social and moral life be shared and accepted. Although MacIntyre does not address care directly, caring relationships can be viewed as an important aspect of the moral life. Accordingly, if one is caring, then one is moral, at least in part. If society cultivates care among its members, then social problems will be mitigated, because the members of society will act out of this virtue.

Another branch in the family tree of care as a virtue can be found in the moral philosophy of David Hume (1711–76). The contemporary philosopher Annette Baier has made the most explicit case for the similarities between Hume's work and care ethics, but Noddings and Rita Manning also make connections to Hume. Ironically, it is Hume's ethics that Kant vigorously denies and responds to in creating the works that have become the guiding ethical approach of the Western world—influencing, among a great many others, Lawrence Kohlberg. Gilligan's response to Kohlberg brings this ethics' historical arc full circle.

Hume's virtue-based morality overlaps with care in numerous ways. Hume describes the moral person as "sociable, good-natured, humane, merciful, grateful, friendly, generous, beneficent."[40] These relational terms describe character or virtues but not specific moral duties. "We are never to consider any single action in our enquiries concerning the origin of morals; but only the quality of character from which the action proceeded."[41] For Hume, moral action is grounded in the natural human proclivity to sympathize. He describes sympathy as a process by which ideas are transformed into impressions. In book 1 of the *Treatise* Hume distinguishes two types of "perceptions." He calls perceptions that are given directly in experience "impressions"; those that are combined or otherwise manipulated in the mind he calls "ideas." Some experience of the world, no matter how remote, always precedes ideas. For Hume, sympathy has the ability to reverse this process and create impressions with the force and vivacity to motivate behavior based on sentiment, or "fellow feelings."[42] Hume recognized the basic role of empathy in human relations: "There is no human, and indeed no sensible, creature, whose happiness or misery does not, in some measure, affect us, when brought near to us, and represented in lively colours."[43] Hume thus begins his moral analysis with the actions and interactions of human beings, not abstract principles of right and wrong. Although neither claims that it is the exclusive domain of morality, both Hume and Gilligan find a central place for empathy. The focus on relationality makes concrete the perception of the moral content.

Baier focuses on the ways Hume's work valorizes those qualities or virtues historically associated with women. According to Baier, Hume's emphasis on emotion, relationality, and concrete context makes him "uncommonly womanly in his moral wisdom."[44] Significantly, Hume's approach makes virtue not a fixed commodity but a complex outgrowth of the society from which it is born: "As every man has a strong connection with society . . . , he becomes . . . favourable to all those habits of principles, which promote order in society."[45] The inherently socially constructed character of ethics is recognized in Hume's work, which matches the type of antiuniversalism found in the writings of care ethicists. Those who write about care universalize the caring or sympathetic impulse without appealing to universal principles of application. Care arises in particular people in particular contexts and relations. Baier finds Hume to be a virtue ethicist with an understanding of the relational: "The status of a character trait as a virtue need not be a fixed matter, but a matter completely interrelated with the sort of society in which it appears."[46] For Baier, Hume's provision for sentiment, emotion, and sympathy gives his work an important commonality with Gilligan's understanding of care.

Manning similarly identifies essential aspects of Hume's work important for care ethics. The first is the experimental aspect of testing moral strategies against experiences. The second is Hume's belief in our ability to sympathize with one another, and the third is care's capacity to elicit action.[47] Manning views Hume and Noddings as sharing an important understanding of the role of moral imagination and its fallibility: "Hume and Noddings are right to suggest that we imagine ourselves in contact with [strangers], that we allow this occasion an emotional response, and that we act, in the full knowledge that our actions, based as they are on insufficient understanding and often less than vibrant sentiment, might not be the right ones."[48] Overall, Manning finds care ethics and virtue ethics to have much in common: "They both emphasize the importance of habit and inclination. Neither pretends to provide a calculus for moral decision making; rather they insist that the context coupled with the character of the actor and some general rules of thumb will provide all the cues."[49]

Noddings, too, draws on Hume's notion of "fellow feeling" as an active virtue in delineating her distinction between natural and ethical caring: "In pointing to Hume's 'active virtue' and to an ethical ideal as the source of ethical behavior, I seem to be advocating an ethic of virtue."[50] Both Hume and Noddings wrestle with the ambiguous relationship between natural inclinations to care and human moral agency. Ultimately, neither Noddings nor Manning is satisfied with subsuming care under virtue ethics; however, they value Hume's virtue ethics because of its insight into what constitutes a moral response.

Rosemarie Tong is dissatisfied not just with the ambiguities of care ethics but also with the polarization in the care-versus-justice schema. She offers a modern theory of care as a virtue. Tong finds care so central to moral functioning that labeling it a virtue is the only way to capture its importance. Nevertheless, Tong has some concerns about the tradition of virtue ethics and any claims that care is a feminist virtue. Tong delineates a continuum of virtue ethics: masculinist, masculine, feminine, and feminist. The ends of the continuum represent forthright and unequivocal positions advocating the superior moral values of their respective genders. For Tong, the significant difference between feminist and masculinist positions is that the latter has held sway in the Western philosophical tradition. The middle categories of the continuum—masculine and feminine virtues —represent a strong sense of different yet complementary moral values. According to Tong, Jean-Jacques Rousseau and John Stuart Mill favor masculine virtues. Nietzsche, however, offers a masculinist view of morality, for in it only men with strong male virtues can be ethical.[51] For Tong, Nel Noddings exemplifies a virtue ethicist who is more feminine than feminist because her version of care lacks a sense of personal empowerment. Although Tong has reservations about Noddings work, she believes the dominance of patriarchal values makes feminist values such as care a modern necessity.[52] The recent emphasis on feminist virtues is a direct result of their omission from traditional virtue ethics.[53]

Some of the steps Tong went through in categorizing care as a virtue may provide insight into the trend in this direction. Tong's primary motivation for associating care with virtue ethics appears to be her discomfort with the ambiguity of care: "I had relatively clear ideas about justice ethics, particularly its deontological and utilitarian versions. I had very unclear ideas about care ethics."[54] Tong creates a category of virtue ethics in which to place care, but her argument in favor of this approach is primarily oppositional. Patriarchal virtues have been so dominant that the current context is ripe for an emphasis on feminist virtues. While this is true, Tong's argument does not elaborate a rich defense of the inherent value of care. For Tong, virtue ethics appears to be the characterization of last resort because no other category adequately fits care.

Like Tong, Ruth Groenhout categorizes care as a virtue, but she, too, offers stipulations before making this categorization. Groenhout describes most virtue ethics as starting with a developed notion of the good human life. Care ethics, however, begins with a personal relationship and posits that right actions will follow. For Groenhout, care theories are less satisfactory than traditional approaches to ethics for the same reason that any virtue ethics is less satisfactory: "the lack of logical entailment between having a certain type of character and knowing what particular action to take in a particular situation."[55] To mitigate this dissatisfaction, Groenhout argues that care ethics requires a well-developed notion of how humans should live, since it cannot provide a clear sense of the good. Groenhout offers mothering practices as the paradigmatic case of healthy, flourishing caring relationships. She believes care theorists need to further explore how humans should live in order to identify the exemplary mothering practices. Groenhout ultimately appears to argue that care ethics resembles but is not the same as virtue ethics. She advocates transforming care ethics further into virtue ethics by asking that a stronger sense of the good be developed, particularly if care is to provide effective social guidance in a pluralistic world.

Michael Slote also argues that care ethics is a radical form of virtue ethics, where motives are the basis for moral evaluation. Slote believes that characterizing care as a virtue or in a "virtue-ethical manner" provides a means for overcoming the common objection that care has insufficient resources to accommodate social morality. According to Slote, a focus on care redirects ethical primacy to personal motivation in acts of care, so that it undergirds a form of agent-based virtue ethics rather than a partialistic form of consequentialism. "[That] caring is morally good or virtuous is a fundamental, intuitive judgment from which other moral judgments derive."[56] Slote claims that moral judgments can be derived from assessing care motivations not only in individuals but also in social groups. Institutions that act out of a caring motivation are virtuous, regardless of the outcome. Again, Groenhout equivocates her characterization by claiming that care resembles, but is distinct from, virtue ethics. To accommodate the uniqueness of care, Slote, like Tong, creates a new category of virtue ethics: "agent-based" ethics. Each of these considerations of care is admittedly awkward. Slote focuses on judging motivations, which is not a traditional method of considering virtue. Groenhout claims that care is inherently teleological, which is another uncommon claim for virtue ethics.[57]

Whether care is considered a virtue, a cluster of virtues, or a synonym for virtue, as Robert Veatch suggests,[58] I agree with the critiques of several feminist ethicists who find numerous pitfalls in associating care with virtue ethics. Virtue ethics is most commonly criticized for being too individualistic, too conservative, and ill equipped to address institutional or social challenges.

Noddings claims that virtue ethics has an individualistic "dark side" that manifests itself if character development is emphasized over relational issues. She uses the example of patriotism, which has been identified as an important aspect of character development by some educators in the United States. Noddings acknowledges that this may be an important individual virtue, but it must be accompanied by a relational analysis if it is to be balanced. The individualistic notion of patriotism can lead to an oppositional divisiveness, pitting individuals with different definitions of citizenship against one another. Noddings writes, "Caring is not an individual virtue, although certain virtues may help sustain it. Rather, caring is a relational state or quality, and it requires distinctive contributions from carer and cared for."[59] Noddings utilizes the language of virtue but does so in a qualified way because she does not wish to replicate traditional individualistic associations. Admittedly, virtue ethics does not have to be interpreted so individualistically, yet it often is. Care is not a virtue that an individual can hope to develop outside relationships to others. Care inherently involves connectedness. Care (like morality) is brought to life through the interaction described by caring habits, caring knowledge, and caring imagination.

A second potential pitfall of associating care with virtue ethics is that the latter remains impotent vis-à-vis social injustice. This position is perhaps best captured by the interrogatives of Claudia Card: "If oppressive institutions stifle and stunt the moral development of the oppressed, how is it possible, what does it *mean,* for the oppressed to be liberated? What is *there* to liberate? What does it mean to resist, to make morally responsible choices, to become moral agents, to develop character?"[60] William Bennett, the former secretary of education and author of *The Book of Virtues: A Treasury of Great Moral Stories,* has championed the notion of personal and civic virtues in the public arena.[61] This personal approach implicitly exonerates communities and social institutions from culpability in regard to today's social ills. The individual moral character is at fault according to this view. The connected or social dimension of morality is deemphasized in favor of personal moral development. On the contrary, I view communities, society, and its institutions as systems of relationships that can exhibit varying degrees of care.

A third critique of virtue ethics lies in its conservative usage. MacIntyre's revitalization of virtue ethics occurred in the context of a communitarian philosophy that attempts to recapture a previous understanding of morality: nostalgia for a moral era gone by. The romanticization of the past, however, may have overlooked the moral pitfalls of history. Hekman argues that a narrow definition of community is employed: "The concept of community invoked by these theorists is a conservative, if not reactionary, one. It is at the very least a concept that, in the discourse of the West, has entailed the inferiority and subordination of women."[62] Laurie Shrage voices a similar critique concerning ethnocentrism in the kind of virtue ethics MacIntyre espouses. She admonishes that to avoid "ethnocentric attributions, it is not sufficient to engage in literary investigations of the virtues as they are conceived by premodern others, as MacIntyre encourages. We also need to consult ethnographic investigations of the virtues as they are conceived by contemporary human others."[63] Conservatism need not be an element of virtue ethics, but the baggage of this association makes one cautious about the link to care.

Because of its individualistic nature, lack of social critique, and conservative tendencies, virtue ethics appears to be an inadequate home for care. While care ethics shares much with virtue ethics, including a deemphasis of the adjudication of particular acts, the assumption of autonomy inherent in virtue ethics is not the starting point for caring reflection.

Care as an Alternative to Justice

While some deny that care adds anything to the moral tradition,[64] most of those writing about ethics accept that Gilligan, Noddings, and other care ethicists have put forth an alternative moral theory. Whether gender specific or not, such care-based theories are largely thought of as distinct but less-developed ethical systems. They are offered as corrective or competing moral approaches with their own means of addressing moral dilemmas. Because care and justice are competing moral principles, much of the focus falls on the differences between the two concepts and the relative efficacy of the two approaches based on them. The lexicon of moral philosophy places justice and care at odds in what is referred to as the "care and justice debate," which unfortunately carries the analogous gendered baggage of a "battle of the sexes." For example, Katha Pollitt writes, "In her immensely influential book, *In a Different Voice*, Carol Gilligan uses [Nancy] Chodorow to argue that the sexes make moral decisions according to separate criteria: Women according to an 'ethic of care,' men according to an 'ethic of rights.'"[65] This all-too-common dichotomous reading of care and justice shortchanges the rich and complex understanding of each.

Gilligan must take some of the responsibility for the binary thinking about care and justice. Although in her later works she moves to reintegrate the two, opposition to justice was initially a means for describing the previously unnamed: care. Furthermore, Gilligan is somewhat vague in her description of justice. Sometimes she identifies justice with rule-based ethics;[66] at other times she associates it with impartialist notions of rights and equality.[67] Her more recent writings still express a certain duality regarding justice and care, but she has reframed these categories around relationality: "Hearing a relational voice as a new key for psychology and politics, I have theorized both justice and care in relational terms. Justice speaks to the disconnections that are at the root of violence, violation and oppression, or the unjust use of unequal power. Care speaks to the dissociations which lead people to abandon themselves and others: by not speaking, not listening, not knowing, not seeing, not caring and ultimately not feeling[,] by numbing themselves or steeling themselves against the vibrations and the resonances which characterize and connect the living world."[68] Although she envisions integration, Gilligan employs language that distinguishes the different voices of care and justice. Gilligan may not have intended to cleanly separate the two, but the subtleties of the continuities and differences are often overlooked, resulting in the interpretation of care and justice as underpinning competing theories of morality.

The philosopher Grace Clement suggests that the present discourse has created two oppositional ideal types.[69] She identifies three common characterizations found among those who pose justice against care. (1) Justice is abstract and theoretical, creating the potential for universalistic claims, whereas care is contextual and grounded in actual experience.[70] (2) The notion of justice presupposes autonomy and, by implication, impartiality, whereas care assumes the connectedness of humanity. (3) The ethics of justice emphasizes some notion of equality as a sustaining priority, whereas care places a rich understanding of relationships as a priority. Clement's ideal types may facilitate comprehension of these abstract ideas, but they are reductionist and tend toward extreme characterizations. The justice ideal type is actually not a single moral theory but an amalgamation of traditional Western moral philosophy. Rights-based, rule-based, and consequence-based ethics are quite different and take numerous forms. These theories generally share tendencies toward abstraction, autonomy, and equality, but with tremendous methodological differences. More important, because they are contrasted with one another, justice and care are often described in extreme terms. The ideal type of justice-based theory is viewed as emotionless, calculating, and completely divorced from the emotive and affective moral resources of care.

For example, Kantian ethics is often portrayed as overlooking relationships altogether, but John W. Lango argues that such an interpretation grossly oversimplifies Kant. Lango agrees that Kant is indifferent to relational *particulars* because of the desire for universalization, but he argues that Kant's ethics is not indifferent to specific relations. Each relationship (parent-child, manager-subordinate, etc.) will elicit certain duties. Lango's interpretation of Kant may not foster the rich notion of moral relationships sought by those interested in care, but it makes the point that stereotypes of justice are problematic.[71] By contrast, care is usually painted as antithetical to autonomy or a sense of fairness.[72] Marilyn Friedman, drawing on and extending the work of Harry Frankfurt, argues that emotion and relationship are resources for autonomy.[73] Applying Friedman's claim may create an argument for autonomy within care that could address some of the concerns about caregivers being lost to those for whom they care. Milton Mayeroff goes a bit further, claiming that caring is not just a resource for autonomy but a prerequisite for it. "I am autonomous because of my devotion to others and my dependence on them, when dependence is the *kind* that liberates me and my others."[74] These examples demonstrate that extreme characterizations of justice and care, while perhaps grounded in some reality, are of limited usefulness and often facilitate reductionist understandings.

Nel Noddings's early writings provide perhaps the strongest suggestions that care and justice operate with little overlap. Noddings does not employ the term *justice* in her book *Caring*, but it is clear that she is often discussing something similar to Gilligan's idea of justice. In describing caring, she makes a number of declarative statements: "I shall reject ethics of principle as ambiguous and unstable. Wherever there is a principle, there is implied its exception and, too often, principles function to separate us from each other."[75] Whereas Gilligan's ethical analyses tend toward the descriptive, Noddings's work is boldly prescriptive, advocating care over traditional impartialist ethics to the point of suggesting the former's superiority, a position that Gilligan never explicitly entertains. Whereas Gilligan ultimately makes overtures toward the interrelationship of justice and care, Noddings appears entrenched in describing their fundamental differences: "I shall also reject the notion of universalizability."[76] Noddings views rules not as absolute mandates but rather as shortcuts that help us make decisions. Rules are not replacements for the moral work of caring. Connection is the ultimate domain of morality, and if we hide behind rules, we insulate ourselves from our ethical obligation to care. Noddings closes *Caring* with the following injunction: "One must meet the other in caring. From this requirement there is no escape for one who would be moral."[77]

Caring defends a care-based approach as an alternative to traditional justice-based approaches more strongly than other works do, leaving it the most vulnerable to criticism, but Noddings's ideas have evolved since the book was written. In a 1990 response directed primarily at Claudia Card's critique, Noddings appears to be open to revising some of her thoughts. "Several thoughtful critics, including Claudia Card and Susan Moller Okin, have suggested that justice and care must be combined in an adequate ethic. These critics might be right, and I want to think through the matter thoroughly. As philosophers we have been trained to defend our positions to the last rhetorical gasp, but as feminists we have taught each other to listen."[78] Noddings acknowledges that part of the early efforts to contrast care to justice was grounded in the need to create a credible intellectual space for discussions of care. In 2002 Noddings published *Starting at Home: Caring and Social Policy,* where she fully integrates justice and care. To accomplish this, Noddings's distinction between "caring-for" and "caring-about" is crucial: caring-for is the direct face-to-face experience of caring that, it is to be hoped, one first experiences at home. Because we cannot care for everyone with the same personal energy and effort, our care is sometimes manifested through indirect channels, such as charitable work, philanthropy, political activism, or voting. According to Noddings, "caring-about may provide the link between caring and justice. . . . caring provides the basic good in which the sense of justice is grounded."[79] While finding care to be foundational, Noddings has abandoned the view that care and justice are mutually exclusive.

Although Noddings's initial work on care may have been too binary (both in its gender orientation and as an alternative theory), she has performed a vital service in advancing a comprehensive phenomenology of care.[80] Whereas Gilligan attends to language in naming the voice of care, Noddings describes the process, agents, and impact of a caring relationship. While avoiding the aforementioned dualism, I will apply Noddings's insight into reciprocity and engrossment when I address the embodied characteristic of care in the next chapter.

Some, such as Margaret Urban Walker and, in a related way, Susan Hekman, find the basis for the difference between care and justice in methods of acquiring knowledge. Walker invokes context, connection, narrative, and communication to provide an alternative model of moral epistemology that is characteristic of care. According to Walker, we come to know or understand particular others through relationships. Relationships imply not an instant in time, however, but a narrative constructed over many encounters. "If the others I need to understand really are actual others in a particular case at hand, and not repeatable instances or replaceable occupants of a general status, they will require of me an understanding of their/our story and its concrete detail."[81] Traditionally philosophy has distinguished sharply between the domains of epistemology and ethics, a distinction facilitated by ethics' abstraction from individuals and relationships. If morality is grounded in context (and in the body), however, it becomes more difficult to maintain these artificial intellectual boundaries. Walker begins with the differences between care and justice to develop an epistemology that undermines the dichotomy itself.

I will not argue that care offers an alternative to justice for building an ethical theory. This argument has lost its usefulness, as many of care's initial proponents have recognized. I will retain the idea that care (particularly the embodied care that I propose) adds content to morality, but I do not view it as underpinning a discrete ethical theory that can be isolated, dissected, and evaluated. Care is grounded in the ambiguity and complexity of the human condition and as such permeates all morality. This conclusion leads directly to the final category of thought on care: care as more than an ethical theory.

Care as More Than an Ethical Theory

Virginia Held, a key figure in feminist ethics, argues that care cannot be compartmentalized in abstract notions of morality. Care is too fundamental to humanity to be so narrowly defined. As have a growing number of theorists, Held has begun to see much more in care than an alternative feminist ethics: "I am coming to the view that care and its related considerations are the wider framework—or network—within which room should be made for justice, utility, and the virtues."[82] In some respects the idea of care as offering more than an ethical theory is not entirely new. In a short book published in 1971, Milton Mayeroff argues that caring is a central aspect of human experience that facilitates the flourishing of self and others. Caring provides the essential context of life: "Man finds himself by finding his place, and he finds his place by finding appropriate others that need his care and that he needs to care for. Through caring and being cared for man experiences himself as part of nature; we are closest to a person or an idea when we help it grow."[83] Mayeroff's work lacks a gender analysis or a significant critique of traditional moral theories, which may help explain why it did not provoke the level of discussion surrounding Gilligan's writing. Nevertheless, Mayeroff often poetically bridges psychology and philosophy, tying the wider significance of care to issues of community, self-development, and autonomy. Mayeroff may have antedated Gilligan with respect to notions of justice and care, but it is clear that he views caring as providing more than an alternative basis for ethics.

In perhaps the most far-reaching exploration of the radical potential of care, Susan Hekman offers a discursive analysis of Gilligan's work. In *Moral Voices, Moral Selves: Carol Gilligan and Feminist Moral Theory* Hekman concludes that care is more than an alternative to justice in creating ethical theory. Justice and care are not independent modes of morality but rather intertwined elements: "Justice and care, the moral voice of autonomy and that of connection, are not opposites at all but, rather, 'inhabit' each other."[84] Given the conventional interpretation of care and justice, Hekman's claim is quite radical. Hekman believes that Gilligan was not fully aware of the revolutionary possibilities of care. Following Gilligan's intellectual trajectory, Hekman claims that care and justice are two voices in the multiple language games of moral discourse. She argues that the real work of morality is to cease the quest for moral judgment and certitude and attend to the plural moral voices found in ethical dilemmas. Hekman finds the care/justice dichotomy unproductive because it only replicates historical arguments: "What I am proposing is not that we should abandon discussions of the ethic of care, but, rather, that we should avoid aping the absolutism of masculinist moral theory and instead discuss different moral voices, not 'the' different voice."[85] Hekman calls for a radical rethinking of underlying assumptions of moral philosophy, including the quest for certainty. Offering *alternative* moral theories presupposes that one will be closer to some objective "truth." Hekman finds this path of inquiry fruitless and believes care ethics allows us to attend to the range of possibilities in a given moral problem.

Whereas Hekman argues for an alternative view of moral theory, Margaret Urban Walker turns to the epistemology that underlies morality. Walker argues that the communication of a narrative activates care and its possibilities, but the significance of that communication is often ignored. Walker constructs the framework of an alternative to the Western tradition of an impersonalist epistemology, which posits an abstract, objective notion of truth. In her attempt to explain the difference between justice and care, Walker shifts the focus from ethics to epistemology. At times Walker suggests something other than a dichotomy: "The result of this alternative epistemology is not, then, an 'opposite number' or shadow image of impersonalist approaches; it is instead a point of departure for a variety of different problematics, investigations, focal concerns, and genres of writing and teaching about ethics, many of which we have not, I suppose, yet clearly imagined."[86] Walker has highlighted the limitations of the label *alternative*. The implication of an alternative ethics is mutual exclusion: a choice. Walker employs the word *alternative* to imply a more radical reshaping of the epistemological landscape.

I suggest that, although morality may be informed by a sense of duty or a concern for consequences or religious convictions, caring habits, knowledge, and imagination are and should be fundamental participants in moral consideration. This is both a normative and a descriptive statement. The confluence of the normative and the descriptive in care means that care flies in the face of what has come to be known as the "naturalistic fallacy." G. E. Moore coined the term in *Principia Ethica*, where he uses it to attack a move commonly made in ethics. Ethicists often use a grammatical form that equates a particular phenomenon with goodness, such as "democracy is good." According to Moore, however, such a statement will always be inaccurate because democracy cannot represent all that constitutes the good.[87] More germane to the discussion of care, questions of moral obligation are always answered with statements of possible actions. Moore found this to be the fundamental error of ethics: to confuse the "is" and the "ought."[88] The influence of the naturalistic fallacy lingers in creating a schism between philosophy, which generally pursues what ought to be, and the social sciences, which inquire into what is.[89] Embodied care finds the human body at the nexus of the is and the ought. As I will show in chapter 2, the habits of the body make it appear to have been "built for care," yet this description does not preclude the normative activity of the caring imagination. Noddings has alluded to a natural aspect to care. Sometimes caring habits come as easily as taking a breath of fresh air. At other times habits of care involve sacrifice, pain, and great effort of will.

The naturalistic fallacy is an example of an artificial philosophical boundary on morality that care breaches. Legalism or formulaic manipulations can result when care is not a participant in a given dilemma. To include care is to attend to the ongoing relationships, individuals, and emotions of all parties. I am making an normative, "ought" claim, but it is also a descriptive, "is" claim. Whether attended to or not, care plays a role in most ethical questions. Few people rigidly adhere to an ethical system without being touched by sympathetic feelings. Confrontations between care and ethical systems offer three possibilities. Individuals will seek to express relations of care within the ethical system, they will subvert the ethical system, or they will suppress the care response.

Although the clusters of thought discussed here display certain continuities among themselves, the idea that care is more than the basis for a theory of ethics will be expanded as I cross certain artificial philosophical boundaries, including ethics versus epistemology, mind versus body, and even the more parochial boundary of Continental philosophy versus American pragmatism. Bernice Fisher and Joan Tronto also identify the need to make radical reconnections: "Caring crosscuts the antithesis between public and private, rights and duties, love and labor."[90] Caring habits, knowledge, and imagination are such basic parts of the human condition that they can help create these fruitful linkages. Held recognizes the philosophical potential of care as rooted in its pervasiveness: "I find care the most basic moral value. Without the actual practice of care, there cannot be human life at all."[91]

Caring as the Body's Habits, Knowledge, and Imagination

The previous discussion of the continuities and discontinuities between my view of care and the views of others indicates the direction this book will take. Allow me to reiterate my definition: care is an approach to individual and social morality that shifts ethical consideration to context, relationships, and affective knowledge in a manner that can be fully understood only if its embodied dimension is recognized. Embodied care centers not on theoretical or abstract understandings of right and wrong but on affective, embodied, and connected notions of morality. Caring violates, or perhaps blurs, many of the established categories of ethics. The morality of embodied care cannot be limited to rules but is not antithetical to them. The morality of embodied care is not solely focused on teleology, but it has a telos of wellbeing or the flourishing of embodied creatures. Nonetheless, the processes and practices of care are as important as the good. Because care is bound up in embodied experience, developing habits of care becomes a normative thrust. These habits are not rote, limiting exercises but dynamic, imaginative responses to the environment.

The possibility of acting morally on behalf of oneself or others is derived from the interaction of caring habits, caring knowledge, and caring imagination. Ultimately rules, consequences, and virtues may inform us, but they will not move us to act morally to the same extent that a personal, affective, embodied caring will. The Douglass speech cited at the beginning of this chapter exemplifies the transformative power of caring. Douglass was not merely passing along data. Rather, by tapping into listeners' caring knowledge and activating their caring imagination, he was eliciting strong feelings of connection even as he appealed to justice. Although the role of care has been historically denied, suppressed, and ignored, particularly in philosophy, it is present in everyday considerations of the ethical. Care is integrated with and arises from relationship—in the knowing and feeling for others. Therefore, considerations of care are bound up in epistemological concerns and cannot be easily segregated from human experience. Because the world is experienced through the body, attending to the corporeal dimension of care and ethics is warranted. The embodied and habitual nature of care should not be confused with mere instrumentality: the physicality of care helps to shape the content and direction of ethical considerations.

In the abstract, care appears ambiguous, particularly when confronted with the justice concern embodied in the question, "What ought I to do?" When placed in context, however, habits of care clarify courses of action. To decide on an action, our caring imagination will draw on embodied experiences, many of which remain unarticulated. For example, when confronted with a new and unexpected situation, such as an unknown, crying child ringing my front doorbell, a series of caring responses can take place. Previous experience (caring knowledge) lets me mobilize habits of care—not as routine but in response to the environment and adjusted to the variables. My tone of voice, my posture, and my comforting hands all go into action. I do not have an explicit rule for this situation, nor can or do I immediately calculate the consequences. I may be very unsure of myself, but I also "know" what to do because of my caring imagination: I do my best to take care of the child.

The values that underlie care also appear vague in the abstract. Fisher and Tronto offer "living well." Human flourishing or living well has both a shared and an unshared element to it in terms of the amount of continuity for which embodiment can account. The extent to which living well is unshared determines the extent to which it will be personally and culturally defined. There is, however, a shared dimension to living well that can be understood across cultures through the common experience of embodied existence. Material satisfactions, freedom of movement and its attendant choices, and friendship are affectively valued phenomena with corporeal resonance. These are real values, although they remain vague until confronted in life. In chapter 4 I will show how Jane Addams offers democracy as a social expression of care. Addams defines democracy not as a mere political system but rather as a method of shared involvement—caring for and about one another—that allows our society to live well and flourish.

A New Methodology for a New Moral Paradigm

> Theorizing connection as primary and fundamental in human life directs attention to a growing body of supporting evidence which cannot be incorporated within the old paradigm.
> —Carol Gilligan, "Hearing the Difference"

Although Gilligan does not identify with radical feminism, care ethics in many ways exemplifies what radical feminist scholarship should accomplish: the questioning of existing institutions. As Virginia Held declares, "Far from merely providing additional insights that can be incorporated into traditional theory, feminist explorations often require radical transformations of existing fields of inquiry and theory."[92] Those who find care ethics inadequate often refer to historical constructions of ethics. As Selma Sevenhuijsen points out, "The philosophical assumptions of liberal ethics, with regard to universality, impartiality, rationality, and equality versus difference, almost inevitably lead to a negative evaluation of the ethics of care."[93] Although care ethics will assist in moral discernment, care is more than an aspect of a decision science. Care is a metaethical aspect of human behavior: it transcends traditional theoretical approaches and permeates human existence and interaction. To grasp the meaning of this, I believe we are going to have to try on new metaphors for ethics. For example, a powerful contemporary metaphor for justice is a scale or balance. For every moral transgression an equal retributive action is required. Whether they represent rules, the good, or the good person, the metaphors we currently use in ethics do not capture caring.

Perhaps an analogous understanding for care is the notion of health. Talk of health evokes a web of meaning both individual and shared. Individuals possess health, but there is a shared yet inconsistent understanding of what it is to be healthy. Health is both natural and artificial, a product of our choices. Our natural inclinations will bring us to eat and provide ourselves with nurturance, but we must choose what we consume if we are to be healthy. Similarly, I will demonstrate that care is natural given the bodies we inhabit, yet it is also a result of specific decisions that we make. Care has both a shared and an individualistic meaning. Like any analogy, the characteristics of health do not perfectly map on to the idea of care, but the notion does gesture toward the kind of new thinking that this ethics requires.

Sara Ruddick offers a metaphor for care that is removed from traditional ethical thinking. She describes care as labor.[94] This metaphor captures the effort and energy necessary to participate in caring relationships and avoids any passive notions that care is instinctual. Women's historical role of performing society's emotional labor[95] has been often justified by ascribing a nurturing character to the female gender. This association betrays the sheer amount of work necessary in many caring relationships. Even among relative equals, caring relationships can be viewed as work. "Happy" or "successful" marriages, for example, result only when both partners work at it. Ruddick's notion of care as labor dramatically demonstrates the inadequacy of traditional moral reflection for capturing the meaning of care. The labor metaphor portrays care as a process.

Caring requires not only new metaphors but also new modes of explication. Fisher and Tronto claim, "We need a vocabulary that reflects our actual caring experience and, at the same time, helps us to project a vision of caring that we want to realize."[96] Traditionally theories have been explained by linear progressions of arguments that appeal to rationality. Because care is more caught up in the concrete characteristics of situations and the human entanglements involved, theoretical treatments are inadequate. Even considerations of cases that ostensibly allow reality to meet theory often simplify the interrelations and details, thus inadequately reflecting care elements. It is not a coincidence that Gilligan identified the voice of care by listening to people's stories and the dilemmas they faced. Care is most adequately reflected in the stories of people's lives, where more is brought to light than the rules or outcomes of a given situation. Those interested in care would do well to investigate literature as well as first-person stories to discover the degree to which care flows through everyday experience.

This claim—that a focus on care is a truly novel approach to morality—is challenging. Authentic paradigm shifts are not easily recognized, understood, or accepted. In trying to place care on the map of ethical theory (a dubious project of assimilation), Veatch states, "Some care theorists may be claiming that there is a new question, not previously on the agenda of moral theorists. If that is the case, then care theorists need to make clear what that new question is and how care provides an answer."[97] This approach is

antithetical to Hekman's. Care is not going to provide answers to questions—
it is going to raise more questions, because it cannot be contained in traditional categories. Those who expect care to resolve traditional ethical questions have not recognized the shift in moral terrain.

In *Rethinking Feminist Ethics* Daryl Koehn lists nine problems with care
ethics, the second of which is that it provides "little guidance in particular
cases." Discussing particular cases, Koehn voices an opinion common in traditional philosophy: "When there are competing claims which cannot both
be honored, there is a need for a weighing process that culminates in a judgment."[98] The following is the longer of the two examples she gives: "An ad-
vertising executive approaches her corporate manager with a request to be
allowed to work out of her home during her pregnancy and for a year following birth of her twins. During the same period, another employee asks
the corporate manager for release time to pursue a MBA. The corporation
does not have a policy in place authorizing extended pregnancy leave or release time for professional development. But the manager has been empow-
ered to work with his employees to make them both more productive and
happier within the workplace. How should the manager respond to these two
requests?"[99] My intention is not to criticize Koehn specifically, but her critique is common. Koehn wants an answer. She wants to know whom the
winners and losers will be. What is the right thing to do? Given our current
understanding of ethical theories, Koehn is responding in a generally compelling and sensible way. Care, however, does not really operate well in a four-
sentence example where no names, history, or relationships are present, because human experience is never so simple. The response can be informed
by policy but also may include many other considerations. Care is not easy.
It is messy and has many entanglements, but it is also imaginative and responsive, and this is its strength as a constellation of morality.

Peta Bowden locates the radical potential of caring in its ability to transcend theory making. For Bowden, care cannot be an alternative theory of
ethics because it is not a theory at all. She claims that care addresses the vague-
ness of human morality because it does not attempt to provide abstract universal solutions:

> No single theory can be created to subsume all instances, no moral concept can
> catch the essence of all of its uses, and no moral judgment can be expected to
> resolve a particular conflict without leaving further ethically significant aspects
> in its train. . . . Ethics is recognized as constitutively contextual and based in the
> actual experiences of actual persons; it is a continuous process of mutual re-
> sponses and adjustments that recognizes the inherent relationship between the
> practical details of that process of mutual response and its ethical possibilities.[100]

The paradigm shift in moral philosophy can be in part described as a move toward a phenomenon more human than ethical theorizing—a move toward an understanding of the basic act of caring.

Perhaps part of the misunderstanding surrounding care results from our being in a transition between paradigms. Thomas Kuhn describes the challenge: "Since new paradigms are born from old ones, they ordinarily incorporate much of the vocabulary and apparatus, both conceptual and manipulative, that the traditional paradigm had previously employed. But they seldom employ these borrowed elements in quite the traditional way. Within the new paradigm, old terms, concepts, and experiments fall into new relationships one with the other."[101]

What is striking about this paradigm shift is that it is a larger issue for moral philosophers than for common folks. In day-to-day interactions everyone understands the significance of caring, without, perhaps, identifying it. Care has always existed, for as I will elaborate later, it is a basic embodied quality. In some ways, the focus on care is not a paradigm shift at all but a rediscovery of something we have all known, perhaps at least in our bodies.

I have so far captured some of the essential themes in the proliferation of writing on care. I have identified a radical dimension to the discussion of care, for it challenges existing ways of thinking about morality, and offered a roadmap through the maze of contemporary characterizations of the concept. In the next chapter I will turn to Continental philosophy, specifically Maurice Merleau-Ponty's thoughts on the body, to identify a phenomenology of corporeal care to support and develop my notion of embodied care.

2. Merleau-Ponty and Embodied Epistemology: Caring Habits and Caring Knowledge

> The body . . . is wholly animated, and all its functions contribute
> to the perception of objects—an activity long considered by
> philosophy to be pure knowledge.
>
> —Maurice Merleau-Ponty, *The Primacy of Perception*

In the middle of his career William Shakespeare wrote *The Merchant of Venice*. Typical of Shakespearean comedies, *The Merchant of Venice* creates merriment through deception and romantic misunderstanding. One of the play's subplots, however, explores human prejudice and the need for revenge. Antonio, the merchant of Venice, is a Christian who lends money without charging interest because of the prevalent Christian belief that the Bible prohibits assessing interest on debt. Shylock is a Jewish moneylender who charges interest, similarly employing biblical grounds to justify his practice. Antonio publicly denounces both Shylock and the Judaism on which his practices are based. Shylock secretly loathes Antonio and seeks an opportunity to exact revenge. Just such an opportunity presents itself when Antonio's relative Bassanio seeks funds to properly woo the fair Portia of Belmont. Shylock offers to lend Bassanio the money if the loan is endorsed by Antonio as security. He demonstrates his good faith by declaring that the loan will bear no interest; should Antonio default, however, Shylock will extract a pound of flesh from him.

Anti-Semitism was rampant in England at the time *The Merchant of Venice* was written, so that a Jewish moneylender made a handy villain. Shakespeare adds complexity to Shylock's character, however, giving the moneylender appealing qualities. Shylock has suffered at the hands of Christians throughout his life, so he elicits a certain amount of sympathy. He garners further compassion by arguing, in one of Shakespeare's most quoted passages, that Jews and Christians share more than they do not: "I am a Jew. Hath not a Jew eyes? Hath not a Jew hands, organs, dimensions, senses, affections, passions? Fed with the same food, hurt with the same weapons, subject to the same diseases, heal'd by the same means, warm'd and cool'd by the same winter and summer, as a Christian is? If you prick us, do we not bleed? If you tickle us, do we not laugh? If you poison us, do we not die?"[1] Ironically Shylock voices this impassioned plea to justify his sadistic revenge against Antonio, but Shakespeare nevertheless constructs a masterful yet brief soliloquy that cuts to a common denominator of humanity: the body.[2] Beyond the socially constructed differences between Jews and Christians is the shared knowledge of embodied experience. Shylock's plea reminds us that everyone experiences and thus understands pain and pleasure. To circumvent the enmity between the Jews and Christians, Shylock appeals to an implicit shared knowledge, thus altering the moral dynamics of his situation. By recalling embodied knowledge, Shylock creates the possibility of shared understanding—a resonance—and therefore an opportunity for his Christian audience to care about him. Those who hear his rhetorical questions, whether they are the other characters in the play or the audience watching the drama, are compelled to answer yes. Shylock crafts an image whereby he is no longer wholly other—a moneylending Jew and therefore despised in a Christian community. He is a fellow human being, and the Christians he addresses can identify with what it is to have a body and feel through that body.[3] The shared corporeal resource to which Shylock alludes does not guarantee that the Christians will care for him, but by attending to and highlighting embodiment, he increases the chances that his auditors will reconsider their moral stance toward him. In attempting to capture empathy from those with bodies and bodily habits like his, Shylock recalls affective knowledge that goes beyond the words uttered. Shakespeare provides insight into the bodily basis of the human capacity to know and care for other embodied beings. The insightful work of Maurice Merleau-Ponty, to which I turn in this chapter, offers rich tools for exploring how the body can ground care.

In the rest of this chapter I will attempt to support three interrelated claims. (1) Knowledge is necessary but not sufficient for caring. (2) What "counts" as knowledge should include what the body knows and exhibits through habits. (3) Merleau-Ponty's corporeal-centered epistemology can be extrapolated to reveal the embodied, habitual basis of care. Ultimately I contend that Merleau-Ponty's epistemology demonstrates care to be a human capacity that can be developed or suppressed through habits, but in either case, care flows from the knowledge manifested in the body.

Phenomenology

> [Phenomenology] is a transcendental philosophy which places in
> abeyance the assertions arising out of the natural attitude, the
> better to understand them; but it is also a philosophy for which the
> world is always 'already there' before reflection.
>
> —Maurice Merleau-Ponty, *Phenomenology of Perception*

Phenomenology can be defined as the study of conscious experience, yet no
brief characterization of it can capture its depths of analysis. Don Ihde claims
that a true understanding of phenomenology can be derived only from "doing phenomenology."[4] It is a practice, a method of viewing or reading the
world, rather than a well-defined theory. As Merleau-Ponty describes it, *"Phenomenology can be practised and identified as a manner or style of thinking . . .
that . . . existed as a movement before arriving at complete awareness of itself
as a philosophy."*[5] Phenomenology is an inquiry into essences that attempts
to recapture primordial experiences by attending to the components and
sequences of action. Like care ethics, phenomenology addresses concrete
experience and therefore relies on description, stories, and observations.

The term *phenomenology* was first employed as early as the eighteenth
century,[6] but it was Edmund Husserl (1859–1938) who transformed phenomenology into a significant field of inquiry and influenced numerous later
philosophers, including Martin Heidegger, Jean-Paul Sartre, and Maurice
Merleau-Ponty. Husserl's view of phenomenology evolved over his career, but
he came to understand it as providing philosophy with a rigorous, system-
atic approach to epistemology.[7] Husserl attempted to eliminate intermediary understandings such that no presupposition is left untested: "Every thing
that makes philosophical beginning possible we must first acquire by ourselves."[8] Husserl offered the "phenomenological reduction" as a method of
looking past the cultural or constructed world to that of immediate experience. This approach requires a certain attitude toward that which is considered self-evident: suspending judgment (especially about the independent
existence of objects) and "bracketing" associated meanings to search for the
essence of phenomena. Husserl came to view phenomenological reduction
as the foundation of both philosophy and science.[9]

Maurice Merleau-Ponty (1908–60) described philosophy as "revealing how
to look at the work . . . [with] attentiveness and wonder . . . , never knowing where it is going."[10] Merleau-Ponty admired and built on Husserl's phenomenology. He shared Husserl's desire to overcome Cartesian and Kantian
subject-object dualism, but he followed his own distinct avenue of phenomenological inquiry.[11] Husserl explored conscious, cognitive acts, whereas

Merleau-Ponty was more concerned with preconscious and noncognitive practices. Although Husserl increasingly investigated the role of the body in overcoming subject-object duality, Merleau-Ponty's emphasis on the preconscious resulted in a more direct inquiry into the body. Accordingly, as much by his own interest as by the general lack of concern for the body among philosophers, Merleau-Ponty established himself as the great modern philosopher of the body. Remy Kwant views Merleau-Ponty as reshaping the field of phenomenology: "Undoubtedly philosophy has exercised great influence on him, but the reverse is also true. Merleau-Ponty's fundamental discovery is, as we have said, his theory of the body-subject."[12] Alphonso Lingis describes Merleau-Ponty's shift to the body-subject as overcoming a unique form of corporeal alienation: "Modern society is a society of alienation, not only alienating man from the instruments and resources of his labor and from the fruits of his labor, but also alienating him from his own body parts, forcing him to sell his arms, his back, his brain, his imagination to another."[13] Phenomenology is not particularly known for its ethical practicality, but here the neglect of embodiment at the theoretical level is tied to its sociopolitical implications.

Merleau-Ponty's work on the body is not without its critics. Elizabeth Grosz points out that a number of feminist philosophers find Merleau-Ponty's insights useful, but they are wary of the "apparently neutral sexuality of his claims."[14] Shannon Sullivan similarly views Merleau-Ponty as characterizing a universal, neutral body that eradicates important considerations of difference and helps support notions of atomistic selves.[15] To be sure, these are important and valid critiques, for Merleau-Ponty does ignore certain specificities of women's embodiment. For my purposes, however, a standpoint approach (and a dose of humility) should help avoid the solipsistic thinking and universalization that worry Sullivan and Grosz. I use Merleau-Ponty's phenomenology of the body not to create a totalizing theory of embodied care but to attend to the corporeal aspects of morality, which heretofore have been largely overlooked. Nevertheless, Sullivan's point should remain in the back of our minds as we review Merleau-Ponty's work: there is no essence of embodiment that can be separated entirely from the body's transactions with society.

Of central concern to developing a notion of embodied care is Merleau-Ponty's expansive treatment of knowledge and the body's role in creating, maintaining, and expressing knowledge through habits. Alternatively, some feminist philosophers, such as Luce Irigaray, Judith Butler, and Iris Young, advocate a reinterpretation of Merleau-Ponty to appropriate his insights, much as feminist have done with Freud and Marx.

Knowledge and Care

Knowledge is necessary for care because it is difficult, if not impossible, to care for someone or something that is entirely unknown. It is not, however, sufficient for care. With knowledge of the other comes only the *possibility* of care. Without some knowledge of the other, however, care is an impossibility.

Knowledge of another person or thing is thus positively correlated with the potential for care. In *On Caring* Milton Mayeroff lists knowing first among his major ingredients of caring: "To care for someone, I must *know* many things. I must know, for example, who the other is, what his powers and limitations are, what his needs are, and what is conducive to his growth."[16] As Mayeroff indicates, care and knowledge are intertwined. The more I know of something, the greater my potential for care; conversely, the more I care for someone, the more I want to know about him or her. International exchange programs are in part based on this concept. The more I get to know an exchange student from China, for example, the more likely I am to overcome preconceived notions about Chinese culture and to care about Chinese citizens as fellow human beings.

This integration of ethics and relational epistemology is consistent with Seyla Benhabib's notion of the "concrete other." Benhabib argues that one of the crucial differences between care ethics and more traditional approaches is that care does not posit an abstract, universal other but is animated by a particular, concrete other.[17] Margaret Urban Walker confirms the role of concretization through her claim that the "adequacy of moral understanding decreases as its form approaches generality through abstraction."[18] The process of concretizing someone is an epistemological move that requires increasing knowledge of an individual other in a relationship. As the details and specific context of people become increasingly known, they "come into view." They are no longer known only as abstract agents who are interchangeable with any others. They become persons with names, faces, bodies, and other aspects to which sympathetic identification gives us a connection. Caring is driven by relationships, and relationships with abstract others are vague. Traditional moral approaches based on principles or consequences have little regard for context or relationships, thus maintaining a level of generalized understanding of the agents involved. An injunction such as "thou shalt not steal" does not take into account the circumstances of the thief or the victim. Walker finds traditional justice approaches lacking in a grounded epistemic position, for abstract, interchangeable moral agents are "none of us at all times, and many of us at no times."[19] The impulse to care is bound up with knowing people such that they are concrete others, whether that concretization emerges from direct or indirect experience.[20]

The knowledge needed to care can be gained directly, as in first-person experiences, or indirectly though books or electronic media. In either case knowledge creates the potential for care. For example, it is difficult for me to care deeply about the general category "homeless people" abstracted from what I know of the homeless. My level of care might be raised through reading accounts of the conditions in which homeless people live. Alternatively, I might directly experience them by volunteering at a homeless shelter. Whether it comes directly or indirectly, as my knowledge of what it means to be homeless increases, my potential for care grows too. Of course, I may care for the homeless without direct or indirect experience, but I probably will not care about them much without the related knowledge to make the word *homeless* tangible for me.

This is an essential aspect of embodied caring: care is not a binary understanding. Although we may express sentiments categorically, saying, for example, "I care" or "I don't care," we seldom have caring feelings that are so discrete. Care exists on a continuum of both knowledge and disposition. I have greater connection to and knowledge of those about whom I care significantly. My experience of them makes them more concrete. Indeed, the kinds of experiences I have and the meaning I attach to them can drastically affect the care continuum. Concrete experiences make the caring choices clearer even in the face of other moral considerations.

An episode of the sometimes philosophically provocative television show *Star Trek: The Next Generation* illustrates the moral implications of concretization. The crew of the starship *Enterprise* belong to an organization governed by a noninterference policy known as the "prime directive": they are not to meddle with the natural and social development of less developed alien species (the antithesis of the Monroe Doctrine). In one episode the crew is studying a geologically unstable solar system.[21] They know that some of the planets have inhabitants that may be imperiled, but in accordance with the prime directive, they do not make contact or intervene. Nevertheless, one crew member, Data—ironically an android with no feelings—unwittingly makes radio contact with an alien child. They begin conversing, and she expresses fear over the geological activity on her planet. Data reassures her and starts up a brief correspondence. The captain is made aware of this violation of the prime directive, and after a heated debate where everyone hears a recording of the alien's voice, he decides to further violate the prime directive by assisting the imperiled aliens. What motivates the crew to transgress their lofty principle of noninterference? The Starfleet officers allow themselves to explore the meaning behind and experience of another being. The child's voice suddenly concretizes what has been an abstract understanding. They are no longer dealing with the abstraction of unknown aliens. A specific embodied subjectivity with a voice and feelings elicits a caring response.

Again, although knowledge is a *necessary condition* of care, it is not a *sufficient condition.* One can learn a great deal about a person (or an idea) without being moved to care or act. For example, one might investigate the life and motivations of a mass murderer. That investigation may lead to better understanding and perhaps even clarify causal linkages. Nevertheless, the knowledge need not lead to care. Knowledge only opens the window to the possibility of care, for as Sarah Hoagland declares, "Caring is a choice we make."[22] The decision may be more or less difficult, but there is always an element of choice.

Knowledge, however, is not homogeneous; there are different sorts. It certainly includes more than what has traditionally been called propositional knowledge, that is, knowledge of discursively statable facts. It further includes the affective knowledge found in our body and its habits. Susan Hekman describes the epistemology that informs modernist moral theories as assuming "a disembodied knower that constitutes abstract, universal truth."[23] Donna Wilshire agrees with this fairly common feminist critique of traditional epistemology, claiming that the Western tradition defines the objects of knowledge as the "publicly verifiable, provable, objective structure of reality (as in mathematics); facts, information."[24]

The body plays little or no part in traditional approaches to epistemology. Mark Johnson describes the "marginalized body" as part of a commonsense view that finds the world to be made up of all sorts of things, each of which is represented by signifiers familiar to our sense. Our minds are capable of manipulating these signs; therefore, knowing and reasoning are mental processes. Johnson finds this epistemology to be "disembodied in that the body has no constitutive role in characterizing the nature of meaning."[25] The traditional approach to epistemology privileges rational outcomes of the mind over what our bodies know. Again, knowledge is a prerequisite for care, but care is embodied, so that any epistemology capable of illuminating care must thus include corporeal knowledge.

A brief review of epistemology helps reveal why body knowledge cannot be ignored. Epistemology addresses both *what we know* and *how we know.* To say what we know is to identify the quality and quantity of our knowledge. To say how we know is to identify the path whereby we acquire knowledge. The what question and the how questions are interrelated in that our method of understanding influences the content of our knowledge. For example, we may experience another person through tactile, olfactory, and visual perceptions that, although we never articulate them, become part of our total understanding of that person. Accordingly, what we know depends on the resources available to our body. Merleau-Ponty goes further, claiming that ideas are body dependent: "The ideas we are speaking of [literature, music, the passions, and experience of the visible world] would not be better known to us if we had no body and no sensibility; it is then that they would be inaccessible to us. . . . they could not be given to us *as ideas* except in a carnal experience."[26]

The body also makes the resources requisite for care accessible. We perceive the world before we know it. The fact that knowledge of the world is filtered through the senses is not particularly controversial, but Merleau-Ponty extends this by positing the body's active role not only in obtaining knowledge but in retaining and using it:

> Knowledge and communication sublimate rather than suppress our incarnation, and the characteristic operation of the mind is in the movement by which we recapture our corporeal existence and use it to symbolize instead of merely to coexist. This metamorphosis lies in the double function of our body. Through its "sensory fields" and its whole organization, the body is, so to speak, predestined to model itself on the natural aspects of the world. But as an active body capable of gestures, of expression, and finally of language, it turns back on the world to signify it.[27]

Merleau-Ponty argues against the dualistic tradition of Western thought that valorizes the mind over the body. He demonstrates that the body is not simply the vehicle for acquiring knowledge but also a participant in creating meaning.

The knowledge necessary for care is more than a collection of discrete, articulated data; it includes a web of entangled feelings and subtle perceptions understood through the body. There is an affective dimension to knowledge that requires both the mind and the body. The affective aspect of knowledge—the unarticulated, felt dimension—makes caring possible. It is the kind of knowledge that makes Shylock's rhetorical arguments plausible. As long as Shylock is limited to the hated category of "Jew," the Christians feel little impetus to care. Once he becomes more than the pejorative moniker, and the Christians confront his shared humanity via his corporeal existence, he is less easily dismissed. Shylock's physical presence contributes to understanding him beyond the label "Jew" through affective resources found in the body. It is the embodied aspect of that knowledge that makes Merleau-Ponty's work so important for care ethics. In what follows Merleau-Ponty's de-

scriptions of bodily processes will reveal the means by which embodied beings have knowledge of the other as manifested by habits that reinforce and
contribute to the possibility of care.

Caring Knowledge and Caring Habits

Although Merleau-Ponty never developed a comprehensive moral schema,
his body-centered epistemology points to an approach to ethics. If "the body
is our general medium for having a world," as Merleau-Ponty suggests, then
the body must be our medium for having morality as well. Moreover, a body-
centered epistemology is incompatible with Western philosophy's traditional
notion of abstract ethics based in universal principles and truths. As Merleau-Ponty describes it, the body is radically contingent: "The things—here,
there, now, then—are no longer in themselves in their own place, in their own
time; they exist only at the end of those rays of spatiality and of temporality
emitted in the secrecy of my flesh."[28] For Merleau-Ponty, the body and the
world are caught up with each other. Merleau-Ponty thus provides the resources for an epistemology that animates the relationality found in care
ethics through habits of the body.

Caring habits can be exercised and broadened, or they can atrophy and
shrink. I have already intimated that the notion of bodily habits as I employ
it is rich and open ended. Consistent with my earlier claim that a focus on
care reframes moral considerations, thinking about habits in terms of embodied care may require setting aside preconceived ideas about the relation
between the mind and body. Merleau-Ponty recognized the radical nature
of his claim regarding the epistemic nature of habits: "The acquisition of
habit as a rearrangement and renewal for the corporeal scheme presents great
difficulties to traditional philosophies, which are always inclined to conceive
synthesis as intellectual synthesis."[29] For Merleau-Ponty, the body captures
meaning in the form of habit. Habit is more than just familiar movement,
however. There is an understanding, although perhaps unarticulatable, attached to the movement. Habits, then, are repositories of knowledge, but they
are also in flux. Habits are enacted in environments that change; thus, they
must adapt. What I have called caring habits comprise all those bodily movements that contain the body's understanding of how to care in and adapt to
new situations.

Three related aspects of Merleau-Ponty's phenomenology of the body help
further explicate his understanding of habit: perception, figure-ground phenomena, and the flesh. Each illuminates the complexity of the body's workings and the conditions that make caring habits possible.

Perception

For Merleau-Ponty, embodied knowledge begins with the centrality of perception. "All knowledge takes its place within the horizons opened up by perception."[30] According to David Abram, Merleau-Ponty understands perception as the "silent conversation" our body has with the world around it.[31] Abram's use of the term *conversation* reflects the interconnectedness that Merleau-Ponty finds in perception. *The Oxford Dictionary of Philosophy*, however, offers a definition of perception that reflects the traditional split between the known and the knower:

> Philosophy in this area is constrained by a number of properties that we believe to hold of perception.
>
> (i) It gives us knowledge of the world around us.
>
> (ii) We are conscious of that world by being aware of "sensible qualities": colours, sounds, tastes, smells, felt warmth, and the shapes and positions of objects in the environment.
>
> (iii) Such consciousness is effected through highly complex information channels, such as the output of the three different types of colour-sensitive cells in the eye, or the channels in the ear for interpreting pulses of air pressure as frequencies of sound.
>
> (iv) There ensues even more complex neurophysiological coding of that information, and eventually higher-order brain functions bring it about that we interpret the information so received.[32]

Note that this definition posits a world separate from the perceiving individual and that the details of perception become increasingly biological. Merleau-Ponty offers a more connected view that breaks down the distinction between the perceiver and the perceived: "Perception is not a science of the world, it is not even an act, a deliberate taking up of a position, it is the background from which all acts stand out, and is presupposed by them."[33] Whereas many philosophers have sought to compartmentalize epistemology with concepts such as perception, Merleau-Ponty is comfortable with the ambiguity that comes with embodied existence. He finds human perceptions to be not discrete but hopelessly interconnected. "Whenever I try to understand myself the whole fabric of the perceptible world comes too, and with it come the others who are caught in it."[34]

For Merleau-Ponty, perception is not an act of the mind separate from the body; subjectivity is physical. His theory of perception is intertwined with his theory of the body. The world cannot be perceived separate from the contribution of the body-subject:

The theory of the body schema is, implicitly, a theory of perception. We have relearned to feel our body; we have found underneath the objective and detached knowledge of the body that other knowledge which we have of it in virtue of it always being with us and of the fact that we are our body. In the same way, we shall need to reawaken our experience of the world as it appears to us in so far as we are in the world through our body, and in so far as we perceive the world through our body. But by thus remaking contact with the body and with the world, we shall also rediscover ourself, since, perceiving as we do with our body, the body is a natural self and, as it were, the subject of perception.[35]

Here Merleau-Ponty summarizes his corporeal epistemology and the central role of bodily perception. Attending to the body is not a process detached from understanding the world. Given his commitment to a phenomenological approach, Merleau-Ponty makes few prescriptive statements. In the preceding passage, however, he connects attending to the body and understanding ourselves. He suggests that we have lost something important by ignoring our corporeal existence. Accordingly, he acknowledges that heeding embodied knowledge is a choice. If we choose to attend to our bodies, we can "reconnect" with the world.

In valorizing the body Merleau-Ponty does not marginalize the mind but instead recasts it as inexorably intertwined with the body. Bodily perception opens the world to us, but the derivation of meaning still requires reflection and interpretation: "A perceived world would not appear to a man if these conditions were not given in his body; but it is not they that *explain* that world."[36]

Noddings claims that relatedness is ontologically basic to human existence.[37] Gilligan found in the different voice of care "the tie between relationship and responsibility, and the origins of aggression in the failure of connection."[38] Merleau-Ponty posits a theory of perception that is inherently sensitive to interconnectedness because perception cannot be separated from the body or the world. Perception thus creates a gestalt that includes explicitly articulated knowledge as well as tacit corporeal understanding. Our bodies' participation in providing the "other knowledge" that remains unarticulated creates attachments or webs of understanding that may be unnoticed but exist nonetheless. The information my body garners when confronting others—knowledge of their expressions, mannerisms, gestures, smells, and sounds—far exceeds what is available to my consciousness and allows me to know others as perceptual wholes. Our perceptions are rich and complex, providing an enormous amount of information and making it possible for us to care.

Merleau-Ponty shows us that moral dilemmas involve a plethora of perceptions, which makes formulaic ethics absurdly reductionist. The entanglements of humanity are simply more complex than justice approaches to morality can accommodate. Embodied care attends to some of that complexity, but there is a trade-off, for corporeal existence creates ambiguity, as Merleau-Ponty repeatedly acknowledges: "Ambiguity is the essence of human existence, and everything we live or think has always several meanings."[39] In *The Merchant of Venice* Shylock attempts to shift the Christians' perceptual focus away from socially constructed differences of religion and toward bodily similarities. At the level of embodied knowledge, Shylock's shift is not a drastic one. The Christians who have interacted with Shylock perceive from the unarticulated interplay of bodies (e.g., shaking hands, walking, standing, and conversing) that bodily continuities exist: Shylock has a human body that acts like any other. His rhetorical move is to point out what they already know and perceive in their bodies—namely, that he is a fellow human being with feelings and desires similar to their own. He wants them to care. Merleau-Ponty's notion of perception, then, is a bedrock concept from which the idea of caring habits can be built. Ultimately the body uses a myriad of habits in helping to create the world that it knows and navigates.

Merleau-Ponty thus provides an account of perception that traverses the classical epistemological divide between the knower and the known. The body, with its ability to collect both propositional and affective knowledge, constitutes the vehicle for the expanded epistemology Merleau-Ponty offers. Understood in this expansive way, perception makes it possible for us to have and utilize caring habits of which we may not be entirely aware. Those who are described as caring in our society are often those people who can "sense" the needs of another and respond accordingly. This sensitivity is not magic but a skill or habit of social interaction that embodied persons can develop. Some have honed these habits of care through modeling or conscious effort. Accordingly, the body perceives the other not just with empirical data but also with affective, disruptive knowledge that can elicit visceral responses leading to habits of care.

What Merleau-Ponty has described as the manner in which the body perceives is a foundational habit of care. It can be built on to create more complex habits of care. For example, the way the body perceives subtleties in others—sometimes from a single instance—can contribute to complex caring responses and habits such as those found in parenting.

Figure-Ground Phenomenon

Merleau-Ponty describes perception as rooted in a figure-ground structure: to perceive an object is to discriminate it from all the perceptible objects presented at a given time. The body not only makes this discrimination possible but also participates in the process by placing itself in either the fore-ground or the background. Given the manner in which the body operates, the historical lack of attention paid to the body's role in perception is un-derstandable. The body, as Merleau-Ponty describes it, "effaces itself" at the moment of perception.[40] The human body is capable of allowing our con-sciousness to attend to immediate activities while remaining oblivious to the finer motor tasks and background activities required. Merleau-Ponty de-scribes this thematization as the figure-ground structure of perception or perceptual focus.[41] The perceptual disappearance of the sense organ is signifi-cant to Merleau-Ponty because it instantiates the subjectivity of the body: "In so far as it sees or touches the world, my body can therefore be neither seen nor touched. What prevents its ever being an object, ever being 'com-pletely constituted[,]' is that by which there are objects. It is neither tangible nor visible in so far as it is that which sees and touches. The body therefore is not one more among external objects."[42]

When I watch fireworks in the sky, I am not thinking about how my eyes are operating; instead, I am caught up in the experience of the event. My body works in the background to place perception at the foreground. Merleau-Ponty observes that "my body does not perceive, but it is as if it were built around perception that draws through it; through its whole internal arrange-ment, its sensory-motor circuits, the return ways that control and release movements, it is, as it were, prepared for a self-perception, even though it is never itself that is perceived nor itself that perceives."[43] This perceptual fo-cus opens the world to the body. It makes externality and therefore our knowledge of the world possible.

The body's recessive quality, its ability to focus consciousness on the per-ceptible world, does not consign it to a passive role. Our body constantly operates to allow us to maintain perceptual focus. These operations of the body that allow us to be in the world also fuel the "other directedness" that is an integral part of care. Nel Noddings describes "engrossment" as an in-tense preoccupation with the other that comes with caring: "I receive the other into myself, and I see and feel with the other. I become a duality."[44] For Noddings, caring cannot occur without such engrossment: "At bottom, all caring involves engrossment. The engrossment need not be intense nor need it be pervasive in the life of the one-caring, but it must occur."[45] Merleau-Ponty's notion of figure-ground interactions provides a useful way of fram-ing Noddings's understanding of engrossment. To be engrossed one must be outwardly focused, not attending to the minutiae of personal bodily habits. The body has the spectacular ability to place itself in the background and put the other in the foreground.[46] It is not that the body does not continue its perceptual dance with the environment; rather, conscious attention is focused outward, making it possible to care for an other.

The phenomena that Merleau-Ponty describes as the body's being built around a perceptual focus also establish the body as built around care. When confronted with another person, my senses focus on the other, and I become part of the background. The other is the foreground, or source of perceptual focus. This transition makes care possible. Earlier I established that knowledge of particular others is important for care. The ability to pick the subjectivity of another embodied being out of a flood of perceptual data is similarly crucial for care. When another embodied being enters the room, he or she immediately stands out as more than just another object in my sphere of perception. Such others are indeed objects, but they also present themselves as sharing the subjectivity I have. Care would be difficult without the foreground-background distinction to restrict the myriad objects that would otherwise equally vie for my attention. Fortunately their embodiment makes them stand out in my perceptual sphere as possible subjects for complex relationships that may include care, differentiating them from, say, a chair, with which I cannot have a rich relationship. The focus phenomenon facilitates many different types of actions, but it is important for caring knowledge because it allows us to attend to other embodied individuals as objects and subjects.

So far I have addressed care only in regard to activities in the foreground, but embodied care can be part of the background, too. In a caring relationship my body collects a variety of sensory information, including visual, tactile, and olfactory data of which I may be largely unaware. My mind-body will fill in missing data about the other. For example, a synchronicity of habitual caring develops between bodies that spend a great deal of time together. Familiar bodies require less of the explicit communication of language as each body "reads" the other's nonverbal communication with increasing nuance. A facial expression or gesture that is ambiguous to a stranger can communicate a specific message between intimates. The perceptual foreground of the other in a caring relationship transfers knowledge to the perceptual background in the silent dance that occurs between the bodies involved. The foreground perceptual focus of a parent and child may be on a bedtime story, but the background interaction of bodies hugging each other tacitly communicates love, tenderness, and security. As Gail Weiss indicates, "To raise a child . . . is not a matter of 'shaping a mind' but rather . . . arises out of an embodied exchange."[47]

The foreground-background phenomenon thus contributes to Merleau-Ponty's corporeal-centered epistemology by explaining how the human body can focus attention and learn about the particularity of other embodied beings. The phenomenon is in a sense a primordial habit of the body that makes other caring habits possible. For example, listening is an important act of caring, and there are numerous subtle habits that both enable and attest to listening. The foreground-background phenomenon is crucial for establishing care in listening. Other stimuli (other conversations or the speaker's loud tie) must be blocked out, as must be internal distractions (my hunger or need to use the bathroom), to make authentic listening possible. Merleau-Ponty's foreground-background focus also explains how the body can nurture a caring relationship through the unspoken background caring phenomena occurring between bodies. The perceptual focus phenomenon is another example showing how the human body is built around the possibility of caring. Without the ability to focus, habits of care would be rendered moot. I must be able to identify my partner as more significant than the chair on which she is sitting or the pencil she is holding and as requiring a more complex set of caring habits than does a chair or pencil. Fortunately, as Merleau-Ponty demonstrates, our bodies help us make this crucial distinction.

The Flesh

Another resource for caring habits found in Merleau-Ponty's work is the slippery notion of the flesh, which overcomes the boundaries of individualistic epistemology in the Western philosophical tradition. Although Merleau-Ponty claims that metaphysics is mere coincidence (because meaning beyond the physical world is tenuous to a phenomenologist), the flesh provides a metaphysical, an epistemological, and an ethical understanding that flows from our corporeal existence but extends beyond it. The flesh is much more than skin. In Merleau-Ponty's words, "The flesh is not matter . . . , not fact or sum of facts 'material' or 'spiritual' . . . [;] the flesh is in this sense an 'element' of Being."[48] The flesh is our entrée into the lifeworld. Part of that lifeworld is other embodied persons. The corporeality of humanity is interconnected and intertwined through the flesh : "There is finally a propagation of these [tactile] exchanges to all the bodies of the same type and of the same style which I see and touch—and this by virtue of the fundamental fission or segregation of the sentient and the sensible which, laterally, makes the organs of my body communicate and founds transitivity from one body to another."[49] Merleau-Ponty here characterizes experience as open-ended both temporally and physically with regard to other bodies. Any experience I have is integrated with previous experiences, giving rise to structures and patterns that are further blended with the experience of others in the ongoing emergence of intersubjective meaning. For Merleau-Ponty, intersubjective meaning gives rise to the possibility of thought: "One must see or feel in some way in order to think, that every thought known to us occurs to a flesh."[50]

The flesh constitutes subject and object in an ambiguous relational moment enabled by human embodiment as experienced, for example, when one of my hands touches the other. My hand can experience both being touched and touching, but this experience is not temporally unified, for I do not perceive touch and touching in the same instance. According to Merleau-Ponty, "It is a reversibility always imminent and never realized in fact."[51] This reversibility creates reciprocity, or "weaving relations between bodies."[52] The flesh, however, also constitutes subject and object in the void between the touching and the touched, between subjective and objective experience. The flesh spans or bridges these experiences to provide us with holistic meaning. "My flesh and that of the world therefore involve clear zones, clearings, about which pivot their opaque zones."[53] According to Galen Johnson, "The genius of Merleau-Ponty's name for Being, Flesh, is that it gives us a flesh-and-blood feel and smell for what Time is. . . . The flesh is flesh and blood Time. It is the explosion of seed pods, united and separated, it is the dehiscence of the colors of fire, it is the labor of pregnancy, the joy and pain of new life and separation, it is the shock of death and the work of mourning and grieving. . . . Flesh is the name for the ontological hinge on which the outside passes over to the inside and inside passes over to outside."[54] Our bodies make participation in the flesh of the world possible.

Every sensory experience I have from birth contributes to my knowledge of my body, both tacit and explicit. I learn habits that allow me to interact and move through my environment, adapting as I go. The flesh as Merleau-Ponty describes it, however, allows for continuity over time, space, and individual bodies. Merleau-Ponty explains, "My body is made of the same flesh as the world (as it is perceived) and moreover this flesh of my body is shared by the world."[55] Because I share a corporeal existence with other beings, we to some extent share sensory perceptions and understandings. This continuity is not a perfect colonization of others' experiences—or as Merleau-Ponty describes it, "not yet incorporeal"—but an extrapolation that is much more than abstraction. It is an "intercorporeal" understanding.[56] The experience of the other becomes a "generalized I" of unrealized potential in all my own experiences.[57] The flesh is a powerful nexus between what it is to be other and what it is to be me. In the words of David Abram, "Humans are tuned for relationship. The eyes, the skin, the tongue, ears, and nostrils—all are gates where our body receives the nourishment of otherness."[58]

What Merleau-Ponty has described in the reversibility and intertwining of the lifeworld through the flesh can be extrapolated to provide a basis for corporeal understanding of care. Because of the ambiguity of subject and object in my body's experience of its perceptual world, I am able to perceive and reflect on my own body. It may slip into invisibility when I focus on sensory experience, but awareness of my own body always resurfaces. The body's reversibility not only allows it to open the world to me but also allows me to view my body as an object in that world. As Merleau-Ponty describes: "There is a circle of the touched and the touching, the touched takes hold of the touching; there is a circle of the visible and the seeing, the seeing is not without visible existence; there is even an inscription of the touching in the visible, of the seeing in the tangible—and the converse."[59] When the flesh confronts other bodies as objects in the world, its reversibility allows for an ambiguous, limited understanding of the other body. The other body that I perceive is also subject and object. I recognize its form (a body) and movement (its habits), and immediately I have a level of shared knowledge that is both tacit and explicit. When my body confronts another, even if it is a foreign body attired and socially constructed differently from my own, there is still a fundamental connection and understanding in the flesh that Merleau-Ponty refers to as the "propagation" of bodily experiences. If a knife accidentally cuts that other body, I do not have to ask whether pain was felt. My own aggregate experiences and the continuity of the flesh tell my body that pain comes with such a violation. An affective or felt response precedes any reflective consideration of the circumstances. I will engage in instinctive bodily responses, such as wincing or gasping, because of the common bond of embodied experience that we share prior to my fully contemplating the meaning of what has transpired.[60] Corporeal knowledge creates the potential of sympathetic perception that makes care possible.

In Merleau-Ponty's notion of the reversibility of the flesh, my body is both subject and object, both active and observed, the toucher and the touched; my disposition toward my body is not neutral. Under most circumstances I do not place my body in harm's way. I do not routinely allow my body to burn itself or cut itself except by accident. I care for my body. Although I make many errors of judgment or give in to excesses from time to time, I generally make decisions for my body's benefit, and my body directs me toward acts that allow it to thrive and flourish. The ambiguous continuity of the flesh extrapolates my positive affective relationship with my body to other "bodied" people. I not only recognize that others will have an analogous regard for the well-being of their bodies but also extend those feelings to other bodies. Merleau-Ponty died before he could fully develop his radical theory of intersubjectivity, but this notion of embodied care appears consistent with his robust notion of our interconnectedness. He claimed that others "are not fictions with which I might people my desert—offspring of my spirit and forever unactualized possibilities—but my twins or flesh of my flesh."[61]

Merleau-Ponty's notion of the flesh, which continues to be a source of philosophical speculation, has intriguing implications for the radical inter-connectedness of the world. The relational knowledge inherent in such a connection of intercorporeality provides another avenue by which the po-tential for caring knowledge and caring habits may be found. Because of the continuity of the flesh, the meaning attached to movements of my body cre-ates the potential for the understanding of others. As the Christians observe Shylock through his soliloquy, they may invest unspoken meaning in his various movements that reveal familiar habits of pain, sorrow, anger, or even revenge. His words are important, but so is the shared grasping of his bodily habits.

Although Merleau-Ponty's concept of flesh is an "ultimate notion" that breaks down discrete categories, such as that of subject and object, it is not intended to elide the alterity of the other. Experience is perceived individu-ally: "I perceive the other as a piece of behavior, for example, I perceive the grief or the anger of the other in his conduct, in his face or his hands, with-out recourse to any 'inner' experience of suffering or anger. . . . the grief and the anger of another have never quite the same significance for him as they have for me. For him these situations are lived through, for me they are dis-played."[62] Between the experience and its meaning for the other, on the one hand, and my grasp of it, on the other, lies a gap I can never entirely ford. As part of the flesh of the world, however, I have an "echo" or "trace" of under-standing. Ambiguity reigns once again. The alterity of the other is preserved, but not in a strictly solitary way.

So the body's ability to focus and differentiate certain objects, such as other embodied creatures, is crucial for caring knowledge to take place, but Mer-leau-Ponty's concept of the flesh takes the focus phenomenon one step fur-ther. Not only is another embodied being different from other objects, par-ticularly in terms of a caring response, but because of the continuity of the flesh, my affective understanding of the embodied being is enormously en-hanced. I know about being cut and bleeding. I know about a comforting hug. I know about hunger. I know about the warmth of a smile. I know about embarrassment. I know about supportive voice inflection. The whole of this knowledge cannot be quantified or easily described in words, but my body knows these things. Given the intertwined nature of the flesh, to a certain degree I know these same things about other human bodies. Because of this knowledge, caring habits are not foreign to me. I can grasp in and for the other what I have grasped in and for myself. There is an internal "logic" to caring habits. They make sense for others because they would make sense for me and my body given similar circumstances. Flesh is thus a significant epistemological component of care, which is why I began this discussion by suggesting it grounds an ethical understanding as well. The intercorporeal epistemology offered by the flesh becomes of moral importance if relationality is the basis of ethics, as it is in care-based approaches.

Caring Habits

Intertwined with perception, foreground-background focus phenomena, and the flesh is Merleau-Ponty's notion of bodily motility and habit. For Merleau-Ponty, movement provides one means for being in the world, and habits are those patterns whereby the body captures movement and, in its interactions in the world, gives movement meaning. Habit is a type of embodied knowledge. My hands have acquired the habit for removing screws with a screwdriver. To remove a screw, you need only apply the screwdriver's blade to the screw's head with sufficient force and rotate the screwdriver in (usually) a counterclockwise fashion. My hands can perform these actions without conscious calculation. The habit has become so automatic that I have forgotten the attending descriptions. If someone asks me the direction one turns a screwdriver to loosen a screw, my hands make the habitual motions, and then I recall that the answer is counterclockwise. Merleau-Ponty claims that "it is the body that 'catches' (*kapiert*) and 'comprehends' movement. The acquisition of a habit is indeed the grasping of a significance, but it is the motor grasping of a motor significance."[63]

This habitual bodily knowledge remains unthematized unless we make the effort to attend to it, yet we cannot navigate in our environment without it. Every day we employ hundreds of habitual activities "known" to our bodies. Merleau-Ponty offers the example of typing: "To know how to type is not, then, to know the place of each letter among the keys, nor even to have acquired a conditional reflex for each one, which is set in motion by the letter as it comes before our eye. If habit is neither a form of knowledge nor an involuntary action, what then is it? It is knowledge in the hands."[64] Unfortunately the language of possession ("I know this or that") is too limiting for what Merleau-Ponty is addressing. The body's affective knowledge is less explicitly discrete than propositional knowledge and therefore often not entirely possessed. Consider, for example, one's knowledge of state capitals: you know either all, some, or none. Compare that to the embodied meaning found in the habits of a handshake or a kiss, for example, which is less articulated than experienced.

Do our bodies also know habitual activities of care? Of course. There are arms that know how to comfort, hands that know how to share joy, and faces that know how to express rapt attention. These are not instinctual activities but learned (and learning) behaviors that exhibit care. Nel Noddings makes a gesture toward habits of care when she addresses skills: "There is a dimension of competence in caring. . . . My engrossment and motivational displacement push me to acquire skills in caring. But it is important to recognize that they *are* skills."[65] Caring habits are often performed without much reflection, but attending to them reveals a richer notion of moral knowledge. If my daughter hurts herself and cries, I comfort her by hugging her body. This is not a habit in the sense of a repeated motion such as typing, but my body has captured the subtle movements necessary to communicate care.[66] My arms do not squeeze her forcefully, as if I were holding a fifty-pound sack of potatoes. My arms do not jostle her as if we were roughhousing. My arms gently caress in a manner that reflects the concern and affection appropriate for the moment. I move into her personal space and apply just the right amount of pressure with my hands and arms to pull her close to my chest. The hug may last only seconds, and few words may pass between us, but important knowledge is transferred. My daughter and I will not consciously attend to all the subtleties of the physical movement. These movements are not overdetermined. My habits of care take on a certain disposition and tone, but they also respond to the situation. I do not announce, "I am putting my arm around you now for the purposes of comfort." My thoughts are all focused on the event that has occurred and the task of comforting my daughter. My tone of voice will reflect my concern. In addition, I not only communicate care but also model a habit that her body catches. If she is exposed to this model of caring repeatedly, she will likely employ this habit when confronted with a similar circumstance. In this manner habits of care pass embodied knowledge from parent to child.

Of course, not all habits are caring habits. For the sake of my analysis, habits can be divided into three categories: acaring, noncaring, and caring. An acaring habit is a morally neutral pattern the body uses to navigate its environment. My aforementioned example of screws and screwdrivers is useful but morally uninteresting. Noncaring habits are those that harm an other embodied being; examples include spousal abuse, child molestation, and acting out road rage. Caring habits are those that exhibit a regard for the growth, flourishing, and well-being of another. Subtle practices such as gentle tactile interactions, a soft tone of voice, or a nod of the head, as well as more complex interactions such as tending to the sick, cradling a baby, or teaching someone to read, can exhibit care. In either case they become habits through repeated use and application to new situations. Nevertheless, disagreements about habits of care can still arise. For example, many parents consider spanking to be an appropriate part of a child's training, while other parents abhor it as an inappropriate use of power.[67]

I earlier argued that caring is a choice, and autonomy remains even with the bodily habits of care just described. Sometimes, as when we comfort a child, caring behavior appears to be more instinctual than chosen, but this appearance is deceiving. There may be situations where I choose not to employ bodily habits of care. If my daughter is testing the boundaries of sympathy, as children are apt to do, and repeatedly cries for trivial reasons, I may decide that I should not be so comforting, although I will continue to care. Under normal circumstances I comply with the impulse of my body, but caring and its commensurate behaviors are always chosen. This example demonstrates the intertwining of embodied and cognitive knowledge. My habitual knowledge of comforting interplays with my cognitive recollections and understanding of cause and effect to shape my behavior.

* * *

A comprehensive study of Merleau-Ponty's insight into embodiment and intersubjectivity could fill volumes. What I have explored here are three central elements of his analysis—perception, the figure-ground phenomenon, and the flesh—which provide a robust understanding of our bodies's capabilities for learning and exercising the habits of caring. Merleau-Ponty addresses the reversibility of the flesh as both subject and object, touched and touching. There is also reversibility in the experience of embodied care. Ideally the earliest experiences of human bodies are those of being nurtured: being fed, burped, hugged, and so on. Although caring for is most pervasive with infants and children, our experiences of another's care for us are often entangled with corporeal interaction such as a touch or a hug. We "learn" the habits of caring for others by being cared for ourselves. As is true of other aspects of our embodied epistemology, some of what we know about caring can be articulated, while other aspects of caring remain a tacit knowledge of the body. In the words of Michael Polanyi, "We can know more than we can tell."[68] If Merleau-Ponty is right about reversibility, then there is a certain necessity about applying what we know through caring habits in interpersonal relations that structure our family, community, and society.

Human interaction thus creates "moments" of care. Situations of dependence, interdependence, teaching, collegiality, and the like can be described as moments when care is possible. Although care can permeate our interactions, it is distinct from interaction and gets its moral dimension at these moments.

To illustrate how care maps onto a particular interaction, I offer the example of teaching my daughter to ride a bike. The knowledge necessary to ride a bike is largely contained in the body and therefore difficult to articulate. The requisite balance, momentum, and coordination needed to ride a bicycle can be learned only through practice and the acquisition of habits. Once the body "learns" to ride a bike, that knowledge is not easily lost. Bike riding offers an interesting case for applying Merleau-Ponty's understanding of embodied knowledge, and it is consistent with many of the examples he offers, but for my purposes I want to focus on the subtle interaction between my body and my daughter's body as she learns to ride. As she first begins pedaling, I stand close by, ready to catch her if she falls. I place my hand on her back, partly to facilitate catching her but also to let her know that I am there. My voice is reassuring yet determined. Our conscious attention is on the task at hand—learning to ride a bike—so that the subtext of the dance between my body and my daughter's goes largely unnoticed. She wobbles and reaches for me, and I grab her. She falls and cries. I hold her, comfort her, and inspect the scrape. My daughter is explicitly learning how to ride a bike but implicitly learning how to care. Her body is capturing the motions and knowledge necessary for bike riding at the same time that it is capturing the tactile and auditory cues for caring knowledge. Because there is a reversibility to care, what my daughter learns from me contributes to her embodied resources for caring for others.[69]

This example highlights how the body adds both content and process to care. Although the body is the vehicle by which we demonstrate care to one another, it is also the primary focus of care. When I am caring for my daughter as she learns to ride her bike, I am caring for her body: trying to keep her from harm while allowing her some independence so her body can learn a skill. This demonstrates the difference between care and overprotectiveness. I could achieve the goal of keeping her from harm by never allowing her to ride a bike, but the opportunity to grow and learn requires risk. Nonetheless, I do not just give her a bike and leave her alone. I facilitate her growth and flourishing at this new skill by providing an early safety net. These values foreshadow the interdependence that will be the hallmark of a caring social philosophy. While learning to ride a bicycle has little moral significance, knowing how to convey care to others is of paramount importance in human interaction. The explicit interaction was merely teaching a new physical skill, but it became another moment for invoking caring habits.

The Knowledge That Animates Care Is in the Body

The factual presence of other bodies could not produce
thought or the idea if its seed were not in my own body.
Thought is a relationship with oneself and with the world as
well as a relationship with the other.

—Maurice Merleau-Ponty, *The Visible and the Invisible*

Gail Weiss argues that morality cannot be reduced to an intellectual endeavor. Although feminist care ethics has offered viable alternatives to rationalist approaches to morality, Weiss claims that "the body's role in calling us to respond ethically to one another has continued to be egregiously neglected."[70] Because Merleau-Ponty calls for philosophers to reacquaint themselves with the body, his work can be an important vehicle for the kind of analysis Weiss desires. It has been my contention that Merleau-Ponty's philosophy of the body provides an epistemological foundation for a notion of embodied care—particularly in what I have called habits of care. More than any other philosopher, Merleau-Ponty demonstrates the crucial role of embodiment in structuring knowledge and deriving existential meaning. Merleau-Ponty describes the bond "between the flesh and the idea, between the visible and the interior armature which it manifests and which it conceals."[71] There is a presumption of knowledge in care ethics, for we cannot care for that for which we do not know. Merleau-Ponty expands the definition of knowledge beyond explicit rational considerations of the mind to implicit knowledge grounded in bodily habits. The elaboration of an embodied epistemology is a significant step in developing a comprehensive understanding of embodied care. Through its habits the body participates in perception and meaning making as part of the flesh of the world. Thus, the body is not merely a vessel for sensory input. Caring habits and caring knowledge are inexorably linked.

The question remains: if embodied knowledge provides the necessary resources for caring, how do we care for "distant" others—those of whom we have little direct experience or knowledge? This leap of care in alterity is the starting point for the inquiry into the caring imagination.

3. Caring Imagination: Bridging Personal and Social Morality

Whether we can conceive of a way to think of morality that extends some form of sympathy further than our own group remains perhaps the fundamental moral question of contemporary life.
—Joan Tronto, *Moral Boundaries*

The moral analysis of the Holocaust can never be exhausted, nor should it be. Although care ethics attests to the notion that morality is more than events, the enormity of the Holocaust's human suffering will continually motivate ethicists to understand the precipitating dynamics and work to ensure that the tragedy is never replicated. Hannah Arendt (1906–75) attempted to make sense of the senselessness of the Holocaust. An activist and philosopher with a tremendous intellectual pedigree (her teachers and mentors included Rudolf Bultmann, Martin Heidegger, and Karl Jaspers), Arendt, a German Jew, narrowly escaped long-term incarceration and possible execution by fleeing to the United States in 1941. She established herself as a scholar in exile, authoring numerous articles and books on the human condition, many of which dealt with the ethics and circumstances of the Holocaust.

Arendt's experience and analysis of the trial of Adolf Eichmann provides a challenging opportunity for understanding the dynamics involved in caring for unknown others. In 1961 Arendt went to Jerusalem to report on the trial of the Nazi war leader for the *New Yorker*. In a controversial report, she judged the term *trial* to be something of a misnomer.[1] Arendt described the unfolding of a grand legal drama prompted by a brutally harmed people seeking vindication. In the words of David Ben-Gurion, then prime minister of Israel, "It is not an individual that is in the dock at this historic trial, and not the Nazi regime alone, but anti-Semitism throughout history."[2] Adding to the buildup and drama over the trial, Eichmann had been captured and extradited from Argentina eleven months previously. Eichmann was alleged to have been the mastermind and administrator of the Final Solution—the extermination of six million Jews in Europe. The trial was expected to bring justice to an evil beast: a larger-than-life monster responsible for one of the worst massacres in modern history. In Eichmann, however, Arendt saw a bespectacled, balding, inarticulate bureaucrat sitting behind a glass booth built for his protection. For Arendt, Eichmann's responses revealed not an evil mastermind but instead someone who did not fathom his situation or its moral consequences. Far from a commanding figure, Eichmann struck Arendt as being intellectually lost outside the rhetoric and culture of the Nazi organization. The Nazis had valorized a way of being—certain habits—that had made Eichmann a leader. Removed from that context, he was rather unexceptional: "Despite all the efforts of the prosecution, everybody could see that this man was not a 'monster,' but it was difficult indeed not to suspect that he was a clown."[3]

Embodied care requires a caring imagination if we are to move beyond caring only for that of which we have direct experience. I will elaborate the caring imagination later, but one of its major aspects is empathy: affective responses to an "other" that integrates knowledge and emotions to better apprehend their situation and feelings. Arendt's account of the Eichmann trial identifies at least two incidents that evoke the caring imagination's role in empathy. One is found in the relationship between Arendt and Eichmann; the other, in the relationship between Eichmann and the Jews. Arendt did not have a face-to-face conversation with Eichmann, but the trial provided a forum to "meet" him through his testimony. Arendt was confronted with a visual and auditory experience of Eichmann.

Applying the work of Merleau-Ponty to Arendt's sensory experience, we can say that she entered into a "sympathetic relation" with Eichmann.[4] The understanding described here is more than what might traditionally be called "rational reflection." According to Merleau-Ponty, "There is a natural attitude of vision in which I make common cause with my gaze and, through it, surrender myself to the spectacle."[5] Because we can know what transpired only through secondary accounts, we are not privy to the unarticulated, embodied dimension of Arendt's experience. Eichmann was confronted as a flesh-and-blood person sitting on trial rather than a mythologized figure of evil. The testimony, combined with her own investigation of his life, elicited in Arendt an empathetic response for Eichmann in the sense that she better understood his feelings and experience. He became less of a mystery and more of a person with a life story or narrative, albeit a reprehensible and unreflective one. Arendt's understanding was not based simply on accumulating facts, although they helped. Arendt made an embodied connection.

Arendt's analysis on seeing Eichmann in person, listening to his voice, and observing the habits of his body confirms my conclusion in chapter 2: an embodied dimension to knowledge informs care. This knowledge is affective and holistic, as Merleau-Ponty claims: "Though perception brings together our sensory experiences into a single world, it does not do so in the way that scientific colligation gathers together objects or phenomena."[6] For Arendt, seeing and listening to Eichmann transformed him from an unknown other, for which wild speculation was possible, to a better-known other who had a face, a body, and certain habits that were in continuity with the rest of humanity and thus shared the subject-object position that all people have. Arendt allowed her imagination to entertain a degree of speculation as to what Eichmann's existence was like.[7] This imaginary speculation is not binary or exclusionary: it does not, for example, negate Arendt's compassionate disposition toward Eichmann's victims. Her understanding of Eichmann does not excuse his atrocities or make him any less culpable; it merely reveals that another human being who shared much of our embodied existence was responsible. Arendt observes, "The deeds were monstrous, but the doer—at least the very effective one on trial—was quite ordinary, commonplace, and neither demonic nor monstrous."[8] Perhaps Arendt's revelation that Eichmann was not exceptional is more horrific than finding an evil, wholly other entity culpable would be, because in the imaginative understanding of Eichmann there is some human continuity: a connection in the flesh.[9]

The question of the caring imagination arises again in the relationship between Eichmann and the Jews. In this case there is a complete failure of the imagination. Eichmann's testimony drove Arendt to see what she refers to as the "banality of evil." Arendt describes this evil as a lack of empathetic reflection: an inability to think through other people's subject position. "The longer one listened to him, the more obvious it became that his inability to speak was closely connected with an inability to *think*, namely, to think from the standpoint of somebody else."[10] An important element of care is missing. Eichmann, of course, had a human body with all its capacities for caring. In addition, court-appointed psychologists declared him mentally fit. Nevertheless, propaganda, bureaucracy, and an underdeveloped imagination truncated his capacities for and habits of caring. Arendt recognized that his imaginative capabilities were somehow defective, preventing him from affectively understanding the enormity of his acts: Eichmann "*never realized what he was doing.* It was precisely this lack of imagination which enabled him to sit for months on end facing a German Jew who was conducting the police interrogation, pouring out his heart to the man and explaining again and again how it was that he reached only the rank of lieutenant colonel in the S.S. . . . . He was not stupid. It was sheer thoughtlessness."[11] Arendt's discussion of the Eichmann trial provides a glimmer of the complexity of embodied care. Certainly Eichmann had experienced enough killing firsthand to have had embodied knowledge of such violence. Nevertheless, an imaginative link was missing, or a tremendous barrier had been built that retarded his caring ability and habits regarding those who suffered around him and those for whom he caused pain. In this chapter I will argue that imagination is a crucial component of caring—an argument consistent with Arendt's discovery of the "banality" or unimaginative aspect of evil.

* * *

My previous phenomenological analysis of the corporeal dimension of care stressed the epistemological aspects of embodied experience that inform habits of caring. Much of the emphasis in this approach is on the direct experience of the other in a relationship that creates the potential for caring. This phenomenological analysis demonstrates how caring is a bodily potential and is therefore a moral resource available to embodied humans through habits that can be developed or left dormant. When considered in isolation, however, a phenomenology of embodied care suffers a significant limitation. If all human caring were reduced to direct bodily experience, then care ethics would be parochial. Caring would at best be limited to those of whom we have direct knowledge. But this is simply not the case. We are capable of caring for the lives of endangered African elephants, young girls who face the horrors of genital mutilation in foreign lands, and people displaced by civil unrest in distant continents. We are even capable of caring for fictional characters, as when the plight of a novel's protagonist brings us to tears. These instances require overcoming great physical, social, or temporal distances, so how is such care possible if the body plays such a prominent role in caring? The *caring imagination* allows us to bridge the gaps between ourselves and unknown others and helps place our caring in psychosocial contexts. This claim need not conflict with the previous chapter's argument that the body plays a crucial epistemological role. Caring imagination is a product of the mind and body working in harmony. The body provides an array of knowledge that creates imaginative possibilities. The type and degree of that knowledge will affect one's ability to imagine. Indeed, our imagination is embodied as well.

Embodied care requires imagination to overcome the limitations of physical existence. As individual human beings with discrete bodies, we are separated from one another by time, space, and socially constructed differences.

Even our closest intimates do not share the same body. We use imagination to traverse those distances and make caring possible. As Merleau-Ponty indicated, my body may apprehend another's habits or movements to reveal that the other is an embodied subject and object like myself,[12] but knowing how another might feel or think or how best to proceed in a given situation requires applying imagination to the information given in perception. There is an imaginative dimension to caring.

The caring imagination includes three aspects: empathy, critical reflection, and psychosocial context. Although care is grounded in embodied experience, it transcends the body through the imagination. This transcendence is not another mind-body dualism; rather, the mind and body work together to inquire into possibilities outside (but known through) direct immediate experience. The three forms of imaginative transcendence will be explored in turn: imagination as empathy, which transcends both physical and social distance; imagination as critical reflection, which transcends time; and imagination as understanding the caregiver's psychosocial context, which transcends the personal subject position. The added understanding of imaginative processes in embodied care will establish an important link between habits of care, discussed earlier, and a social ethic of embodied care, discussed in the next chapter.

Why *Caring* Imagination?

> While the practice [of care] involves moral imagination, this moral imagination is directed by a concern to advance the good of the other(s) in the context of a network of care.
>
> —Rita Manning, *Speaking from the Heart*

What I call "caring imagination" shares much with what many philosophers call moral imagination, and so this chapter will explore various works on moral imagination to help define the connection to care. Still, I selected the term *caring imagination* rather than *moral imagination* to reframe the imaginative processes in terms of an overarching consideration of care, which, as I have argued, is a bedrock of human existence and therefore the foundation of morality. The term accomplishes two purposes. First, it helps synthesize "empathetic" and "rational" approaches to imagination.[13] Some, such as David Hume and Adam Smith, claim that the imagination fosters sympathy or empathy; others, such as Kant, claim that imagination is an extension of reason. I contend that both claims are true of the caring imagination. As a result, such approaches to imagination should not be thought of as mutually exclusive or competing models; rather, they elucidate aspects of the imagination. Second, the term *caring imagination* suggests that embodied care is the "glue" that keeps these approaches to imagination together. Care is a basic aspect of human morality, but (as I will argue in this chapter) so too is imagination. Nevertheless, care and imagination should not be viewed as separate components of morality. Care and imagination are integrated within the body. Habits of care "hold" knowledge of what it is to care, but the imagination is also present, because that knowledge must be applied to new and unknown situations. Care and imagination are closely allied concepts.

To explain more fully what I mean by caring imagination, I will briefly review two major approaches to imagination taken in the Western tradition of philosophy. The first approach is to view the moral imagination as enabling sympathy. Arendt's critique of Eichmann exemplifies this view because she claims that he lacked the imagination to understand what the Jews experienced.[14] Hume and Adam Smith[15] participated in the eighteenth-century fixation on the imagination's role in sympathy. Hume declared sympathy to be "the conversion of an idea into an impression by the force of imagination."[16] For Hume, sympathy is a derivative of the imagination that is crucial for morality. James Engell claims that Hume initiated the eighteenth-century fascination with sympathy that swept philosophy and literature: "Hume jolted the scene. He challenged the concept of thought as distinct from emotion not merely because he reveals that thought calls on emotion and passion, but also because he shows the extent to which thought and feeling—under the sway of imagination—are intrinsically connected."[17] Hume's notion of sympathy, like care, is emotive: a commingling of thought and action. As such, it is difficult to separate sympathy from care. Consider a caring relationship, such as a parent-child relationship: it is difficult to imagine the habits of caring without the integral element of sympathy. Without using the language of care, Hume identified a moral element in sympathetic fellow feelings.[18] The term *caring imagination* explicitly acknowledges the sympathetic element of the imaginative.

Adam Smith similarly finds a sympathetic transference: "By the imagination we place ourselves in [a sufferer's] situation. . . . we enter as it were into his body and become in some measure the same person."[19] Although he does not explore the corporeal possibilities, Smith repeatedly hints at an embodied sympathetic imagination. For Smith, our imaginations can elicit an affective and even visceral response: "The mob, when they are gazing at a dancer on the slack rope, naturally writhe and twist and balance their own bodies . . . as they feel that they themselves must do if in his situation."[20] Smith is not describing a merely mimetic response, a copying of another's behavior. He is referring to the caring imagination working through the body to understand and be concerned for another. Smith and Hume exemplify the sympathetic approach to moral imagination.

Immanuel Kant espoused the second major approach to imagination. As one might expect, given his antipathy for Hume's approach, Kant does not view the imagination as fostering empathy. For Kant, imagination serves reason. Kant attempted to develop a moral philosophy that was entirely a priori: "All moral concepts have their seat and origin entirely a priori in reason."[21] For Kant, reason alone determines what constitutes the ethical. Of course, the fundamental tension in the Kantian approach is that ethics is lived and practiced in the physical world, so how does a priori morality interface with human existence? To solve this puzzle, Kant offers the imagination as the human faculty where an application or schematization can take place: "A schema is a universal procedure of the imagination in presenting a priori to the senses a pure concept of the understanding which is determined by law."[22] For Kant, the imagination does not invoke sympathetic feelings, but it does allow for the rational application of principles. Imagination provides the crucial structure mediating between a priori rules and lived experience. Kant's view of imagination differs markedly from Hume's and Smith's; Kant's approach is rational, not affective or embodied. Nevertheless, it highlights another form of imagination in the application of the abstract to sense experience. The connection between care and sympathetic imagination is more readily apparent, but a caring imagination need not preclude the imaginative consideration of moral context in the manner that Kant formulates it, albeit without the disembodiment that Kant espouses.

These two views of imagination fit a pattern of binary understanding: emotion versus reason, Hume versus Kant, feminine versus masculine, body versus mind. I propose a caring imagination that transcends such dichotomies. The caring imagination integrates the emotive possibilities of sympathy and the reflective application of reason, just as embodied care combines the physicality of caring habits with the affective responses to others.

The Caring Imagination: An Integration of Three Roles

Like care, imagination is an often-overlooked aspect of ethics. Despite the previously cited excerpts from Hume, Smith, and Kant, the Western canon of philosophy centered on teleological, deontological, and virtue ethics seldom employs imagination in any significant way. A close examination, however, reveals that imagination plays a crucial role in animating morality and, in particular, in our ability to care for unknown others.[23] Again, one function of imagination is creating the possibility for *empathy*. As I propose it, however, the caring imagination does more than just permit empathy. It has at least two other functions. One is a *critical thinking and critical application* function. Caring responses are not always prereflective. Recall Noddings's distinction between natural and ethical caring. For Noddings, ethical caring involves reflection and decision. In many cases the caring imagination allows the mind to carry out possibilities in the moral context of a given situation, thus transcending the moment. Rules and consequences may be considered in this process, but care is always present. For example, as a caring father I am predisposed to keep my daughter from physical and psychological harm. For the past several years my daughter has chosen to sing in school talent shows. I initially wanted to discourage her because of all the anxiety and potential for public embarrassment. I wanted to protect her from harm. On reflection, however, I realized that personal growth comes only with a certain amount of risk. As a caring parent I of course should encourage her to take such chances, all the while being available to support her along the way. My caring imagination had to play through the scenarios and their attending implications to choose a course of action. Consequences were considered, but care was always present.

Caring imagination also provides a sense of balance among competing emotive pulls. Critics of care ethics often worry that caregivers can be lost in the impulse to provide for others, resulting in an unhealthy and perhaps exploitative situation for the one giving care. Historically this has been the case for women, who most often assume, or are saddled with, the role of caregiver—many times at the exclusion of other possibilities. As I will argue later in this chapter, a caring imagination allows for the self-reflection that can view caring in the context of a web of relationships, not with an objective, God's-eye view, but with a healthy sense of ego and balance. As Merleau-Ponty points out, we have the ability to see ourselves as both subject and object. As an object I can have a sense of my place within a given context. The caring imagination can allow caregivers permission to care for themselves. I will refer to this as the *psychosocial role* of the caring imagination.

Caring Imagination as Empathy: Transcending Distance

The human imagination is complex and embedded with metaphysical qualities. It is capable of reaching out through time and space. In this section I will address one aspect of that reaching out: our ability to empathize with those outside our immediate experience,[24] where the imagination transcends distance to help create the potential for care through empathy. The distance to which I refer is both physical and social. When significant physical distances are involved, creating the potential for care can require imaginative intervention, as when North Americans come to care about those affected by famine in Ethiopia. At other times the gulf may be not physical but social, as in the misunderstandings between the Korean and African American communities of Los Angeles. Extending care into new particularities or new situations often requires a translation, but not the one-to-one correspondence of a phrasebook. When we come to care about that which we have experienced only indirectly or not at all, the caring imagination draws from its wealth of tacit body knowledge to make the connecting leap. In Merleau-Ponty's words, the imaginary "finds in the body analogues of itself that incarnate it."[25] Although Merleau-Ponty does not address empathy directly, his phenomenology of the body implies the presence of empathy. For example, the continuity of the flesh implies a fundamental connection among similarly embodied beings that creates the possibility of empathy.

Several feminist philosophers identify the empathetic aspect of the imagination and make the connection to care. For example, in *Care and Moral Motivation* Debra Shogan views imagination as crucial for empathy. The imagination, in her view, allows us to understand what it is like to be someone in a given moral circumstance. She distinguishes between objective imagination and subjective imagination. The former involves, say, visualizing the physical characteristics of someone or something; the latter involves trying to understand what it is to be a given person in a given situation.[26] Subjective imagination includes trying to understand how someone feels, thus highlighting the emotive aspect of caring. To a certain extent Arendt attempts to subjectively imagine what it was like to be Eichmann. Recall that she claims he "never realized what he was doing"; Arendt could not know this with certainty, but her imagination made this projection based on her response to his words and habits. Shogan acknowledges the epistemic aspect of embodied imagination because she notes that it is much more difficult to imagine what it is like to be strangers than it is to imagine what it is like to be family or friends. "Subjective imagination is limiting when it comes to imagining what it is like for a particular person to flourish if one does not know what counts as flourishing for that individual."[27] The proximate knowledge breeds clearer imaginative possibilities.

Again, Hume's extensive exploration of the imagination as empathy exhibits some concerns similar to those that surround embodied care. Hume claimed that moral sentiments or fellow feelings were natural: "When I relieve persons in distress, my natural humanity is my motive."[28] Yet Hume found that people do not always act on their moral sentiments. He acknowledged a gap between the "extensive sympathy on which our sentiments of virtue depend, and that limited generosity which I have observed."[29] Similarly, in chapter 2 I characterized care as a human potential that stems from embodied existence but insisted that caring actions are always a choice (i.e., we do not always act on our caring inclinations). Although Hume recognized that moral sentiments involve imagination, he was dubious about our ability to care for distant others. "We sympathize more with persons contiguous to us, than with persons remote from us: With our acquaintance, than with strangers: With our countrymen, than with foreigners."[30] The idea that we could care for distant others was such a barrier to Hume that he limits his theory of moral sentiments to interpersonal relations and develops a separate social-political philosophy. As Joan Tronto observes, "Indeed, the problem of distance and of increasing distance is so serious for Hume that it gives rise to one of Hume's most important contributions in political and moral theory: his account of the nature of justice, and its relation to benevolence."[31] Hume gave imagination an important role in the empathy needed for morality, but his caring imagination has significant limitations.

Considering embodied care as previously developed, Hume's doubts about the extent of moral imagination are understandable. For example, Hume states that "the imagination is more affected by what is particular, than by what is general."[32] This is consistent with what I have claimed about the embodied epistemology of care. Sense perceptions provide the particular experiences from which the imagination can extrapolate. This also fuels the idea that we empathize with those close to us more easily than we do with those at a great distance. Although the language of imagination permeates Hume's notions of moral sentiments, it is a limited imagination that requires the intervention of a system of justice to account for distant others. Hume also lacks any attachment to the embodied aspect of morality. Nevertheless, Hume was one of the first philosophers to consider the link between empathy and imagination.

Edith Stein (1891–1942) employed a phenomenological approach to identify the corporeal aspect of empathy. Stein was Edmund Husserl's prize student and assistant. She is most often remembered because of her conversion to Catholicism, her death at Auschwitz, and a subsequent beatification process that was the subject of some controversy. In any event, she wrote several significant philosophical works, including her dissertation, *On the Problem of Empathy*, in 1917.

The motivation for Stein's work can be traced to Husserl's dialogue with Theodor Lipps. According to Lipps, three categories of knowledge exist: self-knowledge, knowledge of objects, and knowledge of human beings. Lipps claims that self-knowledge is attained through reflection, and knowledge of objects comes through sense perception, but knowledge of other human beings requires empathy, which he described as an instinctive projection of personal experiences into an external body. Husserl rejects the idea that sensations can be experienced immediately without first experiencing the other as a body-subject with a point of view. Husserl's notion of empathy evolved later in his life, and part of that evolution included extensive interaction with Stein. Although Stein and Husserl agreed on methodology, Stein was more interested in creating a philosophical anthropology. Her project was to develop a theory of personhood foregrounding empathy as the structure of intersubjective experience. The similarities and differences between Husserl and Stein came to light in Stein's dissertation. Although she employs "eidetic reduction," the phenomenological search for essences, she does not entirely suspend existential considerations in her approach to empathy. Stein wished to discover what empathy is, not how humans derive empathetic awareness:

> Let us take an example to illustrate the nature of the act of empathy. A friend tells me that he has lost his brother and I become aware of his pain. What kind of an awareness is this? I am not concerned here with going into the basis on which I infer the pain. Perhaps his face is pale and disturbed, his voice toneless and strained. Perhaps he also expresses his pain in words. Naturally, these things can all be investigated but they are not my concern here. I would like to know, not how I arrive at this awareness, but what it itself is.[33]

In her analysis of the empathetic phenomenon, Stein distinguishes between "primordial" and "non-primordial experience."[34] The friend's pain is primordial for the friend but not for me, because I did not experience the pain directly. On Stein's account, however, the empathy that I feel for my friend's pain is primordial for me. We can never experience another person's pain primordially because that would require a single identity: we would then be that person.

For Stein, empathy makes intersubjective experience possible:

> Were I imprisoned within the boundaries of my individuality, I could not get beyond "the world as it appears to me." At least it would be conceivable that the possibility of its independent existence, that could still be given as a possibility, would always be undemonstrable. But this possibility is demonstrated as soon as I cross these boundaries by the help of empathy and obtain the same world's second and third appearance which is independent of my perception. Thus, empathy as the basis of intersubjective experience becomes the condition of possible knowledge of the existing outer world.[35]

Stein's argument supports my contention that empathy as part of the caring imagination makes care possible. Because the other's experience is not primordial to me, my imagination must create empathy to bridge the gap of alterity. That empathy does not arise magically but is grounded in my own experience and caring habits. Stein does not employ the term *imagination* as Hume does, but the language of transcendence is implicit in the previously quoted passage. According to Stein, imagination lets us transcend our individual experiences or "boundaries" to empathize with others. The mind and body work together to make this imaginative leap, or transcendence, possible. My body has primordial experiences that provide the imaginative basis for affectively understanding possibilities.

Whereas Hume argues for the role of the imagination in empathy, Stein reasserts the role of the body in claiming that all psychic phenomena are bound up with embodiment.[36] Each of these approaches contributes to understanding the caring imagination. Feelings and experience interact at the body's zero point: "We always experience general feeling as coming from the living body with an accelerating or hindering influence on the course of experience."[37] Feelings are expressed through the body and ultimately motivate action.[38] Imagination, accordingly, is not simply a creative faculty but a fully cognitive process that emerges from our lived and affective experiences. For Husserl and Stein, embodiment becomes important in the epistemological significance of empathy in two ways. First, it is the sensory cue for a subjective other or ego stream. One cannot see another's ego, but one can see another's body. Second, the body becomes the nexus of experience as both object and subject in the lifeworld. Intersubjective experience without corporeality is unimaginable; no longer is a disembodied Cartesian thinker possible. The *cogito* is incarnate in phenomenology. Embodiment is a necessary condition of the ego.[39] Given the ontological and epistemological significance that Stein ascribes to the body, it follows that the body should play an important role in ethical theory, too.

Although Stein was not interested in showing how empathy arises in individuals, Mark Johnson's work on moral imagination helps explain how the body makes the translation between what Stein called primordial and nonprimordial experience. Whereas Hume places imagination at the forefront and Stein emphasizes the body's role, Johnson addresses both. Johnson cites empirical evidence that "the embodiment of human meaning and understanding manifests itself over and over, in ways intimately connected to forms of imaginative structuring of experience."[40] Human imagination needs a basis for organizing meaning, and it finds a starting place and structure in the body. The perceptual interactions, spatiality, and motility of our bodies within our specific environments provide that structure through "image schemas." Johnson posits metaphors as the principle cognitive method for extending embodied structures to abstract concepts. The body's physical experience of the world provides certain structures of understanding. For example, our bodies contend with gravity from birth. Much of our activity is associated with standing up or otherwise resisting gravity. Our bodies understand what it is to move vertically.[41] Johnson contends that our imaginations use this embodied knowledge, which I have claimed is contained in caring habits, to comprehend other aspects of our experience. For example, verticality can be mapped onto morality: we speak of "high" and "low" moral characters.[42] Metaphor enables our imaginations to transcend domains in the application of meaning. The use of linguistic metaphors provides a clue to the deeper metaphoric structures of the imagination.

With respect to understanding the caring imagination, Johnson's notions of mapping and domain transfer are more significant than is his moral theory per se. Because caring offers more than just another moral theory, Johnson's approach to metaphorical understanding need not be incompatible with care. The idea of domain transfer fills an important gap in the notion of embodied care that enables empathy. Johnson has demonstrated how our bodies structure information in meaningful ways and how, through metaphor, those structures provide meaning to phenomena outside the originary experience. This domain transfer can be extended to care. The body's experiences of care within its physical sphere can sometimes be mapped on to knowledge of distant events in a metaphorical manner. For example, numerous programs across the United States pair troubled, incarcerated youth with animals.[43] The young people are usually asked to care for the animals long enough to form a relationship that elicits affective responses. Such programs do not seek to train future farmers or veterinarians. In effect, these kids are purposefully given an opportunity to experience embodied care so that they can apply the structures of experience or habits of care developed with animals to other situations. Such children, who otherwise lack analogous caring experiences, can thus experience the care and understanding of animals as an embodied metaphor for caring for people.

Johnson describes moral development as rooted in the emergence of prototypes within human experience.[44] A prototype is a member (e.g., beagle) of a category that is an imaginative concretization of that category (e.g., dog). These prototypes can become linked to essential moral concepts, such as justice and fairness. Prototypes almost always develop from experience to concept; one usually experiences a particular dog before understanding the general category of dog. Johnson's notion of prototype can be applied to care.

Children directly experience care prior to developing the concept of care. One does not attempt to teach children an abstract definition of care, because there is too much tacit and affective knowledge tied up with the prototype of care. Instead prototypical experiences of caring habits ("Remember how I took care of you when you were sick?") are used to flesh out an understanding of care. Johnson notes that these prototypes are not static: "A central part of our moral development will be the imaginative use of particular prototypes in constructing our lives. Each prototype has a definite structure, yet that structure must undergo gradual imaginative transformation as new situations arise. It thus has a dynamic character, which is what makes possible our moral development and growth."[45]

The human capacity for moral imagination allows for the extension and expansion of ethical prototypes manifested in the body as caring habits. The capturing of a caring habit is not merely a rote skill of repetition, such as juggling or tying shoelaces. The caring habit is integrated with imagination to make it adaptive to new situations. When activated by empathy, the imagination applies prototypical caring habits to a new situation. I may never have been sexually abused, but when confronted with someone who is telling me his or her story of abuse, my imagination calls on the bodily resources I do have to give me a glimmer of understanding. The encounter may elicit a set of caring habits that affect my eye contact, facial expressions, posture, tone of voice, and words that I use. If my imagination can make the empathetic linkage, then my prototypical caring habits can be adapted to the situation. I may make mistakes. I may feel awkward, but I will adapt my caring habits the best that I can. Merleau-Ponty writes of an imagination intertwined with the body—a bond between the flesh and the idea.[46] David Abram refers to the integration of imagination and bodily habits as transcendence: "a capacity of the physiological body itself—its powers of responding to other bodies, of touching, hearing, and seeing things, resonating with things. Perception is the ongoing transcendence, the ecstatic nature of the body."[47] We cannot dissociate the creative capacity of the mind from the body's ability to radiate beyond itself.

The empathetic component of a caring imagination is crucial in extending care to those for whom we have little knowledge. The move from the known to the unknown is an important component of moving embodied care from a personal ethic to a social ethic. If we cannot employ imagination and metaphor, then care cannot underpin a viable social ethics, because members of a society are constantly confronted by new and unknown others on whose behalf they must consider acting. Whether the context is voting, social work, or merely social discussion, citizens confront issues concerning others who identify with different races, classes, conditions, and experiences. If we cannot imaginatively empathize, then we will have great difficulty understanding and caring about these foreign others. Even though there had been a thriving Jewish population in Germany, Eichmann and the other Nazis viewed the Jews as distant others to whom their caring imaginations did not extend. Empathy did not take place; caring habits were not engaged.

Distance is only one dimension our imagination can traverse; there is also the challenge of time.

Caring Imagination as Critical Reflection on Moral Context: Transcending Time

Not only can we empathetically imagine what it is like to be another person (although never with perfect precision); our imaginations are capable of numerous other simultaneous activities, too. One such capacity is our ability to reflect on moral context. This imaginative reflection includes the consideration of socially constructed ethical systems, such as rules and rights. For these systems to be fully considered, present events must be projected forward in time. The caring imagination will temper these reflections in regard to the central concern for relationship. In this respect the caring imagination bears some similarity to the Kantian notion of imagination, whereby an application of moral rules can take place. Nevertheless, although the caring imagination can consider rules and consequences, such considerations never supersede care and its agent, empathy. As part of the imagination's ability to critically reflect on a situation, these considerations are not an abandonment of the body. Even today, the long shadow of Descartes means that considerations of the mind and considerations of the body are often taken as mutually exclusive. Merleau-Ponty, who posits an intertwined flesh of the world, finds the need for meaning derived from reflection: "A perceived world would not appear to a man if these conditions were not given in his body; but it is not they that *explain* that world."[48] Human bodies help constitute meaning, but that meaning is not always immediate or complete, thus warranting further reflection.

Consider the example of the prohibitively expensive drug referred to in chapter 1 (the "Heinz" case);[49] if I, as the husband, steal the drug, how will my actions affect my wife and my relationship with her? To better understand the people involved, I can empathize with their feelings and situation. Depending on how well developed my imagination is, I can consider any number of paths. The imaginative consideration of consequences or rules does not negate embodied care. Care is always present as the foundation of my ethical consideration, but it does not preclude me from considering established ethical systems. As Manning indicates, "Even where we can adopt a model of caring, we are morally permitted and sometimes obligated to appeal to rules and rights."[50] In the Heinz case my primary concern is for my wife, but I do not exist in a moral vacuum. I recognize the druggist and any other party to the situation as agents who deserve my consideration as well.

Critical reflection in the context of a caring imagination can take the form of considering creative alternative actions or applying moral theories, but the subtext is care. This discussion of critical reflection and care is consistent with Virginia Held's claim that "care and its related considerations are the wider framework—or network—within which room should be made for justice, utility, and the virtues."[51] Again, care offers more than just the basis for a competing moral theory. Our imaginative capacity to consider the moral context, including justice, utility, and virtues, within a caring perspective is consistent with that view. In the Heinz case caring can structure and inform the reflection but does not preclude my weighing of socially established ethical approaches. Of course, a caring approach will eliminate certain courses of actions. For example, killing the druggist to obtain the drug would be inconsistent with embodied care. It would satisfy my impulse to help my wife, but it would violate my intersubjective corporeal continuity with the druggist. When it comes to rules and consequences, I do not violate social standards willy-nilly, yet they do not supersede my embodied care. For example, I do not wish to trample on the socially established property rights of the druggist; however, I will not let rules or consequences have final moral authority. As previously mentioned, embodied care is not a moral theory, so that applying it to a particular case often frustrates the traditional search for a cut-and-dried answer. As the subsequent chapters' discussions of Addams's social theory of care and same-sex marriage will show, care hints at relevant issues instead of providing universal causes of action.

The critical reflection aspect of caring imagination takes the long-term view without losing sight of immediate needs. Whereas empathy is often reflexive, critical reflection on the moral context extends the caring over time to consider other results.[52] Sometimes the empathetic response is enough; indeed, sometimes it must suffice because immediate action is required—rendering first aid, say, to someone just injured. At other times the caring response may require some reflection on alternative courses of action. For example, social issues such as teenage drug abuse are complex and require some consideration of the moral context. The caring imagination can play out various scenarios into the future to determine the most appropriate response.

Among others, Hume claims that imagination allows us to bridge time.

We can forecast what will happen if present events run their course and act out of the compassion that such imagined situations elicit: "'Tis certain, that sympathy is not always limited to the present moment, but that we often feel by communication the pains and pleasures of others, which are not in being, and which we only anticipate by the force of imagination. For supposing I saw a person perfectly unknown to me, who, while asleep in the fields, was in danger of being trod under foot by horses, I shou'd be actuated by the same principle of sympathy, which makes me concern'd for the present sorrows of a stranger."[53] Here Hume addresses the role of imagination in projecting into the future. He can see that the course of events left uninterrupted would result in the crushing of the sleeping stranger. What Hume does not mention is that the imagination also serves an empathizing and affective role in the recognition of physical continuity. Hume does not have to wonder whether the stranger lying in the field will be hurt and feel pain. As Merleau-Ponty's intertwining of the flesh indicates, the man watching the field knows implicitly, in his own body, that it is another embodied creature like himself who will suffer terribly if there is no intervention. Sympathy as Hume describes it transcends time, but only if present circumstances are known. In the example given, the knowledge is proximate, derived from the physical presence of the observer. Hume makes the epistemic connection found among later feminist philosophers, "'Tis certain, that the imagination is more affected by what is particular, than by what is general."[54] As we move away from our present circumstances in time, space, social standing, and so on, the imagination must work harder to sympathize with the other.

Hume observes that people often sympathize with others yet do not act on their behalfs. There is a pragmatic element to Hume's understanding of imagination's relation to morality. Although the imagination allows us to make causal connections, thus helping sentiments move us to action, it can also limit us by bringing social standards to bear on our moral reflection. If, for example, I see another person's car has broken down, my imagination helps frame the situation. Reason is mingled with imagination, but all are circumscribed by care. Do I have a duty to help, or are the consequences too risky? I care about what happens to this unknown person, but I care for myself, too.

Reflection on moral context influences caring habits just as caring habits influence moral reflection. Action and reflection reside in a dynamic, reciprocal relationship. Again, care ethicists valorize context and experience, and this is reflected in the caring imagination and the resulting habits. For example, Robert Balmer, engaged in some public reflection on caring in an editorial that appeared in the *Oregonian:* "Why I Stopped Giving Money to

Panhandlers."[55] Balmer recounts giving money to a stranger who showed up at his house one day. Balmer felt very positive about the interaction until the man began returning, some times inebriated, asking for additional funds. After numerous unsavory encounters, Balmer resolved never again to give money to panhandlers. Balmer's original actions reflect caring habits: Balmer treated the stranger as someone he knew and trusted, and he sought to help him out of a difficult situation. The unpleasant result, however, influenced his reflection on such caring acts. This experience jaded his imagination, and giving money will not become a habit for him. Balmer has determined that the negative consequences are too steep: he took a risk and got hurt. While it may be unfair to judge every request for money from an unknown other based on one experience—a kind of ethics by anecdote—it does demonstrate how caring habits and the imagination mutually influence each other. This is a dynamic relationship, and another experience may someday alter what Balmer imagines as the possibilities for panhandlers. For the present, Balmer does not see money as contributing to the growth and well-being of the other, so giving money is not an act of care for him.[56]

The caring imagination's ability to reflect critically on the moral context demonstrates that embodied care is not antithetical to ethical systems, but it does balance them against supererogatory considerations.

Caring Imagination as Addressing Psychosocial Context: Transcending the Personal Subject Position without Negating It

One criticism of care ethics stems from the primacy of relationship. Some feminists are concerned that women or members of other oppressed groups that emphasize care may fall into the trap of being so other directed in their caring that they will not act strongly enough on their own behalfs: a kind of selfless behavior to which social constraints have often limited women in particular. For example, Sarah Hoagland is unimpressed by Nel Noddings's claim that we must care for ourselves. "Although Nel Noddings argues that we take care of ourselves, the moral basis for this is to become better onescaring. Thus we have an other-directed justification for self concern that can encourage false information about what counts as health as well as what counts as moral good."[57] Hoagland contends that reciprocity in caring relationships is romanticized and that the current understanding of care as a feminine characteristic supports oppressive social systems. The caregiver (often a woman) may put a great deal of time and effort into caring for another without ever receiving any care in return. For Hoagland, the one-sidedness of care is personally and politically dangerous: "The unidirectional nature of the analysis of one-caring reinforces oppressive institutions."[58] Hoagland refers to care as an ethics of agape, borrowing the ancient Greek notion of brotherly love. She finds agape to be directionally distinct from eros, which she defines as self-centered love. Hoagland fears that care has the potential to maintain an oppressive gendered division of labor because it encourages love of others over love of self. Hoagland is not anticare per se, but she believes it carries historical baggage that is difficult to shed.

Michelle M. Moody-Adams offers a similar concern: "A conception of the self as defined not through separation from but through interconnection with others is oddly unhelpful in deciding what is morally wrong with rape, abuse, and sexual harassment."[59] Moody-Adams is concerned that a morality based on relationality offers insufficient protection for individuals, unlike rights based ethics, for example. The presumption in all these criticisms is that an ethics based on relationality and caring for others lacks the resources for a healthy ego and motivation for action on behalf of the self. This is an important concern, particularly considering how women have historically been asked to put others first.

I believe Hoagland's and Moody-Adams's concerns can be addressed by a well-developed caring imagination, which can transcend the personal subject position without sacrificing the self. That is, the caring imagination lets us view ourselves as both subjects and objects and thus see ourselves as objects of care.

As the earlier discussion of Merleau-Ponty's phenomenology of the body indicated, we can perceive ourselves as both subjects and objects, the toucher and the touched. The perceptual framework of our bodies makes the double understanding of the subject-object position of human beings possible. This perceptual double standpoint opens up the potential for reflexivity. If we can perceive ourselves as both subjects and objects, then we can also reflect on ourselves as both subjects and objects. Just as my perceptual awareness of other human beings triggers an understanding of their potential needs and opens the possibility for my caring for them, my awareness of my own body allows for imaginative consideration of my needs and how I might care for myself. Moody-Adams's and Hoagland's concerns are legitimate, but a self-reflective caring imagination can diminish the possible loss of self in caring because my embodied self is a primary object of my care. Shannon Sullivan argues that proper attunement to the body breaks down the dualism between caring for oneself and caring for others. According to Sullivan, caring only for others is a self-defeating proposition: "Self-neglect not only prevents one from caring for oneself, it also prevents one from effectively caring for others."[60] Part of that attunement to the body is an imaginative empathy for oneself.

Edith Stein's work on empathy, too, is useful in understanding how a caring imagination can transcend the personal subject position without getting caught up in caring for the other. Stein's concept of empathy does not negate the self but actually strengthens self-concept: "We also see the significance of knowledge of foreign personality for 'knowledge of self' in what has been said. We not only learn to make us ourselves into objects, as earlier, but through empathy with 'related natures,' i.e., persons of our type, what is 'sleeping' in us is developed. By empathy with differently composed personal structures we become clear on what we are not, what we are more or less than others. Thus, together with self-knowledge, we also have an important aid to self-evaluation."[61] The interplay of subjects in empathetic relations allows for continual self-assessment and self-development. If a close friend loses a loved one, my empathetic responses may tell me something about myself. I may have a variety of caring responses, but I can have several self-reflective ones as well. For example, I may ask myself if I am taking my loved ones for granted. The caring imagination integrates concern for others with concern for self. There is no reason caring habits cannot include caring habits for oneself. Stein's analysis shows that a caring imagination need not result in the loss of self. Although Stein does not intend to explore moral implications, if the empathy that accompanies intersubjective experience results in the stronger development of self, and if this is considered a good, then it would follow that we should seek out intersubjective experience to facilitate this process. In the next chapter I explore the work of Jane Addams to develop this theme.

Nevertheless, claiming that a healthy imagination should include considerations of the self cannot assuage Hoagland's politically charged concerns. Hoagland would likely grant that a caring imagination can include the self but add that social structures have historically closed this possibility to women. Hoagland views a capitalist, patriarchal society as positioned to exploit those who care. For example, Hoagland describes the "double bind of heterosexism" as the expectation that a woman must "attend to everyone else's projects... [but] has no final say in how they are realized."[62] Hoagland's concerns are certainly valid, as history evinces them to be, but she appears to assume that care is limited to personal morality. True, a personal approach to care morality can be subsumed and appropriated by an overarching system of justice. As Gilligan has argued, when care is understood within a justice framework, it simply supports justice with notions such as mercy, which leave the justice system intact and unchallenged.[63] Nevertheless, embodied care can be understood as the basis for a viable social ethics that can reshape how we understand social institutions, as the next chapter, on Addams, will demonstrate. In other words, care can be understood not as a tool for the status quo but as disruptive moral knowledge that can infiltrate and transform existing social systems in the form of social habits. Addams's philosophy and activism thus contribute a social dimension to care that can address Hoagland's critique.

I mentioned earlier that the caring imagination is a complex interplay of many faculties, including empathy, critical reflection, and psychosocial concerns. The American pragmatist and social psychologist George Herbert Mead provides a link between empathy and psychosocial concerns. Mead offers a method for understanding the self as an object of imagination in his notions of "play" and "game." Mead refers to play as an imaginative empathizing technique that we employ at an early age to try out roles. Caring for others includes an element of play, where we "try out" the other person's feelings and perspectives (often with visceral responses). As Mead points out, such play need not result in a loss of self: "The process is one which develops, to be sure, into a more or less definite technique and is controlled; and yet we can say that it has arisen out of situations similar to those in which little children play at being a parent, at being a teacher—vague personalities that are about them and which affect them and on which they depend. These are personalities which they take, roles they play, and insofar control the development of their own personality."[64] According to Mead, this imaginative exercise has an internal and external function. By "trying out" the role, we gain insight into our own personalities, including our preferences and needs. At the same time, we develop an appreciation or insight into those who occupy these roles. This is also true of imaginative flights of care. In caring and empathizing with others, we appreciate their positions while gaining insight into ourselves. An example of this can be found in the contemporary novel *Brothers and Sisters,* by Bebe Moore Campbell.[65] The two protagonists of the novel are upwardly mobile single women living in post–Rodney King riot Los Angeles. Esther is black and Mallory is white. They form a friendship that results in greater caring and empathy for each other. As part of their growing friendship, Mallory explores why Esther is so passionate and sensitive about her African American heritage. In the process Mallory imaginatively "plays" at being Esther in an effort to understand her better. Mallory ends up examining her own latent racism. Mallory's caring resulted in a better self-understanding and a stronger self.

Mead reminds us that play is accompanied by the "game": "The fundamental difference between the game and play is that in the former the child must have the attitude of all the others involved in that game. The attitudes of the other players, which the participant assumes, organize into a sort of unit, and it is that organization which controls the response of the individual."[66] The game demonstrates and develops the imagination's ability to hold all the players together in relation. The self is seen in a web of interactive relationships and not merely subsumed by the others. The game demands imaginative absorption so that everyone can play his or her part,[67] but any child should be able to leave the role once the imaginative exercise or game is over. Analogously, a caring imagination that empathizes with others should not imply a loss of self under normal circumstances. A healthy imagination should move between caring for others and caring for self in ways that benefit both self and other.

Offering an example that resonates with Mead's notion of play, Rita Manning shows how a caring imagination includes considerations of the self:

> Perhaps I am contemplating a divorce. First, I imagine how I would respond as one caring; I think about the situation with moral imagination, becoming sensitive to the emotions that color my response, trying to understand the perception of the other and the effect on us both of any possible response. But now I recognize that it is not just we two or three, but we as members of a family. Now I must reflect on our shared history. This helps me to understand our present conflict. I try to become conscious of the expectations that color our reactions to this episode. Finally, I reflect on the effects on the larger family. All of this reflection takes place in the shadow of my commitment to caring as an ideal, and with the recognition of myself as deserving care.[68]

Manning does not immediately conclude that a divorce is not the caring solution. Her imagination's ability to play at a number of roles allowed all parties, including herself, to be taken into consideration. Manning exhibits a caring approach and a healthy imagination that does not lose sight of caring for self.

As Noddings indicates, the caring individual may have to engage in engrossment. The perceptual-focus phenomenon of the body may direct my attention on the one for whom I care, but the sense of self, or "self cared for," should not be lost on the caring imagination. On the contrary, according to Mead's model, reflective insights stemming from the empathetic process should help develop a stronger sense of self. For example, one may become engrossed in the process of caring for an ill parent and spend a great deal of time providing care. Nevertheless, moments of reflection may include thoughts such as, "How would I react if I were ill?" "How might I reduce the chances of having a similar fate?" These reflections are not contradictory to caring for the parent but rather indicate a caring imagination that is concerned about the self.

The ability to empathize, to visualize moral contexts, and to understand and care for one's position in the environment are intertwined with one's corporeal existence. As Johnson suggests, if our embodiment were different, our imaginative processes would likely be different. We know, however, that cultural diversity and socially accepted norms of behavior prevent generalizing the caring imagination across humanity. Caring is manifested in different ways and to different degrees in contingent norms of language, gesture, physical distance, and so on. The common ground of embodiment nevertheless remains. Caring, whatever form it takes, will come through the body of the caring person and be experienced through the body of the cared-for person. Thus far, the discussion of caring imagination has been largely descriptive. Next I explore what can be done to improve the caring imagination.

Why Do People Fail to Care?

Thus far I have focused on internal resources for care while largely ignoring the power dynamics and social forces that can work to promote or inhibit care. In chapter 2 I argued for the embodied nature of care, and in this chapter I have discussed the imagination's ability to overcome impediments to care such as time and distance. Given all these resources for care, why do we observe so much noncaring activity in the world? Eichmann, for example, identified with a powerful Nazi supremacist discourse that painted the Jews as less than human and as a pernicious evil, not worthy of care. The enormity of the Final Solution makes it an important yet extreme case to consider. I will briefly consider a more personal and ambiguous case of apparent noncaring that unfolded in a documentary film.

In a troubling scene from Michael Moore's film *Roger and Me,* a woman who is eking out an existence in economically depressed Flint, Michigan, advertises her new business with a sign in front of her home that reads, "Rabbits: Pets or Meat."[69] Moore interviews her, and while she is discussing her business, she strokes the rabbit in her arms as anyone would, reflecting habits of care for pets. Anyone who has ever spent time with a dog, cat, rabbit, or other mammal can identify with the habit of stroking a pet. The contact associated with stroking an animal is an example of reciprocal care in that it is soothing for human and animal alike. The film takes a somewhat unexpected twist, however, when the woman kills the rabbit with a hammer so that she can sell the meat. The transition from stroking to killing jars the viewer. The woman was clearly capable of engaging in embodied practices of care with the animal, but she was also capable of hurting it without provocation or regret.

Is this a damning counterexample demonstrating that a caring imagination is a myth because the business owner made no connection between stroking the animal and killing it? Alternatively, is this an example of a failed imagination? To a certain extent it is impossible to know the answer. It is no mere coincidence that Merleau-Ponty is considered a philosopher of both the body and ambiguity. There is a great deal of indeterminacy between the caring body and the caring imagination. When mapping one experience onto another, the correspondence is not always precise. Life's complexity and many dynamics can prevent caring in one arena from translating into caring in another arena. Nevertheless, Moore's film provides a clue at least to what Moore views as the motivation behind this act of violence. Moore is a savvy film director who would not include such a scene for shock value alone. His film painstakingly demonstrates how the large-scale General Motors auto plant shutdowns affected residents of Flint. The business owner is only one of the film's numerous subjects whose lives have been disrupted by the plant closures. It is difficult to overestimate the impact of these layoffs. Jobs are not just a source of money; they also contribute to people's identities. At the social level, a great deal of strife ensues when a community cannot absorb all the labor made available by numerous layoffs. On the individual level, dignity and self-worth suffer. "Downsizing" serves as a reminder that many corporations view people as objects who are valuable only as long as they are productive. Such objectification takes a potent psychological toll. In the "pets or meat" scene, Moore depicts a microcosm of this objectification: a play within a play. This former General Motors employee is forced to subsist on the income generated by operating a business out of her home, where she breeds rabbits that can be pets or food. A powerful discourse of human objectification (the disposable laborer) that she has experienced is in turn being replicated with her rabbits. Because her own survival is at stake, she wards off her embodied connection to the rabbits (depicted by the stroking) to use them as a means to an end rather than treat them as subjects of ongoing care. Her actions are supported by existing norms, which construe rabbits as an acceptable food source. That is, most people assign animals an agency and a subject position inferior to that given to people. Carol Adams contends that people use language in a manner that "distances us further from animals by naming them as objects, as 'its.'"[70] This objectification makes it easier to kill and consume animals because they do not enjoy the moral status that humans do. Since most people eat meat, the business owner is engaging in a socially legitimate activity. What makes the actions of the displaced General Motors worker so shocking, even to meat eaters, is the swift transition from care to violence, as well as the juxtaposition of the choice: pets or meat.

Again, habits of care can be reciprocal and modeled for others, but habits of noncare, too, can be practiced and learned. Hitting a rabbit on the head with a hammer may be necessary for survival, but it does not demonstrate care for the rabbit. Because the rabbit is objectified as a means to an end, and the breeder has repeated this act many times, the violence against the rabbit becomes something of a habit. Recall that care is not necessarily antithetical to principles and consequences. The business owner may have decided that raising and slaughtering rabbits was necessary to produce the income she needs. Given what I have established about embodied care, we should not simply judge the rabbit breeder but consider the wider implications of this scene. If Merleau-Ponty is correct about the interconnection of the flesh and body's capturing movement in habits, what does it mean to move so swiftly from habits of care to an act of violence? What habits are being manifested in the body? What habits are being modeled for others? To what extent do these habits contribute to the growth and the flourishing of the bodies involved, of those who have relationships with the individuals involved, and of the larger community?

The "pets or meat" scene from Moore's film illuminates this chapter's transitional nature. The imagination provides the vehicle for moving from the inward examination offered in chapter 2 to the outward analysis found in chapter 4. This transition is analogous to the relationship expressed in the old feminist adage "the personal is political." Moore has confronted us with an individual's behavior, but every individual act of morality can have wider social implications.

Developing Caring Habits through Exercising the Imagination

The prescriptive commitments of embodied care are slowly coming into focus. Earlier I introduced Merleau-Ponty's phenomenology to highlight the need to attend to the role of the body in ethics and, more specifically, to care. Because the body has been largely ignored in moral theorizing, I argued that attending to and reinforcing the habits of care can inculcate a caring disposition in our comportment. A similar claim can be made in regard to imagination. Our imaginative faculties have been largely ignored in moral theorizing, yet they can be developed or "exercised" to increase our capacity to care for little-known others. For example, Virginia Held offers an "exercise of the imagination" by applying the mother-child relationship to strangers: "I suggest that in trying to understand social relations between persons we should think about how they would look if we used as a model the relation between a mothering-person and child instead of the more usual model of contracts between self-interested strangers, my point is to suggest the alternative model as an exercise of the imagination."[71] Held is not suggesting that we should treat unknown others maternally. She is attempting to push us to imagine changing the dominant discourse from one where society consists of a collection of autonomous agents who have nothing but contractual relations to one where a society consists of agents connected in a web of interdependent relationships. Held understands that imaginative shifts can facilitate caring.

Rita Manning views the development of a moral imagination as the hard work necessary to overcome the simplistic belief that morality encompasses nothing more than the application of rules and principles. "The person with a rich moral imagination works very hard at developing such an imagination and never allows her rules to become inflexible. Instead, she is sensitive to the actual situation in which she finds herself."[72] A metaphor for the caring imagination that arises from Manning's and Held's analyses is that of a muscle. Caring imagination must be used and exercised to be stronger and therefore more useful. The lack of attention paid to the caring imagination has led to a kind of atrophy of this faculty.

Martha Nussbaum also believes that a moral imagination is a faculty worthy of development. In *Poetic Justice: The Literary Imagination and Public Life,* she claims that a literary imagination is an essential component to social ethics. For Nussbaum, literature is not philosophically incidental but rather an essential tool for stimulating our moral imaginations: "Unlike most historical works, literary works typically invite their readers to put themselves in the place of people of many different kinds and to take on their experiences. In their very mode of address to their imagined reader, they convey the sense that there are links of possibility, at least on a very general level, between the characters and the reader. The reader's emotions and imagination are highly active as a result, and it is the nature of this activity, and its relevance for public thinking, that interests me."[73] Fiction can expose me to a variety of otherwise unknown others. This is not a substitute for lived experience, and Nussbaum does not claim that novels are sufficient for constructing social justice.[74] Nevertheless, fictional experiences can be integrated with my embodied experiences to give me a richer epistemic position from which to imaginatively care. Recall the previous chapter's argument that knowledge is a prerequisite to care. This enrichment can occur in complex ways with causal relationships that are not always clear. On hearing the news of a violent crime, for example, I tend to sympathize with the victim and not with the alleged perpetrator. Having read Toni Morrison's *Beloved,* however, I am probably more aware that violence may result from unjust and oppressive institutions and circumstances. I know this not simply because I know more facts but because I have an affective experience through the characters portrayed in the novel. The novel's contribution to my caring imagination is complex. Just because I read a certain novel does not mean that there is a direct empathetic association. For example, it is unlikely that I will come across the circumstances of slavery faced by Sethe in *Beloved.* Still, the novel does add one more set of affective experiences to my knowledge base. Nussbaum recognizes that fiction is compelling in part because it engages specific circumstances while allowing the reader to be sufficiently removed from the situation to allow for reflection: "This play back and forth between the general and the concrete is, I claim, built into the very structure of the genre, in its mode of address to its readers. In this way, the novel constructs a paradigm of a style of ethical reasoning that is context-specific without being relativistic, in which we get potentially universalizable concrete prescriptions by bringing a general idea of human flourishing to bear on a concrete situation, which we are invited to enter through the imagination."[75] What Nussbaum describes is a process similar to embodied care. We move back and forth between the specifics of our own embodied experiences and more general connections to other embodied beings, creating possibilities to care for others known and unknown. Imaginative explorations such as those suggested by Nussbaum add to our potential to understand and care for unknown others. Nussbaum hints at what Addams will make explicit: that taking embodied care seriously compels us to experience others widely, directly, and imaginatively.

Eichmann's uncaring behavior may have resulted from underdeveloped habits of care (as a result of abuse, distant relationships, etc.), developed habits of noncare (reinforced or enabled by habits of violence), or a diminished imagination preventing the exercise of caring habits (possibly as a result of identification with destructive social narratives such as Nazism). We can view the events of the Holocaust as an active attempt to squelch the caring imagination. Although the Nazis had their own internal ethical imperative, they failed to critically view their beliefs in a larger moral context. They did not empathetically imagine the Jews in continuity with their own corporeal existence. Eichmann was no less human than anyone else was, but neither were the Jews he tortured and killed less than human. He was not intrinsically evil—he was intrinsically human. Eichmann was immersed in and embraced an environment that damaged his capacity to care. Just as the economic conditions of Flint, Michigan, damaged the rabbit breeder's ability to make caring connections, the relentless rhetoric of anti-Semitic hate obstructed Eichmann's ability to empathize with the Jews.

The move to valorize a caring imagination is not a contradiction to the embodied characteristic of care but an inseparable part of it. To care is to draw on embodied knowledge in imaginative ways. Enhancing care involves attending to the ways our body constructs knowledge and exercising our imagination so that it can better empathize, contextualize, and balance our caring efforts. The kinds of caring habits we have, as well as when and where they are deployed, result from our caring imagination. This model of embodied care has thus far been applied at an interpersonal level. In the next chapter I examine the work of Jane Addams to suggest that habits of embodied care can be applied at the social and political levels, too.

4. Jane Addams and the Social Habits of Care

> Far from being romantic, an ethic of care is practical, made for this earth.
> —Nel Noddings, *Caring*

In 1871 the feminist author Elizabeth Stuart Phelps penned the novel *The Silent Partner,* which critiques industrial capitalism and the social distance that accompanies class stratification in the United States. The protagonist is Perley Kelso, whose father owns a stake in a textile mill. Kelso is an upper-class woman engaged to one of the mill's other owners, but beyond spending summers in the mill town, she has had little to do with the company. Early in the novel Kelso's father dies, and leaves her his interest in the mill. When she attempts to participate in operating the business, however, the company's other partners invoke the sexist norms of the day and refuse to allow her any role larger than that of "silent partner." In an important narrative thread Kelso befriends one of the mill workers, Sip Garth. The relationship between the two is rocky and uncomfortable, particularly at first. Garth and Kelso occupy different ends of the social hierarchy, and each carries the prejudice of labels often given to unknown others. Their first meeting is a fluke encounter in a rainstorm when the carriage carrying Kelso stops and the door is left open. Kelso observes Garth struggling in the rain. Garth catches Kelso staring and confronts her. The class differences are apparent from the start. Kelso explains her gaze:

> "I think I must have been sorry for you . . . that was why I looked at you. You seemed cold and wet."
> "You're not cold and wet, at any rate."[1]

Garth's response puts Kelso on the defensive because of her material advantage. Nevertheless, Kelso initiates the process, albeit awkwardly, of getting to know this working-class other whose existence is foreign to her: "I do not often see people just like you. What is your name?"[2] Kelso's expression "people like you" reveals the tremendous social distance between the characters. This initial meeting comes to an abrupt end, but the two see one another again at the mill. Although Garth is a blue-collar worker with little education, she has insight into the nature of class relations. In their second meeting Garth is surprised that Kelso remembers her: "'I knew you,' said the girl abruptly, still without turning her head. 'I didn't suppose you'd know me. You needn't unless you want to.'"[3] One of the trappings of wealth is greater selectivity in whom one knows and cares about. Typically Kelso's social standing would not compel her to remember the working-class Garth. Nevertheless, Kelso does want to know and care about Garth, but she struggles to find the experiential resources to make the personal connection. She does her best to express this to Garth: "I want you to talk without being questioned. I don't like to question you all the time. But I want to hear more about you, and—you didn't speak of your mother; and where you live, and how; and many other things. I am not used to people who live as you do. I presume I do not understand how to treat you. I do not think it is curiosity. I think it is—I do not know what it is. I suppose I am sorry."[4] Because of her interaction with Garth, Kelso slowly gets to know the other laborers in the mill, and a relationship is formed with a growing level of trust. Kelso is able to obtain some concessions on behalf of the exploited workers, but as a silent partner, she has little direct influence.

Along with offering class analysis, Phelps weaves into her novel an implicit understanding of the relationship between epistemology and care ethics. At one point Garth becomes impatient with the detachment of the wealthy and lashes out at Kelso: "They don't none of 'em know. That's why I hate your kind of folks. It ain't because they don't care, it's because they don't *know;* nor they don't care enough *to* know."[5] Garth recognizes how important knowledge is for caring and, more important, how the lack of knowledge reveals a type of erasure. The poor do not even warrant a passing concern.

Phelps also highlights the role of the body in differentiating social class. For example, *The Silent Partner* uses a great deal of hand imagery to foreshadow plot developments as well as to provide insight into the characters Kelso confronts. When Kelso contemplates the social world outside of her upper-class existence by observing people on the street, she declares of that world, "It conceived such original ways of holding its hands, and wearing its hats, and carrying its bundles."[6] Although the rich and poor share the same embodied existence, Kelso begins to see that class difference can be observed in bodily comportment.

The relationship between Kelso and Garth can help us confront socially

constructed barriers that separate embodied beings. Merleau-Ponty's phenomenological reduction suspends reflection on socially inscribed differences
to focus on the basic commonality of the body. That suspension is crucial in
developing the idea that the body is "built" with the potential to care. But
that suspension cannot last. A morality that deals with real-world experiences
must return to considering social differences that impinge on morality. I have
suggested that the caring imagination can be a vehicle for overcoming such
differences, yet these social constructions must be addressed directly. In *The
Silent Partner* Phelps portrays the rich and poor engaging in different corporeal habits emerging from their stations in life. When Kelso speaks with
Garth at length for the first time, their hands become a focal point of class
difference. Kelso asks, "Don't you earn enough to buy yourself gloves?"[7] Garth
evades the question, but it is clear that her hands are those of a working-class
woman. As they converse, Garth is "chafing her purple fingers."[8] Later in the
novel Phelps deals more explicitly with the experience of laboring in the mill.
Phelps again chooses to use the body as the signifier for class difference: "You
grow moody being 'a hand' at Hayle and Kelso's [mill]. . . . [You] find pains
in your feet, your back, your eyes, your arms; feel damp and sticky lint in your
hair, your neck, your ears, your throat, your lungs; discover a monotony in
the process of breathing hot moisture."[9] These bodies know what it means
to be exhausted from physical exertion. Phelps chose to communicate to her
reading audience a social message of care using a vehicle that both crosses
and highlights economic class: the body. Wendy Sharer finds Phelps's corporeal language to trigger the caring imagination of her audience: "Her physical descriptions and body metaphors imprint themselves on the minds of
the readers and better enable those readers, from their positions 'on the parlor
sofa, in clean cuffs and . . . slippers,' to experience what is outside their typical realm of experience."[10] Phelps frames her social message by exploring
specific relationships and their bodily aspects. In their afterword for the 1983
edition, Mari Jo Buhle and Florence Howe identify care in Phelps's social
agenda: "The 'feminine strength' of women, the caring quality that Phelps
admired in her mother, is present throughout. As Perley 'cares' for Bub [a
child laborer] and sees him home, and attempts to inquire into the conditions of work for eight-year-olds more generally; as Sip cares for Catty [Sip
Garth's physically challenged sister], and for other young women in her
purview; and as these women care for each other, Phelps portrays the reality
of women as she sees them: the strong caretakers."[11] For Phelps, social
change—better working conditions for blue-collar workers—is tied to a sympathetic knowledge elicited through an embodied understanding of care.
Similarly, Jane Addams addresses the role of sympathetic knowledge in the

relationship between direct individual experience and wider social concern and social change. Addams begins with what she knows from speaking with and tending to the marginalized members of society. Her caring imagination helps to transform a collection of experiences into theories about improving society. Like Phelps, Addams finds that the personal is political, despite overwhelming social forces that attempt to disconnect them.

* * *

At this point one might wonder how caring knowledge, habits, and imagination in the individual can coalesce into a social or political philosophy compatible with embodied care. Initially I explored the ultimate common denominator of human experience, the body, through the work of Maurice Merleau-Ponty to establish that caring knowledge and caring habits are a foundational aspect of embodied existence. I then developed the notion of the caring imagination to explain how we transcend our embodiment to care for others. Our caring imagination can extend in any number of ways, but how can those extensions coalesce into a social or political philosophy compatible with embodied care? Jane Addams's writings provide an answer to this question by making a significant contribution to what might be called the demand of care: to seek out experiences of others toward the possibility of building a better society through caring. Addams calls for particular practices of care for the betterment of society, or what can be called the social habits of care.

While this chapter is an appropriate conclusion to the theoretical development of embodied care from individual phenomenology to social habits, it is also motivated by the common concern that care, although perhaps applicable to personal ethics, is insufficiently developed to contribute to social morality. For example, in reviewing Virginia Held's work, Ann Cudd writes, "Care is not what most normal adults need or want from most others in society."[12] Laurie Shrage suggests that care is too limited to support a viable social ethics: "Care theorists have the basic problem—that of defining the boundaries of care."[13] Shrage worries that care lacks the resources to address social problems. I contend that Addams's work at Hull House reveals particularly viable social habits of care. Care can contribute to the morality of both the private sphere and, through habits of listening, participation, involved leadership, and activism, the public sphere.

I previously established care as emerging from knowledge contained in the body using Merleau-Ponty's phenomenology, an approach generally associated with Continental philosophy. This chapter turns to American philosophy to explore how embodied care manifests itself in a social and political sense. Philosophical projects rarely combine phenomenology and pragmatism because the two approaches differ widely in both canon and method, if not fundamental worldview. Nevertheless, cross-disciplinary awareness has been making for fruitful interconnections, such as this one.[14] The insights of phenomenology help us understand the workings of care in the body, just as the insights of pragmatism help us understand how embodied care can frame a social or political philosophy. The latter move is significant because one of the persistent criticisms of care ethics is that it is more effective as personal morality than as social ethics.

The writings and activism of Jane Addams not only exemplify embodied care but, more important, contribute a theoretical framework and illustrate practices necessary for a social-political philosophy of caring. In other words, Addams practiced a social-political ethic of embodied care long before the term *care ethics* existed, but she did so in a way that adds significantly to modern concepts of care. Addams believed that certain habits of caring—of active listening, participation, connected leadership, and activism—will allow society to flourish and grow. I begin by exploring the commitments of the American pragmatist tradition, of which Addams was a part. Then I will explore the multifaceted American heroine and philosopher who was Jane Addams. Finally, I will discuss Addams's unique contribution to a social ethics of embodied care. Her philosophy and practices regarding the social habits of democracy and citizenship demand that we seek a broad experience of a wide variety of others.

American Pragmatism

> The distinctive appeal of American Pragmatism in our postmodern moment is its unashamedly moral emphasis and its unequivocally ameliorative impulse.
> —Cornel West, *The American Evasion of Philosophy*

In the following brief introduction to pragmatism I seek to illuminate the tradition in which Addams arose, highlight the connections between care ethics and pragmatism, and explore the emphasis on habit found among these American philosophers. As one might expect, different scholars define pragmatism differently, but Scott Pratt describes four commitments on which most can agree: interaction, pluralism, community, and growth.[15] American pragmatism has traditionally been portrayed as originating in the Metaphysical Club of Cambridge, Massachusetts, in the 1870s and was given concrete form through the works of Charles Sanders Peirce, William James, and John Dewey.[16] Nevertheless, many rightly wish to expand and diversify what constitutes it to include Native American, African American, pragmatic feminist, and early colonial philosophies.

As the moniker *pragmatism* indicates, the commitment to interaction is associated with an instrumental understanding of meaning. William James argues that "we disbelieve all facts and theories for which we have no use."[17] John Patrick Diggins describes American pragmatism as helping "people deliberately reflect about what to do when confronting 'problematic situations.'"[18] This instrumentality, or thinking with a purpose, includes placing experience at the forefront of reflection. Peirce goes so far as to develop a "pragmatic maxim" that validates theories and concepts if they are connected to experience.[19] Accordingly, experience, not abstract theories or frameworks, provides the starting point for pragmatism. James argues that the pragmatist "turns his back resolutely and once and for all . . . from abstraction and insufficiency, from verbal solutions, from bad *a priori* reasons, from fixed principles, closed systems, and pretended absolutes and origins."[20] Pragmatists view experience to be not just something that happens to passive subjects but rather a means for actively participating in life. As John Dewey proclaims, "Experience becomes an affair primarily of doing."[21] According to Cornel West, pragmatism employs its instrumentalism "as a weapon" for effective action.

The second commitment Pratt discusses is that of pervasive pluralism, which is "ontological, epistemological, and cultural."[22] Because pragmatism is not grounded in a conception of knowledge as absolute truth, there is a recognition that various methods of inquiry can lead to different understandings. Knowledge is neither static nor monolithic. The pragmatist approach can be applied to care. Earlier I emphasized the epistemological basis for embodied care: knowledge is a prerequisite for care. I cannot care unless my body and mind obtain knowledge, and they require experiences to do so; if other bodies care, they too will require knowledge. Two bodies cannot inhabit the same physical space, however, which means that they can never have precisely the same experiences; as a result, a collective intelligence made up of a plurality of individuals will be superior to a singular one. Addams makes the latter point when she claims that "those who desire [a moral ideal] must be brought in contact with the moral experience of the many."[23] Far removed from the subjective focus of some philosophical traditions, as in Descartes's *cogito,* pragmatism's commitment to pluralism recognizes the value of a social epistemology as a basis for morality.

Pragmatism's third commitment is that of community, which is a central concern of this chapter. This commitment emerges from the concern for interaction and pluralism in recognition of the tension between the one and the many. Despite its valorization of multiple perspectives and multiple solutions, pragmatism always seeks the commonality of community. Care mimics this tension. As I have argued, care has a personal, embodied dimension, but embodied care exists only as a potential until it is brought out through social interaction.

The final pragmatic commitment Pratt lists is to growth.[24] Consistent with the previous commitments, growth is understood not as a movement toward a shared, absolute truth but as individual development that will vary by circumstances. Democracy becomes a framework for individual participation that allows for both individual and communal growth. Individuals and the community must be connected if growth is to take place. Addams refers to such growth as "lateral progress" that necessitates ever-deepening cocommitments. For example, in *Democracy and Social Ethics* Addams uses the case of "a little Italian lad of six" to demonstrate the negative impact of child labor. According to Addams, such labor harms the child by making him overly conscious of material concerns. She finds that the adult cares of subsistence foisted on the child retard his caring imagination: "He is not able to see life from any other standpoint."[25]

Addams finds the stifling habits that child labor fosters to raise concerns at the social as well as the individual level. She claims that such labor may lower overall wages, add an illiterate member to the community, and stifle the development of someone who might otherwise have contributed more to society.[26] For Addams, the boundary between individual morality and social morality blurs as personal stories aggregate into communal concerns. Care can be seen as an important aspect of the integrated involvement of the community that facilitates individual freedom and growth.

These commitments have methodological implications. Pragmatists emphasize methods and practices that, particularly for Dewey, translate into adopting the experimental spirit of scientific inquiry. Such an approach valorizes both fallibilism, because every truth claim can be superseded when new or better evidence is presented, and pluralism, because human endeavors are similar to scientific ones in that experience is complex and multiple perspectives bring greater insight. Dewey believes that fallibilism is inevitable; because "we live in a world in process, the future, although continuous with the past, is not its bare repetition."[27] Consistent with this fallibilism, pragmatist solutions are considered context dependent and revisable. The pluralism found in this approach is an important outgrowth of the notion of interconnectedness. A pragmatic solution to social challenges seldom addresses only a single variable. Making the case in the extreme, James states, "Not a sparrow falls to the ground but some of the remote conditions of his fall are to be found in the Milky Way, in our federal constitution, or in the early history of Europe."[28] Unlike some other philosophers, pragmatists do not shy away from social concerns, because ultimately they believe philosophy is a means for making the world a better place.

Pragmatism thus provides an ideal framework for synthesizing embodied care and the caring imagination into a social philosophy of care. Again, I turn to the idea of habit as a galvanizing concept. Although he does not provide a phenomenological analysis like Merleau-Ponty's, John Dewey recognizes the human body to be a central part of human existence that is organized around habits: "We are . . . likely to have a conception of habits which needs to be deepened and extended. For we are given to thinking of a habit as simply a recurrent external mode of action, like smoking or swearing, being neat or negligent in clothes and person, taking exercise, or playing games. But habit reaches even more significantly down into the very structure of the self. . . . Habit covers in other words the very make-up of desire, intent, choice, disposition which gives an act its voluntary quality."[29] For Dewey, habits reflect the agency of the individual. In Shannon Sullivan's words, "We are our habits."[30] Unlike Merleau-Ponty, Dewey explicitly connects habits and the moral imagination: "Only the man whose habits are already good can know what the good is."[31] Dewey conceives habits not as rote physical acts but as structures capable of fueling the imagination. Habits are physical anchors that can be used as launching points for the imagination. For example, once I have mastered the physical habits necessary for tending to a baby, my imagination can extend that experience to others who must tend to babies. Dewey claims that every habit "takes its turn in projecting itself upon the screen of imagination."[32] In *The Silent Partner,* Perley Kelso is unfamiliar and uncomfortable with numerous subtle habits that separated the social classes, such as the ways the poor hold their hands, wear their hats, and carry their bundles.[33] Her growing friendship with Sip Garth gives her a better opportunity to understand those habits and provides her imagination the affective knowledge necessary to care about the poor. While numerous American pragmatists address habit, Jane Addams actualized her commitment to interaction, pluralism, community, and growth through her work and writing at Hull-House.

The foregoing description is too brief to fully characterize the rich tradition of American pragmatism, but it provides a basic understanding of the intellectual milieu that Addams helped to shape and from which her ideas would evolve. Pragmatism is particularly well suited for my project of moving care from considerations of individual relationships to addressing wider social issues. The commitments of interaction, pluralism, community, and growth not only are compatible with care but, through Addams, will add an important social dimension to care.

The Ethics of Jane Addams

> You are not like the rest of us, who see the truth and try
> to express it. You *inhabit* reality.
> —William James to Jane Addams

The accomplishments of Jane Addams (1860–1935) would be remarkable under any circumstances, but given that her achievements occurred at a time when the separation of private and public spheres gave few women social leadership opportunities (or even the opportunity to vote), they are truly spectacular. Addams helped to found the American Civil Liberties Union, the National Association for the Advancement of Colored People, and the Woman's Peace Party. Her efforts to help poor immigrants and establish child labor laws, as well as her efforts on behalf of world peace and for women's suffrage, brought her the Nobel Peace Prize in 1931. Perhaps her most well known accomplishment was Hull-House, which Addams and Ellen Gates Starr founded in Chicago in 1889.

Hull-House became (and continues to be) the flagship of the settlement movement in North America, which tried to overcome the disconnections created by class and race in large urban areas. Eleanor Stebner describes the settlement movement as "a conscious attempt of middle- and upper-middle-class folks to cross boundaries of class and ethnicity, and to connect with others usually identified as different from themselves on a human everyday basis."[34] Addams intended Hull-House to be a place where the privileged and educated could live and work among the poor in a community dedicated to the betterment of the neighborhood, but it never was a highly structured organization. Hull-House evolved and responded to the needs of the community, becoming an institution without being institutionalized.[35] If a kindergarten was needed, Hull-House offered it. If recent immigrants needed English classes, Hull-House provided it. If the community needed political leverage to get trash picked up, Hull-House advocated for them.

Hull-House was many things to many people. One of its important roles was as an epistemological portal into urban life; nevertheless, the neighborhood did not perceive Hull-House residents as social scientists or rich white women alleviating social guilt (although Hull-House was the first settlement to house men and women, it remained a women-centered endeavor). The Hull-House community was part of the neighborhood and exhibited embodied care. As Addams recounts, the tasks were sometimes political, but often they were quite basic: "From the first it seemed understood that we were ready to perform the humblest neighborhood services. We were asked to wash the new-born babies, and to prepare the dead for burial, to nurse the sick, and to 'mind the children.'"[36] Hull-House residents gained credibility and trust through close, physical interaction helping people with the most basic of needs.

Addams encouraged the caring social habits of listening, participation, connected leadership, and activism. Accordingly Addams combated habits that retarded the growth and flourishing of the neighborhood. Child labor, prostitution, and exploitation of workers counted among the practices she fought. Firsthand knowledge exchanged between Hull-House members and the community fueled the caring imagination to find human connection, which transcended the social distance of class and culture and resulted in caring social habits. Addams recognized the connections taking place:

> We were constantly impressed with the uniform kindness and courtesy we received. Perhaps these first days laid the simple human foundations which are certainly essential for continuous living among the poor: first, genuine preference for residence in an industrial quarter to any other part of the city, because it is interesting and makes the human appeal; and second the conviction . . . that the things which make men alike are finer and better than the things that keep them apart, and that these basic likenesses, if they are properly accentuated, easily transcend the less essential differences of race, language, creed and tradition.[37]

This language recalls my earlier discussion concerning the caring imagination: physical presence and a willingness to address basic needs allowed people from very different social backgrounds to interact, understand, and ultimately care for one another. The Hull-House residents had made a caring connection that would provide mutual benefits.

Addams did not just "go to work" at Hull-House; she lived there with a community of college-educated men and women who wanted to make a difference. Visitors included Dewey, Susan B. Anthony, Charlotte Perkins Gilman, Richard T. Ely, and a who's who list of progressive intellectuals and politicians. But for its physical location in a working-class neighborhood, the intellectual and cultural life created by the Hull-House community was much like that in a university. Addams's Hull-House experience is significant for my project because it is impossible to separate her experiences and activism from her ideas on morality. In many ways it was Addams who pushed American pragmatism out of the universities and onto the streets. As Charlene

Haddock Seigfried observes, it was the women pragmatists "who took [Dewey's] argument one step further by adopting the radical position that scholars ought to be or become members of communities plagued by the problems their theories are supposed to solve."[38] Hull-House was the vehicle for Addams and her cohort to physically confront the outcast "other" of her day (e.g., the immigrant other, the working-class other, the poverty-stricken other, the prostitute other). These "others" were the by-products of the Industrial Revolution and the commensurate rise of big cities.[39] According to Dewey: "The work of such an institution as Hull House has been primarily, not merely in the arena of formal discussion—for argument alone breeds misunderstanding and fixes prejudice—but in ways where ideas are incarnated in human form and clothed with a winning grace of personal life. Classes for study may be numerous, but all are regarded as modes of bringing people together, of doing away with barriers of caste, or class, or race, or type of experience that keep people from real communion with each other."[40]

As a public figure Addams was praised and at times lambasted for her various social endeavors.[41] What is less well known about Addams is that she wrote twelve books and hundreds of articles that form a wellspring of social philosophy in the American pragmatic tradition. Although modern philosophers have given her little attention, Addams's contemporaries recognized her intellectual contributions. William James described Addams's first book, *Democracy and Social Ethics,* as "one of the great books of our time,"[42] and John Dewey described her essay on the Pullman strike of 1894, "A Modern Lear" (which was not published until 1913 because it was so controversial), as "one of the greatest things I ever read both as to its form and its ethical philosophy."[43] Nevertheless, until recently a combination of sexism and a bias against activism in some philosophical circles has caused Addams's philosophical work to go largely unnoticed.[44] Few anthologies of American philosophy seriously consider Addams's writings, but feminist philosophers are beginning to rediscover the richness of her work. For example, Marilyn Fischer argues that Addams "anticipates perspectives commonly found in contemporary feminist ethics."[45] It is my contention that Addams makes a unique contribution to American philosophical discourse by offering a social-political philosophy of embodied care. To make the case for Addams as a care ethicist who implicitly understood the moral significance of human embodiment, I will examine her notion of sympathetic knowledge, her relational approach to morality, and her valorization of context.

Again, knowledge is a prerequisite for embodied care because one cannot care for something about which one knows nothing. Addams also believed that morality could not be abstracted from the quality and degree of our knowledge of one another. To know about someone is to open the possibility of caring for them. Addams referred to this as "sympathetic knowledge." According to Addams, knowledge, empathy, and action exist in dynamic relation to one another. For example, in addressing prostitution Addams finds personal understanding indispensable: "Sympathetic knowledge is the only way of approach to any human problem, and the line of least resistance into the jungle of human wretchedness must always be through that region which is most thoroughly explored, not only by the information of the statistician, but by sympathetic understanding."[46] For Adams, sympathetic knowledge is not only important for interpersonal morality, but for social ethics as well. Seigfried finds Addams's notion of sympathetic understanding critical for her social program: "Through the mediation of sympathetic understanding, a space can be opened in which the viewpoint, values, and goals of others can become part of moral deliberation and social transformation."[47]

Addams's embodied epistemological methodology is a significant aspect of sympathetic knowledge. Real examples, many drawn from personal experiences at Hull-House, accompany most of Addams's philosophical writings. For example, her comprehensive plan to address prostitution found in *A New Conscience and an Ancient Evil* refers to a number of prostitutes that Addams met at Hull-House. Addams had direct experience with women forced into sexual labor, often sitting face to face as she listened to their stories. Prostitutes were not wholly unknown others for her and therefore not reduced to the labels given to them as moral outcasts of society. They were met as individuals with bodies and feelings continuous with those who would listen. Addams created the opportunity for care and caring action by being physically present to others. Physical presence breeds embodied knowledge. Addams was able to capture the habits, movements, and other physical cues that carried enormous information about the other because she was there as an active member of the neighborhood, reflecting what Noddings refers to as the "I am here" response of the carer for the cared-for.[48] Addams's caring imagination could take this information to create better generalizations of the prostitutes in her social critique and her search for solutions.

The importance of Addams's physical presence through the social experiment of Hull-House cannot be overstated. The Hull-House community employed embodied care practices that provided a forum for experiencing others. This is not to say that direct experience should be the only source of knowledge. Addams also refers to accounts written by others who had direct experience with prostitutes. Much like Martha Nussbaum, Addams recognizes that literature can enliven the caring imagination, leading us to care through vicarious experience.[49] In *Twenty Years at Hull-House*, Addams includes a chapter entitled "Arts at Hull House," which not only recounts their forays into drama, music, and painting but also argues the significance of the arts for developing a caring imagination. Addams viewed the stage as a "reconstructing and reorganizing agent of accepted truth"[50] because it gave the settlement community an opportunity to step back and witness ethics in action. Drama provided a moment of reflection on the human condition and its morality. The arts were not a substitute for experiencing others widely, but neither were they a mere luxury. They provided another means for confronting others' experiences.

Much of Addams's writing grew out of sympathetic knowledge garnered through her physical involvement in the Hull-House community. This sympathetic knowledge is consistent with the epistemic requirement of care and is the foundation of a relational approach to morality. Like care ethics, embodied care is inherently relational and therefore animated through intersubjectivity. A care orientation is grounded in a concern for the way decisions affect the relationships involved. In her most comprehensive theoretical work on social morality, *Democracy and Social Ethics*, Addams attends to the quality and quantity of relationships as having significant moral importance. Along with many thinkers in the post-Darwin era, Addams viewed social morality as evolving for the better. She believed that the individual moralities of the past could not satisfy the communal needs of society in the present. Without explicitly employing the terminology, Addams held the new morality needed in her day to be a care orientation that she believed everyone could adopt, even though many had lost touch with it.[51] Addams's view is consistent with understanding embodied care as a foundational moral orientation of the body. We can "lose touch" with care by squelching or denying the caring impulse, or we can attend to and cultivate the drive to care. For example, Addams claimed that social systems such as charitable organizations are sometimes poor substitutes for "the natural outgoing of human love and sympathy which, happily we all possess in some degree."[52] These institutions lacked a caring orientation. Another care inhibitor is wealth. Addams found that the ability to insulate oneself makes it easier for those of means to lose touch with their ability to care for others in society, yet Addams's life and writing is a testament to the idea that everyone of whatever social standing has the capacity to care.

Addams's various extended examples in *Democracy and Social Ethics* reveal her bias toward finding connection and balance in relationships. In a chapter titled "Filial Relations" Addams addresses young middle-class women caught between the desire for positive relations with their families and the call to serve society in the spirit of the democratic impulse. Addams declares,

"The attempt to bring about a healing compromise in which the two shall be adjusted in proper relation is not an easy one."[53] Yet this is precisely what Addams sets out to do. She does not offer a radical reconceptualization of the family but instead attempts to rectify the relation: Addams wants to avoid viewing the family as an isolated unit. The family should evolve as society has evolved in recognizing the need for a social ethics—a concept of right relationship broader than the concerns within the household. Addams acknowledges that such change will provoke misunderstanding and pain for those in traditional families, but a new morality of connection can mitigate that pain: "Wounded affection there is sure to be, but this could be reduced to a modicum if we could preserve a sense of the relation of the individual to the family, and of the latter to society, and if we had been given a code of ethics dealing with these larger relationships, instead of a code designed to apply so exclusively to relationships obtaining only between individuals."[54] Addams could have made her point about evolving social needs and the family in many different ways, but she chose to focus on achieving a balanced relationship. *Democracy and Social Ethics* is replete with examples concerning what constitutes a balanced, caring relationship, whether it is a domestic servant and her employer (chapter 4), business management and labor (chapter 5), or King Lear and his daughter (chapter 2). For Addams, the democratic spirit is a complex weaving of morality and relationality that closely resembles the modern understanding of a care orientation.

In addition to advocating sympathetic knowledge and a relational approach to morality, Addams places a great emphasis on context and experience, as her concern for the working poor exemplifies: "There is a pitiful failure to recognize the situation in which the majority of working people are placed, a tendency to ignore their real experiences."[55] An ethics of care privileges the tangible and the concrete over the abstract and the absolute.[56] This is equally true of embodied care, which takes as its starting point the context of one's own body. Addams also values the reality of context in ethical matters. This contextualization of morality is perhaps most clearly revealed in Addams's understanding of social progress and evolution. Addams does not view the morality governing the democratic impulse as derived from static principles found in religious canons or elsewhere.[57] Her social morality is historically contingent: "Each generation has its own test, the contemporaneous and current standard by which alone it can adequately judge of its own moral achievements, and that it may not legitimately use a previous and less vigorous test."[58] For Addams, morality is an open-ended inquiry that requires scrutiny and continual revision. As such, ethics is situated within each society and age but informed by the morality that precedes it. Once again, Addams addresses ethics in evolutionary terms: overall morality improves with each generation.

While placing morality in a historical context, Addams recognizes that social situatedness will reveal great differences within each age. In a chapter of *Democracy and Social Ethics* titled "Charitable Effort," Addams appeals for understanding morality in its contexts—in this case, social classes. The charitable visitor represents middle-class values that are, in part, dictated by the comfort and security of relative material abundance. The family in need of social service not only lacks materially but also operates with different social values Addams calls the "neighborhood mind": "The neighborhood mind is at once confronted not only by the difference of method, but by an absolute clashing of two ethical standards."[59] Here Addams, although critical of charity's institutionalization of caring, does not adjudicate between the moral orientations of the middle class and the working poor. She recognizes that circumstances have dictated divergent standards of morality.[60] Material well-being is a concrete factor and not inconsequential in moral understanding for Addams. She does not attempt to impose a universal ethical principle but instead focuses on the dynamics between moral orientations in an attempt to understand and rectify the problems in the relationship.[61] Her understanding and use of context and examples is consistent with embodied care, which grounds moral knowledge in what the body knows.

I have suggested that Addams's understanding of sympathetic knowledge, her relational approach to morality, and her focus on context resonate strongly with embodied care. In addition, Addams provides what care ethics has often been accused of lacking: a strong social-political element.

According to Addams, "it is most difficult to hold to our political democracy and to make it in any sense a social expression and not a mere governmental contrivance, unless we take pains to keep on common ground in our human experiences."[62] This quote typifies Addams's effort to connect social ethics to shared and diverse experiences: the "common ground." An embodied ethic of care relies on experiences of the other and habits of caring to provide the corporeal resources for the possibility of empathy and action. Part of these corporeal resources are the caring knowledge and the habits of care: the subtle movements known to the body that express meaning through the eyes, facial expressions, and touch. These corporeal resources, built up through interpersonal interaction, are not lost on the caring imagination when the wider social environment of norms, rules, and laws are considered. The embodied beings that engage in individual personal relationships are also citizens of a larger community that are often asked to consider issues of social policy. In her philosophical writings Addams repeatedly refers to the moral necessity of social experience—a demand not made by modern care ethicists. For example, in *Newer Ideals of Peace* Addams claims that "it is not so much by the teaching of moral theorems that virtue is to be promoted as by the direct expression of social sentiments and by the cultivation of practical habits."[63] Addams views a diverse experience of others as essential for actualizing the sympathy needed in the democratic impulse. Here Addams links the simple, subtle habits of care with more complex habits of care found in social practices.

Modern care ethicists have been so careful to distinguish care-based approaches from justice ethics that they have shunned mandates, rules, or principles. For example, Nel Noddings describes how we must care for those who come within our sphere of knowledge: "[The caring person] would prefer that the stray cat not appear at the back door, or the stray teenager at the front. But if either presents himself, he must be received not by formula but as individual."[64] Noddings is arguing that care cannot be reduced to a formulaic duty but must be an intersubjective response that is unique to the person and circumstances. But note the tacit passivity in Noddings' claim. The other— stray cat or stray teenager—comes to the caregiver, who "receives" the one to be cared for. Noddings describes an embodied experience, but the other's coming to the caregiver activates it. Addams, however, whose starting point is the commitment to the improvement of society, reconfigures embodied care as an active process. She addresses "social settlements" and the "cultivation of habits" as a responsibility of the caregiver. Addams argues for a proactive embodied care that involves certain habits of interaction.

Addams goes so far as to state that to choose the habits of an insular life is to shirk one's social and ethical responsibility. She integrates an understanding of embodied care with a valorization of a caring imagination, but she finds in this integration a duty or obligation to act:

> We have learned as common knowledge that much of the insensibility and hardness of the world is due to the lack of imagination which prevents a realization of the experiences of other people. Already, there is a conviction that we are under a moral obligation in choosing our experiences, since the result of those experiences must ultimately determine our understanding of life. We know instinctively that if we grow contemptuous of other fellows, and consciously limit our intercourse to certain kinds of people whom we have previously decided to respect, we not only tremendously circumscribe our range of life, but also limit the scope of our ethics.[65]

Addams transforms an embodied ethic of care from a reactive perspective of one body confronting another to a proactive transaction dictated by a caring imagination in developing a social-political understanding.[66] Care ethicists share her belief that experience is a necessary condition of empathetic caring, but Addams goes further by claiming that avoiding the experiences of others violates the democratic spirit, squelches our own nature (because we all possess "the natural outgoing of human love and sympathy"),[67] and limits our caring imagination. Addams implicitly invokes the caring imagination: by choosing the type of experiences we have, we feed our imaginations in certain ways. *To choose to experience others in diverse social conditions, including when others are in pain and misery, for the expressed purpose of learning and caring about them*—this is a demanding moral imperative. The choice to care means summoning the energy necessary to enter relationships that may require emotional, material, and temporal involvement. Noddings refers to the depth of our caring relationships as forming concentric circles, with the proximate relationships (family) calling forth the greatest care. For Noddings, there is an ambivalence about meeting unknown others whose newfound relationship may make new requirements of care: "Indeed, the caring person, one who in this way is prepared to care, dreads the proximate stranger, for she cannot easily reject the claim he has on her."[68] Addams contributes a proactive bias to care in asking that we expand our caring circles and seek out the unknown other: "a new demand involving a social obligation."[69] By developing habits of care that include experiencing diverse social interactions, Addams implies that we can build a more caring society. Thus, for example, if my community includes a burgeoning group of people who differ from me racially, religiously, or otherwise, it is not just "nice" if I get to know something of their interests, values, and history; it is a moral obligation for me as a member of the community. This demanding social habit of care will invoke both my corporeal engagement through all the habits of care that interaction requires and an engagement of my caring imagination to understand and empathize with the plight of others.

Addams defies the traditional notions of rugged individualism and its dicta of autonomy, such as "do not harm" and "do not disturb the privacy of others," as well as the self-centered material concerns of capitalism. Fischer describes Addams's understanding of society as "organically interconnected," linking economic conditions, political operations, and civic infrastructure through her intimate understanding of the lives of the people in her neighborhood.[70] Jean Bethke Elshtain finds the organic connection valued by Addams to be reflected in a positive human ontology: "Addams's evolutionary optimism is tied to her conviction that human beings are more similar than they are different. It follows that what unites us is stronger than what divides us."[71] When Perley Kelso makes the difficult decision to get to know

Sip Garth better, she, too, begins to see the interconnectedness of society. Their personal, embodied interaction gives Kelso's caring imagination the affective knowledge of the hardship Garth experienced, both physical (as revealed by her hands) and psychological (as suffered by any oppressed mill worker). Kelso's social position does not require her to make this connection, but according to Addams's understanding of caring citizenship, she does have a moral obligation to reach out and try to know Garth.

The long remark by Addams quoted previously connects well with the trajectory of this book. Notice that Addams finds most people's moral imaginations to lack something that experience of others could alleviate.[72] I have thus far claimed that care involves embodied habits supported by a moral imagination that draws from the knowledge of others found in the body. Addams sees similar linkages and therefore argues that more diverse experiences of others will give us more information to feed our imaginations, creating the possibility for greater understanding of and sympathy for them, as exemplified by this statement concerning the social classes: "Nothing so deadens the sympathies and shrivels the power of enjoyment as the persistent keeping away from the great opportunities for helpfulness and a continual ignoring of the starvation struggle which makes up the life of at least half the race."[73] Note that Addams blurs the boundary between personal and social morality. For Addams, individual interactions with diverse others help weave the social fabric.

Although sometimes criticized for being moderate, Addams acknowledges that what she advocates—making efforts to meet and experience unknown others—is radical. In a moment of eloquence, Addams revels in the idea of diving into the murky waters of human experience: "Thus the identification with the common lot which is the essential idea of Democracy becomes the source and expression of social ethics. It is as though we thirsted to drink at the great wells of human experience, because we knew that a daintier or less potent draught would not carry us to the end of the journey, going forward as we must in the heat and jostle of the crowd."[74] While care ethicists have been careful not to mirror justice-based approaches by attaching principles to care ethics, Addams's mandate to experience others seems fitting if care is to be more than parochial. The claim is neither universal nor absolute. As a pragmatist, Addams would not ask that we experience everybody or even all categories of people. Nonetheless, if we are to have the necessary internal resources to work for one another, to vote for representatives and bills that affect us all, and to care for one another, we will need to know each other in a more direct way. Addams calls for members of society, including its leaders, to be actively involved with one another, for otherwise it is difficult to know and care for one another. Addams's demand for connection seems even more imperative today, when technology and transportation give us a capacity for isolation greater than anything we have experienced previously.

From what we know of her writing work at Hull-House, Addams was clearly a care ethicist who recognized the embodied and imaginative aspect of care; furthermore, she transformed embodied care by adding the social mandate that we seek out others to know and care for. It is important to emphasize that Addams does not simply call for us to experience others randomly or without purpose. Addams employs a rich and complex understanding of democracy to frame the practices of embodied care.

Pragmatism's commitments to interaction, pluralism, community, and growth are present in Addams's understanding of democracy and the roles of citizens. Good citizens in a caring community must develop habits of interaction, including caring habits, in a way that maintains an understanding and respect for diversity and pluralism.[75] "It is inevitable that those who desire [social morality] must be brought in contact with the moral experiences of the many in order to procure an adequate social motive."[76] For Addams, community cannot be built without what might be termed "deep interaction": meaningful time spent with diverse people in the community that fosters understanding and the potential for care. "We realize, too, that social perspective and sanity of judgment come only from contact with social experience; that such contact is the surest corrective of opinions concerning the social order, and concerning efforts, however humble, for its improvement."[77] Here Addams links the values of interaction, pluralism, community, and growth. We cannot begin to have a democratic, caring, helping community without experiences of one another that let us better understand the plurality that exists among us. For Addams, democracy describes both our present experience of citizenship and an ideal of human interaction marked by a caring citizenry that works toward mutual benefit. Social morality and democracy go hand in hand.

The individual and communal growth that Addams sought for society bound personal relationships, local communities, and national concerns to one another. At Hull-House she worked to effect local changes in habit as well as national changes in policy. Addams believed something was amiss when communities were left behind or disconnected from social progress. She advocated "lateral progress," where advancement involves extending society's material, cultural, intellectual, and spiritual goods to all, realizing the reformer's belief that

> if in a democratic country nothing can be permanently achieved save through the masses of the people, it will be impossible to establish a higher political life

than the people themselves crave; that it is difficult to see how the notion of a higher civic life can be fostered save through common intercourse; that the blessings which we associate with a life of refinement and cultivation can be made universal and must be made universal if they are to be permanent; that the good we secure for ourselves is precarious and uncertain, is floating in mid-air, until it is secured for all of us and incorporated into our common life.[78]

Addams felt that no one should be left behind, and to that end she worked with and wrote about the marginalized of society. Addams's own body was in a sense a nexus for lateral progress, because she modeled habits of moving between the personal and the political to achieve lateral progress. Addams embodied care. By examining some specific habits of Addams's embodied care that are framed by the value of democracy, as well as the goal of lateral progress through the commitments to interaction, pluralism, community, and growth, we can begin to piece together the value that practices of embodied care have for a social philosophy.

The Social Habits of Embodied Care

In what follows I will address some of the specific habits about which Addams writes, as well as the practices she modeled, that support or extend her call for a wider experience of one another in the creation of a social ethics. These habits include active listening, participation (the democratic spirit), connected leadership, and activism. These practices provide the contours of a social-political embodied ethics of care.

While serving her community by working at Hull-House, Addams modeled an essential habit of embodied care: active listening. This habit can be viewed as a complex of simpler habits. What Merleau-Ponty has described as the body's ability to perceive another embodied being holistically, to focus on one individual out of a field of sensory input, and to recognize the continuity of embodied experience in the flesh are foundational aspects of the social habit of active listening.

For Addams, listening is much more than a passive, polite act of civilized individuals. Listening is the starting point for political action. Listening is how members of the Hull-House community came to interpret their neighbors and their needs. As Elshtain describes, "The mutual process of interpretation that takes place at Hull-House challenges and quickens human sympathies and is a powerful form of social learning."[79] By leaving the extent of their involvement open, Hull-House residents made a commitment to listen and learn. The paternalism of institutional charitable organizations that Addams criticized did not afford the kind of listening that made Hull-House flexible and trusted in the neighborhood. It was not a passive listening—waiting until the neighbors had something to say. Individuals in the Hull-House community assertively crossed class and racial boundaries to be physically present, living in the poverty-stricken working-class neighborhood and listening to its denizens. This physical presence makes a crucial difference in the quality of listening and the associated care.

Although the literature on care does not address it in depth, listening is a significant component of embodied caring. Authentic, active listening is a necessary condition for the attention (or Noddings's "engrossment") inherent in a caring relationship. If one is not open to understanding what the other has to say, it is difficult to characterize that relationship as caring. Physical presence enhances the caring in immeasurable ways. Much of what is communicated between people is found in the subtleties of facial expressions, hand gestures, posture, inflection, and eye contact. When one is actively attending to someone else face to face, these subtleties can be absorbed consciously and subconsciously through the body. Hull-House allowed Addams to be physically present and thus to listen actively to the stories of the poor and oppressed in a way that an outside visitor would have a difficult time replicating. Addams used what she learned through listening to people's stories to inform her writing and activism. Marilyn Fischer views Addams's physical presence in the community as integral to her philosophy: "Because she lived in the midst of Greek, German, Russian, Italian, Irish, and Polish immigrants, Addams accumulated vast, detailed knowledge of their daily lives. She uses this contextual knowledge repeatedly to show society's organized interconnectedness."[80]

Addams listened, but not to create ethnographies of the neighborhood inhabitants. She used what she learned to help meet the needs of the neighborhood. It is clear that Addams could not stray far from what she learned by listening to others' experiences at Hull-House, because in most of her books and articles she uses anecdotes and recollections from people she has met. For example, in *The Long Road of Women's Memory* Addams finds a social organizing function and present-day lessons in listening to the stories told by the elderly. In *Peace and Bread in Time of War* Addams credits listening to the immigrant community of Hull-House during the conscription for World War I for having shaped her commitment to peace.[81]

Susan Hekman identified one of the differences between Lawrence Kohlberg's and Carol Gilligan's work as arising from the way the two researchers employed their interpretive frameworks while listening to the stories of men and women. Whereas Kohlberg was "listening" for abstract principles, Gilligan was less presumptive in her listening. What emerged for Gilligan was the different voice of care. Although Hekman believes Gilligan was making a radical departure from the rationalist tradition by interpreting women's (and other oppressed peoples') stories as moral stories, she does not draw out the corporeal dimensions and political implication of this methodological shift. Addams employed the sort of methodology that Gilligan uses in nonjudgmentally listening to people's stories, but she added a social-political dimension to the process. Addams was physically present and listened to the unheard and oppressed of society not at a safe distance but face to face. In *The Silent Partner* Kelso maintains superficial understanding of the poor and Garth has an equally superficial view of the rich until they actively listen to each other. At Hull-House Addams chose to enter caring relationships that were mutually beneficial, but she used the knowledge gained to ameliorate the plight of neighborhood residents. Addams demonstrated that physically being present and actively listening to people constitute important habits in the social-political ethics of embodied care.

Cross-cultural communication has been the topic of tremendous discussion in postcolonial studies. Many rightly worry that people in positions of power can practice limited or selective listening. The potential for claiming ownership of or otherwise misrepresenting someone else's position increases when the relevant cultures are bound together in asymmetrical power relations. Although it is beyond the scope of this book to take on a comprehensive analysis of this important discussion, I can at least briefly examine how Addams's approach to active listening fares in regard to the standards put forth by Maria C. Lugones and Elizabeth V. Spelman in "Have We Got a Theory for You! Feminist Theory, Cultural Imperialism, and the Demand for 'The Woman's Voice.'" This article addresses some of the pitfalls that confront white women and women of color who attempt to write theory together. One of the particular concerns is whether the voices of women of color are lost or distorted. The authors identify the dichotomy of the "outsider" and "insider" to describe the theorizer's subject position: "Only when genuine and reciprocal dialogue takes place between 'outsider' and 'insiders' can we trust the outsider's account."[82] Given her Hull-House experience, Addams would be labeled the outsider in the working-class neighborhood, but she clearly acted to create the "reciprocal dialogue" that Lugones and Spelman describe.

For example, in *Twenty Years at Hull-House* Addams relates an incident when striking shoe factory workers met at Hull-House.[83] Addams and the other residents of Hull-House listened to the striking women, who told them that the workers who lived in rented apartments were the most vulnerable because they had to make monthly payments. The group decided to create a boarding club that would accommodate working women and provide flexibility in rent collection in the event of hard times, such as a strike. A dialogue between community members sparked this venture and saw it through to fruition. Hull-House established the "Jane Club," providing seed money and organizational support for start-up, but the operation was then turned over to the working women to manage. The openness to new ideas and the lack of paternalistic control suggests that Lugones and Spelman would approve of this venture as meeting the criteria for reciprocal dialogue.

Spelman and Lugones also call for friendship when women of color and white feminists attempt to work together. "If you enter the task out of friendship with us, then you will be moved to attain the appropriate reciprocity of care."[84] The proactive embodied care practiced by Addams inevitably leads to the formation of friendships. Hull-House fostered numerous opportunities for human connection both internally and externally. Internally Hull-House provided a unique structure for a woman-centered activist environment that brought together some of the great minds of the time. One of the extraordinary photographs reprinted in *100 Years at Hull-House* depicts Jane Addams dining with the accomplished physicians Rachelle Yarros and Alice Hamilton at either side of her.[85] There were probably few venues where women of such achievement worked, lived, and socialized together. Eleanor Stebner suggests that friendship was an important aspect of Hull-House's success: "The friendships made and fostered at Hull House enlarged the personal worlds of each woman. They helped each woman identify her unique vocation, and served as a basis for her social and political involvement."[86] In her philosophic exploration of friendship, Marilyn Friedman proposes that friendships are crucial for moral development: "Friendship provides us with an inclination or invitation to take our friends seriously and to take seriously what our friends care about."[87] The personal relationships among Hull-House residents fueled their activism and modeled the spirit of connection they sought with the neighborhood at large. One of their efforts to connect the community was a series of social clubs whose activities centered on the arts, education, politics, or many times simply socialization. Addams describes the underlying theory of the social clubs: "Through friendly relations with individuals, which is perhaps the surest method of approach, they [people from all over the city] are thus brought into contact, many of them for the first time, with the industrial and social problems challenging the moral resources of our contemporary life."[88] This statement suggests how savvy Addams was about the value of friendly relations. She recognized that caring relations were important for understanding serious issues in the community. The comfortable atmosphere of a social club, while appearing as a mere social opportunity, provided an opportunity for direct embodied experience across social barriers. This experience included active listening, which would facilitate understanding and possibly activating care. For example, the Working People's Social Science Club was one of many Hull-House clubs that were committed to the free exchange of ideas even when the speaker was controversial. As Addams describes it, "Although the residents of Hull-House were often baffled by the radicalism within the Social Science Club and harassed by the criticism from outside, we still continued to believe that such discussion should be carried on."[89]

Given the history of disfranchised peoples in Western civilization, suspicion of listening across cultures or social classes is understandable. Although the preceding discussion only scratches the surface, Addams's commitment to promoting social relationships to those who are mutually involved, interactive, and caring makes active listening a central concern.

Addams's proactive embodied care mandates that we seek out a variety of experiences of others. These experiences are crucial for her notion of democracy and the interconnection of people supporting a caring society. Addams's proactive bias fuels her advocacy of social and political participation. Fischer describes Addams's understanding of ethical action as coming through "widespread, cooperative, highly participatory efforts, rather than through individually directed activities."[90]

Regarding every aspect of society—political, economic, and social—Addams believes that where possible, people should be physically present and involved: a caring habit of participation. For Addams, participation is an active, embodied habit of care. It involves a physical presence and an active engagement, and indeed, Hull-House's physical presence led directly to its residents' participation in the surrounding community. Participation can take many forms, but as a social habit, it involves the development of numerous interpersonal habits of communication, collective effort, and strategic thinking that are strengthened through practice. Participation improves the quality and quantity of relationships, which in turn builds corporeal resources or caring knowledge, providing more bases with which a caring imagination can work. As Addams says, "Unless all men and all classes contribute to a good, we cannot even be sure that it is worth having."[91] To demonstrate Addams's practice of participation, I will briefly explore the economic critique in her analysis of the Pullman strike of 1894.

In *Democracy and Social Ethics* Addams recounts the Pullman strike of 1894 to make a point about the need for participation in social organizations. The Pullman Palace Car Company manufactured rail cars in an assembly plant near Chicago. Workers lived in a company town, and "Pullman" was a household name at the time. When economic hard times hit in 1893, the company eliminated workers and reduced wages. Subsequently a strike was called. The strike was eventful, for the U.S. Army intervened following allegations of violence and the union leader, Eugene Debs (a Hull-House visitor), was thrust into the national limelight, later becoming the leader of the Socialist Party of America. Addams viewed the disconnection between labor and management to be one reason for the strike.

Addams was not just interested in the quantity of relationships; such relationships are important to ensure diverse experiences, but their quality is significant as well. Specifically, she advocates connected, involved social relations. In discussing the Pullman strike, Addams invokes the democratic ideal as one that calls for "representation in the administration of industry."[92] She views the new democratic spirit as one that mandates participation throughout society, including the management of businesses. She couches the Pullman conflict in terms of more traditional "individual or aristocratic management" versus democratic management. Although removed from Marxist analysis in many ways, Addams did believe that a more socialistic form of organization is an inevitable part of social progress.

Addams views traditional business organizations as anything but the free associations they claim to be. In reality, economic conditions pressure people into entering the "undemocratic conditions of the factory organization."[93] For example, in *A New Conscience and an Ancient Evil* Addams lays partial blame for the rise of prostitution and white slavery on an economic system that lacks an effective support system and pays women low wages.[94] Addams claims that the business environment is much less free than the rest of social life and that the tradition of autocratic management is flawed and contributes to workers' oppression. "The man who disassociates his ambition, however disinterested, from the cooperation of his fellows, always takes this risk of ultimate failure."[95] In this case, George Pullman was that man.

In *Democracy and Social Ethics* Addams critiques patriarchal institutions such as capitalism by imploding underlying premises from within the structure of relationships created by social institutions rather than by attacking their external manifestations. Instead of confronting issues of the distribution of wealth, private property, or even worker rights, Addams questions the types of relationships capitalism creates. She is concerned that it is easy for the capitalist to make decisions on behalf of many who have no voice in the strict contractual nature of the marketplace.[96] The concern is that capitalism can squelch certain habits of participation and communication. Much like Phelps in *The Silent Partner*, Addams focuses not on abstract theories of economic operation but on the real experience of people in a business organization as exhibited by the Pullman strike. In her earlier treatment of this incident, "A Modern Lear," Addams chastises those, such as anarchists and socialists, who focus on freeing wage workers from oppression without considering the full impact of "human affection" and "social justice" on those in power.[97] Her notion of participation cuts to both sides of labor-management relations. Addams desires greater worker participation in decision making and greater management participation in the employees' work lives to foster understanding and care.[98]

One method of accomplishing this goal is to increase people's reciprocal embodied experiences of one another. By connecting her economic critique to notions of democratic participation, Addams taps into values within the American tradition, making it difficult to marginalize her views as being those of an outsider or antithetical to the American ethos.

As her analysis of the Pullman strike demonstrates, Addams puts a great deal of emphasis on habits of participation in decision making and leadership. Participation is integral to what she refers to as the democratic spirit. For Addams, the democratic spirit encompasses a moral dimension but most essentially involves changing the way people relate to one another. This transformation requires widespread participation. Although participation can take many forms, a physical, embodied dimension is a major component. Habits or practices of being physically present to workers, being physically present to voters, and being physically present to those in need bring embodied knowledge that cannot be fully replicated in any other way. Their shared disconnection with what is dear to them in part motivates Addams's comparison of George Pullman to King Lear. Lear is disconnected from his daughters, and Pullman has lost touch with his workers. Had Pullman taken the time to listen and be present to his workers, he might not have been as shocked by the growing labor discontent. For Addams, democracy implies a system of relationships where people genuinely care for each other and adopt habits indicative of their willingness to act on those sentiments. Pullman, however, failed to connect and care: "To follow the path of social morality results perforce in the temper if not the practice of the democratic spirit, for it implies that diversified human experience and resultant sympathy which are the foundation and guarantee of Democracy."[99] In this instance Addams makes a relatively clear statement about the connections among experience, sympathy, and democracy. Two causal links are offered. First, we must experience one another, and in this interpersonal experience, we develop sympathies, or what could be termed empathy or understanding. Second, our developed sympathies from our diverse experiences undergird a democratic spirit, which will govern our decisions and actions. Addams reaffirms this formula in the negative a few pages later: "Much of the insensibility and hardness of the world is due to the lack of imagination which prevents a realization of experiences of other people."[100] When we cannot realize the experiences of others—when our imagination prevents an affective response—the result is insensitivity.

For Addams, democracy is not a set of abstract principles but a guide for action and a statement about fundamental beliefs in the goodness of others. She integrates morality and human ontology: "We are thus brought to a conception of Democracy not merely as a sentiment which desires the well-being of all men, nor yet as a creed which believes in the essential dignity and equality of all men, but as that which affords a rule of living as well as a test of faith."[101] In the final chapter of *Democracy and Social Ethics* she equates those who are frightened by democracy as "losing their faith in the people."[102] For Addams, the democratic spirit entails believing in the underlying goodness of people, thus making the democratic impulse an active and participatory search for living in right relation to others.

In 1932, a few years before Addams's death, the American theologian and social commentator Reinhold Niebuhr published his influential work *Moral Man and Immoral Society.* Niebuhr believed it was up to individual morality to overcome the inevitable foibles of social morality.[103] Although Addams shared Niebuhr's confidence in individual morality, she did not share his pessimism about society. Addams repeatedly argues that society can improve the lives of its constituency if a democratic spirit of active participation in the lives of all is fostered. This is not a utopian fantasy, such as those of the Social Gospelers, which became the foil for Niebuhr's realism. Addams's vision for society was practical, as her successes at Hull-House exhibited, yet hopeful about what a participatory society could accomplish.

Although Addams favors the engaged participation of group members, she is not adverse to leadership. Consistent with her notions of active listening and participation, however, leaders should be well connected to their constituency: "The real leaders of the people are part of the entire life of the community which they control, and so far as they are representative at all, are giving a social expression to democracy."[104] Connected leadership is another advanced habit of care that coalesces a number of bodily habits to form a complex practice. In this context *connected* is an epistemological term referring to a level of understanding that includes caring knowledge of the body. Without caring knowledge, the leader will suffer from incomplete understanding—missing the affective and emotive knowledge found in the body—and therefore disconnected from the group she or he leads. This lack of caring knowledge will give the caring imagination less to work with and increase the chances that actions and policies undertaken will not reflect the group's needs, feelings, and well-being. In the chapter of *Democracy and Social Ethics* titled "Political Reform," Addams finds a surprising example of connected leadership in the civic leaders of Chicago.

Addams battled the political machine in Chicago for many years. This city government was notorious for its cronyism, vote buying, backroom deals, and other questionable activities. Although Addams recognized the inherent corruption in this system, she came to appreciate what made many political bosses so popular: their connection to people's lives. Granting that Chicago aldermen are "corrupt and often do their work badly,"[105] Addams provides example after example showing how these politicians maintained strong local connections to provide assistance when needs arose. Practicing habits of connected leadership, the aldermen knew how to work the neighborhoods by forming associations, attending local organization meetings, and generally being visibly present to community members. Their physical presence in the neighborhood gave people a tangible connection to their leaders: "Men living near to the masses of voters, and knowing them intimately, recognize this and act upon it; they minister directly to life and to social needs."[106] The motives of these politicians may not have been pure, but voters were willing to ignore excesses if they believed their leaders were listening to them and cared enough to act on their behalf. Addams sought political reform, but she believed the only way to achieve it was for the reformers to be grounded in the experience of the people to the extent that the corrupt local aldermen had been.

These local officials were perceived as having a tangible relationship with their constituency. Addams argues that their physical presence in the community—their connection to the community—demonstrated moral responsiveness that outweighed abstract theoretical notions of social or political ethics: "Ethics as well as political opinions may be discussed and disseminated among the sophisticated by lectures and printed pages, but to the common people they can only come through example—through a personality which seizes the popular imagination."[107] Nevertheless, many of the aldermen exhibited superficial embodied care. Under the Chicago system care was politicized to procure favors and to facilitate power advantages. Addams observes, "All this [usage of alderman influence] conveys the impression to the simple-minded that law is not enforced, if the lawbreaker have a powerful friend."[108] If the aldermen had nothing to gain from the demonstrations of care, the acts would cease. What made the embodied care of Hull-House residents different from that of the Chicago aldermen is that they sought no such material reciprocity. Although there is always mutuality involved in care, the aldermen exacted a steep price for theirs.

The Chicago aldermen enjoyed success antithetical to what Addams found in the leadership of George Pullman. Although he had provided his workers with many services, Pullman failed to maintain contact with their lives and needs. Pullman's benevolence was derived from an abstract knowledge of his workers, not a direct relationship that could have created better understanding. The aldermen had developed habits of connected leadership, whereas Pullman had not.

In arguing for habits of grounded or connected leadership, Addams makes a claim that is both continuous with but separate from the call for participation. Whether one is running a business or running a government, participation is a critical prerequisite for the democratic spirit to flourish. Workers should have a voice in the operations of a business, just as citizens should have a voice in the choices of their government. Grounded leadership takes the notion of participation one step further. According to Addams, leaders should stay in contact with their constituencies, with such participation becoming an ongoing element of their leadership.[109] Listening plays a vital role in this type of leadership as social habits of care overlap one another. The connection created by listening makes a statement about the quality of the ongoing relationship between leaders and their constituencies. According to Addams, the democratic spirit transforms the leader-follower relationship, breaking down the social distance between the two poles. The implication is that the leader should not only be available to listen and care about those in his or her charge but literally be present and emerge from the people in a highly connected manner.

Just as the settlement movement broke down the physical distance that accompanied the gap between classes, Addams sought a social morality that will break down the social psychology of the power distance between leaders and nonleaders: "In this effort toward a higher morality in our social relations, we must demand that the individual shall be willing to lose the sense of personal achievement, and shall be content to realize his activity only in connection with the activity of the many."[110] Addams exemplified this belief in her own habits of leadership at Hull-House. Addams was pragmatic enough to recognize that Hull-House and its many projects needed bold leadership, despite the criticisms of some who believed the settlement should exemplify a utopian vision of leaderless equality.[111] Nevertheless, her leadership was clearly grounded in the neighborhood in which she lived and the community that surrounded her. Rather than set a rigid plan of services it would provide, Hull-House residents consistently attempted to meet the needs that arose around them.

Habits are established practices of the body. They count as caring habits if they promote the growth, development, and flourishing of the one to whom care is given, be it self or other. These caring habits do not occur in a vacuum but result from the interplay of caring knowledge in the body and the caring imagination. Caring habits can be described as actions directed toward the well-being of self or others. Addams's view of social ethics has a strong bias toward habits of taking action: "For action is indeed the sole medium of expression for ethics."[112] Addams did not write out a theory of social engagement prior to her involvement with the settlement movement. Her social ethics is derived from her experiences and actions at Hull-House. I have already quoted her statement regarding the moral obligation to choose life experiences that will allow the widest range of contact and understanding of human existence. Prior to confronting moral dilemmas, Addams has tipped her hand in favor of the active over the passive. Rather than allow life's experiences to come as they may, Addams favors plotting a course that will bring one into interaction with people of various lots to promote understanding and ultimately action on their behalf. In a cycle of social habits, action begets experience that begets further action.

Like an open inquiry, Addams's habits of social action are fluid and reciprocal.[113] Action changes both the environment and the individual: "The young woman who has succeeded in expressing her social compunction through charitable effort finds that the wider social activity, and the contact with the larger experience, not only increases her sense of social obligation but at the same time recasts her social ideals."[114] Addams describes social ethics in terms of *praxis,* with theory and action operating in a dynamic relationship of influence. This approach is consistent with Addams's Hull-House experience of acting to meet the day-to-day needs of the community while formulating a philosophy of connection. Her habits of action and her philosophy informed each other.

In *Democracy and Social Ethics,* linking her notion of participation to action, Addams argues that a group's clumsy and ineffective efforts can be more socially valuable than the more effective action taken by an individual. She regards the process of collective action to be as significant as its outcome. In *Newer Ideals of Peace* Addams recalls the French *l'impérieuse bonté* as the irrepressible impulse toward compassionate conduct. She is not satisfied in leaving this as an individual concept, however, and questions whether the current context calls for a collective expression of this impulse.[115] For Addams, social action, like the experience of caring, has a transformative quality whereby working together toward a goal may spread the democratic spirit, which in turn will affect future actions.

Addams concludes *Democracy and Social Ethics* with an emphasis on caring habits of taking action. Her words recall the significance of concretizing experiences of the other in a care orientation. When one acts, morality can no longer be abstract. To act is to confront a reality and generate an experience: "We continually forget that the sphere of morals is the sphere of action, that speculation in regard to morality is but observation and must remain in the sphere of intellectual comment, that a situation does not really become moral until we are confronted with the question of what shall be done in a concrete case, and are obliged to act upon our theory."[116] While theorizing about morality presents little personal risk, acting is risky. Addams is willing to embrace that risk as part of the democratic spirit.

The End in View: Lateral Progress

A careful analysis of Addams' writing reveals that what was often dismissed as sentimentality was actually a politics of connection that gives care ethics a viable sociopolitical dimension. Her social ethics holds a vision of a democratic spirit that can lead to human flourishing. Addams offers a means for realizing the value of care at the social level. By calling for and practicing habits of embodied care, Addams began with a local epistemology of interpersonal relationships, listening to those around Hull-House and understanding their plights. She took that knowledge and experience and developed a series of practices that placed direct physical interpersonal involvement at the forefront of changing society for the better. The caring society Addams envisioned is not a clear utopian image but a less well defined "end in view." This tentative telos is not out of reach, yet it remains a great social challenge. Addams's end in view is comprehensible given the moral imagination and the embodied resources derived from experience. Addams had experienced the closeness of community and the attending affective responses of reciprocal caring. She knew that such caring could make an appreciable difference in the lives of people both psychologically and materially. Addams wished to extend this caring to society in what she called "lateral progress." The person who practices a proactive embodied care "has to discover what people really want, and then 'provide the channels in which the growing moral force of their lives shall flow.' What he does attain, however, is not the result of his individual striving, as a solitary mountain climber beyond the sight of the valley multitude, but it is underpinned and upheld by the sentiments and aspirations of many others. Progress has been slower perpendicularly, but incomparably greater because lateral."[117] This lateral progress is the idea that true advances are evaluated for their contribution to the whole of society rather than to a select few who are the best and brightest (as supported by social Darwinism). Without advocating a utopian notion of perfect equality, the commitment to lateral progress demands a certain valorization of equality. Fischer argues that Addams "saw the failure of American commitment to equality in criminally unsafe factories, inadequate wages, and the simple refusal of the well-to-do to associate in friendship and fellowship with the poor."[118] For Addams, developing social habits of care and connection will yield lateral progress that can benefit all.

If embodied care is part of our vision for the lateral progress of society, then we must determine how to organize society to achieve this goal. For example, how could we structure schools to place care as a high priority? Addams provides one model. Active listening, participation, connected leadership, and activism can be used to create schools that are responsive to the needs of students and society. Furthermore, care could be elevated to a foremost objective in education. Noddings, who is a professor of education, contends that "we should educate all our children not only for competence but also for caring. Our aim should be to encourage the growth of competent, caring, loving, and lovable people."[119] If such a goal were adopted, then opportunities for students to develop caring habits would be an important means to that goal. Education is just one institution of society, but the practices of law, medicine, and politics can all be examined in regard to their social application of the habits of care. Returning to my claim in the first chapter, if care is indeed more than the basis for just another ethical theory, if it is something foundational to embodied existence, then we need to mitigate what inhibits habits of care and foster what facilitates them, as Jane Addams did.

A Genealogy of Care

The social philosophy of Jane Addams brings us to the latest generation in a particular genealogy of what I have called embodied care. This genealogy traces its roots to treatments of morality in the spirit of Hume and Adam Smith, but it finds its first developed expression and character in the writing of feminist care ethicists such as Gilligan and Noddings. Care ethicists perform the essential function of naming the previously unnamed: an approach to morality that is relational, emotive, contextual, and lacking in a dependence on rules or formulaic considerations of consequences. Surprisingly, little attention has been given to the corporeal dimension of care.

Earlier I described care as not yielding just another moral theory (care ethics) but as an approach to morality that is more foundational than a theory and that can be understood fully only if we attended to its embodied aspects. The phenomenological reduction of Merleau-Ponty allows us to address basic workings of the body in perception, focus phenomenon, flesh, and habits that reveal how the body can maintain caring knowledge and caring habits. Whereas Merleau-Ponty claims that the body is built for perception, however, I extend that claim to suggest that the body is built for care. The activities of the body, including its knowledge and habits, make care possible—hence the term *embodied care.* The body provides resources in imagination, knowledge, and habits that make it possible to transcend time, space, and social situation to care for others. This care is not a totalizing impulse, claiming to occupy another's subject position, but rather an extension of the flesh that allows for a level of understanding. Caring imagination, caring knowledge, and caring habits are enmeshed in a dynamic relationship. The works of Addams demonstrate how care is essential for building community and developing social policy. Addams was not a disconnected social leader or theorist. She actively confronted the outcast of society to help and care for them as well as to inform her activism and political strategizing. Addams's work contributes complex social habits of care that are rich in meaning and involve the orchestration of many caring habits developed through personal interaction. Social habits of care perform embodied care at the institutional level without losing site of the significance of care as a response to individuals.

In the following chapter I will briefly examine the difference embodied care makes to moral inquiry by exploring a contemporary social issue: same-sex marriage.

5. What Difference Does Embodied Care Make? A Study of Same-Sex Marriage

Widows and Children First, the third play of Harvey Fierstein's *Torch Song Trilogy,* relates the tale of Arnold Beckoff, a gay man who has recently lost his partner of five years, Alan, in a brutal hate crime. Arnold struggles to convey his grief to his mother, who has recently lost her husband of thirty-five years to an illness. In one scene Arnold tries to explain to his mother why he is participating in a foster-parenting program, and the conversation turns into a examination of the feelings of homosexuals in a committed relationship.

Arnold: Because I was tired of widowing.

Ma: Wida-whating?

Arnold: Widowing. Widow-ing. It's a word of Murray's.

Ma: And a nice one at that. What does it mean?

Arnold: You know.

Ma: No, I don't know.

Arnold: Widowing . . . feeling sorry for myself, cursing every time I passed a couple walking hand in hand, watching Tear Jerkers on T.V., knowing they could only cheer me up. Christ, of all the things going down here I was sure that was the one thing I wouldn't have to explain.

Ma: How should I know about Whatchmacallit? Did you ever say a word to me?

Arnold: I didn't think I had to. Christ, it's only been three years since Daddy died.

Ma: Wait, wait, wait, wait, wait. Are you trying to compare my marriage with you and Alan? (*Haughty and incensed*) Your father and I were married for thirty-five years, had two children and a wonderful life together. You have the nerve to compare yourself to that?

Arnold: That's what I mean, I'm talking about the loss.

Ma: What loss did you have? You fooled around with some boy . . . ? Where do you come to compare that to a marriage of thirty-five years?

Arnold: You think it doesn't?

Ma: Come on, Arnold. You think you're talking to one of your pals?

Arnold: Ma, I lost someone that I loved very much . . .

Ma: So you felt bad. Maybe you cried a little. But what would you know about what I went through? Thirty-five years I lived with that man. He got sick, I brought him to the hospital and you know what they gave me back? I gave them a man . . . they gave me a paper bag with his watch, wallet, and wedding ring. How could you possibly know what that felt like. It took me two months until I could sleep in our bed alone, a year to learn to say "I" instead of "we." And you're going to tell me you were widowing. How dare you![1]

Mrs. Beckoff is aghast at the comparison between her marriage and her son's relationship with his lover not simply because of the different lengths of the two relationships but because, for Mrs. Beckoff, a homosexual relationship cannot be anything like a heterosexual relationship ("you fooled around with some boy"). This dialogue presents an interesting dilemma for embodied care. In the *Torch Song Trilogy* we confront a mother and a son angrily comparing their grief. These are not the "unknown others" I addressed in previous chapters. The predisposition for care and empathy should be high given the proximal familial relations of parent and child. Nevertheless, Mrs. Beckoff refuses to acknowledge the depth of her son's grief. There is a barrier to care that may arise in part from social norms that marginalize homosexuals and render their relations illegitimate. Arnold recognizes the duplicity:

Arnold (*Over her speech*): Listen Ma, you had it easy. You have thirty-five years to remember, I have five. You had your children and friends to comfort you. I had me! My friends didn't want to hear about it. They said, "What're you gripin' about? At least you had a lover." 'Cause everybody knows that queers don't feel nothin'. How dare I say I loved him? You had it easy, Ma. You lost your husband in a nice clean hospital, I lost mine out there. They killed him there on the street. Twenty-three years old, laying dead on the street. Killed by a bunch of kids with baseball bats. (*Ma has fled the room. Arnold continues to rant.*) Children. Children taught by people like you. 'Cause everybody knows that queers don't matter! Queers don't love! And those that do deserve what they get![2]

Arnold twice invokes what he perceives as socially prevalent beliefs: "Everybody knows that queers don't feel nothin'" and "Everybody knows that queers don't matter." He expresses the turmoil that he supposes his mother faces but will not say directly. She is grieving for her husband, so she should understand how her son feels, yet she is insulted that a homosexual relationship could be compared to her marriage. For Mrs. Beckoff marriage is a sacred, legitimate expression of a commitment between a woman and a man. Arnold and Alan could express no such commitment.

In the eyes of society, in the eyes of the law, and in the eyes of Arnold's mother, homosexual relationships are inferior to married, heterosexual relationships. Given their parent-child relationship, however, she should understand Arnold and his feelings as well as anyone can. Here embodied care confronts socially constructed limitations that leave the observer believing that Arnold's mother could understand his grief if only she could get past the stigma attached to the word *gay*. As Hume would argue, Arnold's grief should invoke analogous feelings in her,[3] yet a powerful force blocks sympathetic understanding. It would be too easy to claim that Mrs. Beckoff simply needs to be more sympathetic toward her son's grief. Such a position would dismiss her socially constructed value system and her experiences. Nevertheless, caring is not without its commitments. Our connectedness is one important commitment. A great opportunity for caring would result if Arnold were to listen to his mother's pain and connect it with his own. Caring is always a choice, however, and there is no guarantee that the barriers will be overcome. Still, unless the relationship has been abusive or oppressive, it should provide the mother and her grown son significant resources, including embodied ones, for rekindling their mutual care.

Fierstein uses his craft to elicit an affective response from his audience. Drama, like all other fiction, can move people to care to a degree not usually attained through moral theorizing. As Noddings claims, "Real literature tells existential stories and moves us in ways that philosophical fiction cannot."[4] Unlike propositional knowledge, the pleas of Arnold Beckoff can spark emotions in the readers or the audience that mere facts or rational arguments about the rights of homosexuals cannot. Mrs. Beckoff's indignation also draws forth from the audience an understanding of the frustration she feels given the changes in her life as well as the shifting norms and values around her. Through our vicarious participation in the lives of the characters, we can feel their pain and joy. Indeed, theatrical productions are usually designed to involve the audience's emotions. We come to care about what happens to the characters. The caring imagination allows the audience to feel continuity with complex and realistic characters, such as Shakespeare's Shylock or

Fierstein's Arnold and Mrs. Beckoff. The audience can empathize with Arnold's solitary grief and Mrs. Beckoff's violated morality. We are confronted with human suffering, much of it unnecessary.

Jane Addams's social mandate seems to make passive empathizing with fictional characters insufficient. According to Addams, "A situation does not really become moral until we are confronted with the questions of what shall be done in a concrete case, and are obliged to act upon our theory."[5] Nevertheless, experiencing the literary arts can contribute to our diverse knowledge of others and is therefore an important social habit of care, as Nussbaum has suggested.[6] Watching a drama unfold can help instill habits of empathy and caring. If lateral progress is to take place, however, there must be the kind of domain transfer that Mark Johnson describes, where our embodied experiences in one domain are metaphorically mapped onto other aspects of our lives. In other words, we must be able to leap imaginatively from art to life. The disruptive and affective dimension of an embodied experience of the arts can change our lives, sometimes significantly. A new range of habits opens to us if we allow the drama into our existence. Of course, not every experience of art will have this impact, and perhaps few can change our lives profoundly. Nonetheless, art does more than just imitate life; it can challenge the living to see, feel, and hear with one another. If art is indeed more than amusement and escapism, then the theatrical experience should also have the power to elicit an affective response that motivates us to further alter social habits for the betterment of our society.

* * *

This chapter will conclude my exploration of embodied care by discussing the current issue of same-sex marriage. It seems only fitting that an approach to ethics that is embodied and contextual delve into a concrete contemporary issue. Embodied care can be applied to any situation, but I selected a controversial issue that is somewhat unique to the present;[7] moreover, the recent rash of legislation on gay marriage makes this an opportune moment for such a discussion. For Addams, writing in the early twentieth century, prostitution, child labor, worker exploitation, and the specter of war provided plenty of concrete material for ethical analysis. Given that feminism not only initiated discussions of care but also has provided a safe space for lesbian issues and theory, same-sex marriage is an appropriate topic for applying embodied care to a real-world issue.

The first of this chapter's three principal sections will briefly address the difference embodied care makes in the consideration of moral issues. The second will address how some of the arguments surrounding same-sex marriage are framed. Particular attention will be paid to the moral language used to support and oppose gay marriage. The third and central part of the chapter addresses how an emphasis on embodied care transforms the discussion of same-sex marriage. This analysis will require that we revisit certain theoretical matters and examine how the process of moral consideration is transformed, as well as how values are changed, by attending to what it means to care through the body.

The Difference That Embodied Care Makes

Embodied care alters the way we approach ethical issues. This occurs in at least two ways, epistemologically and axiologically. Again, embodied care expands the knowledge base "brought to the table." People considering controversial issues generally want to know the facts of the case: who, what, when, where, and how? Such information is indeed important, but embodied care also valorizes the affective knowledge that is continuous with the facts: feelings, passions, and sympathies. This broadened notion of moral epistemology resonates with Margaret Urban Walker's claim that "morality needs to be seen as something existing, however imperfectly, in real human social spaces in real time, not something ideal or noumenal in character. And both the understandings of morality within societies and the understandings of morality in moral philosophy need to encompass many kinds of information about human social worlds and many forms of interpersonal recognition in thought, feeling, and response."[8] For example, my body knows an array of feelings that can help me empathize not only with the positions concerning an issue but with the affections and relations that accompany the position. Suppose a man expresses moral outrage over the idea of allowing same-sex marriage, and I see his facial expression, his flushed cheeks, and his sweaty brow; my body has the resources to understand, at least in part, what it is to be this passionate about an issue. My body captures an implicit understanding of the other.

This is where an emphasis on embodied epistemology transforms the ethical approach. My embodied knowledge does not necessarily help me resolve the issue, but it does help me understand the advocate of a particular position. Solving the problem is the traditional focus of those concerned with moral dilemmas. As Walker laments, "I have come to wonder, or rather to worry about, why it is so important to know whether 'we' are right and 'they' are wrong, tout court."[9] Care acknowledges that resolving the issue is not the whole of morality. I need to maintain my dignity and my relationship with the agents involved. Gilligan began the discussion of care ethics by pointing to an alternative moral voice of connection that has been ignored in philosophical discourse,[10] and a focus on embodied care reinforces interconnection by starting with our shared embodiment. Here the underlying value of interconnectedness comes to the fore. This interconnectedness begins with our shared embodiment. It is fostered and extended through our caring and is a means for structuring social relations.

Embodied care also reframes the values involved in ethical analysis. Recall that I define care as providing an approach to personal and social morality that shifts ethical considerations to context, relationships, and affective knowledge in a manner that can be fully understood only if its embodied dimension is recognized. Care is committed to the flourishing and growth of individuals yet acknowledges our interconnectedness and interdependence. The notion of embodied care reveals that moral principles are not themselves of ultimate value. Rules and the consideration of consequences are ethical aids, but they are not the whole of morality; in the rush to adjudicate acts, people and context can be lost or forgotten. To employ habits of embodied care, such as listening and encouraging active participation, is to value individual beings, including their relationships and context. Even with a caring approach, we may decide that following the rules or choosing the best consequences is the right decision in a particular case—but then again, we may not. The issue of same-sex marriage will provide an opportunity to apply these distinctions.

Same-Sex Marriage

The specific issue at stake here is whether it is morally licit for two men or two women to participate in a marriage that has the same social and legal status as heterosexual marriage. No nation allowed gays and lesbians to wed until 2001, when the Netherlands became the first. Several countries now recognize legal partnership status, however, and the legal recognition of the rights of same-sex partners is on the rise worldwide.[11] Because marriage is usually a state-sanctioned public ritual, it is difficult to separate the moral from the legal issue. I will limit my discussion to the topic of same-sex marriage in the United States. Although this chapter focuses on marriage, heterosexual and homosexual couples can of course choose other arrangements, such as cohabitation without a marriage ritual. Nevertheless, marriage in Western culture has come to be an important signifier beyond the domestic union of two people. Heterosexual marriage is used as a unit of study in the social sciences, as an important category for tax and insurance purposes, and as a normative assumption in many people's lives.[12] Although less so than in the past, children and young people are often treated as if they are expected to marry someday, with speculations about their adulthood beginning, "When you grow up and get married . . ." Part of that assumption is bound up in the social norm of heterosexuality.

The current public discussion of gay marriage was precipitated when three same-sex couples applied for state marriage licenses in Hawai'i in 1990. They were refused, but a 1993 Hawai'i Supreme Court ruling, as well as a 1996 Hawai'i circuit judge ruling, suggested that denying same-sex marriage licenses might be unconstitutional. That statement sent political shockwaves across the country. Antigay "defense of marriage" laws were proposed in several states, and many were enacted. The turmoil pointed to an intriguing conflict in public thinking on the subject of gay rights. A May 1996 *Newsweek* poll found that 58 percent of respondents believed gay marriage should be illegal (versus 33 percent who thought it should be legal), but 84 percent of Americans believed there should be equal employment rights for gays.[13] This poll indicates that same-sex marriage strikes a nerve in a population that is otherwise predisposed to gay rights in the economic arena.

The issue of same-sex marriage is enmeshed in important symbolic concerns. Jonathon Goldberg-Hiller describes the reaction against same-sex marriage as indicative of a "long-simmering culture war" that emerged in part as a response to gay activism and visibility.[14] Andrew Sullivan views same-sex marriage "as the only [homosexuality-related] reform that truly matters" because of its importance as legitimizing homosexuality in society.[15] It appears that same-sex marriage is the line drawn in the sand with respect to gay rights.

In a 1996 midnight signing President Clinton wrote the Defense of Marriage Act (DOMA) into law. DOMA defines marriage as a union between a man and a woman and gives states the right to refuse recognition of same-sex marriages granted in other states. Although not banning same-sex marriage outright, DOMA eliminates federal spousal benefits for same-sex couples. After a brief lull the controversy over gay marriage erupted again when, on December 20, 1999, the Vermont Supreme Court ruled that same-sex couples have the same rights as heterosexual couples and ordered the Vermont legislature to craft laws to recognize the equality. On April 25, 2000, after four months of rancorous debate, the Vermont House of Representatives passed a progressive bill acknowledging civil unions between same-sex couples and giving them the most extensive rights in the nation.

Nonetheless, same-sex couples were still not allowed to marry. In the state that started the current spate of controversy, Hawai'i, citizens enacted a constitutional amendment defining marriage as a union between a man and a woman, supporting the measure two to one. The Hawai'i Supreme Court was then forced to declare its previous ruling on same-sex unions moot, which it did on December 9, 1999. At the federal level a definitive Supreme Court ruling has not taken place, and the public debate continues. Some conservatives fear that DOMA will be overturned as unconstitutional, leading them to support a campaign to pass an amendment to the U.S. Constitution that would define marriage as a union of a man and a woman.[16]

In addition, the issue involves more than just homosexuality, for some have questioned whether marriage itself is a desirable goal. There are some gays and lesbians who view marriage as an anachronism or at least a concept heavily burdened by historical baggage (e.g., high divorce rates, asymmetrical power relations, and domestic violence).[17] Given this history, some believe that either no marital signification or an alternative symbol of commitment is a superior choice to marriage. For example, one criticism of heterosexual marriage is that it implies ownership rights of one spouse over the other.[18] Still, although there is much to support a critique of romanticized notions of marriage, others argue that marriage is a symbol of legitimation that the gay community sorely needs given today's rampant homophobia. Such arguments not withstanding, studies indicate that 75 percent of lesbians and 85 percent of gays would marry if given the opportunity.[19] I will explore same-sex marriage with the understanding that it is not a panacea or every couple's goal, but it is a choice that a majority of same-sex couples would like to have.

Framing the Arguments

Applying traditional ethical categories, we can divide the majority of current arguments concerning same-sex marriage into deontological arguments based on principles, rules, or rights and teleological arguments based on consequences or outcomes. I will briefly examine these frameworks prior to exploring how an embodied ethic of care changes the analysis.

One approach in the former category focuses on the definition of marriage. Some make the claim that because "marriage" is understood as a particular kind of relationship—between a man and a woman—the term *gay marriage* is an oxymoron.[20] This linguistic argument seeks definitional authority as a kind of moral authority. For example, *Webster's Encyclopedic Unabridged Dictionary of the English Language*'s first definition of marriage is "the social institution under which a man and woman establish their decision to live as husband and wife by legal commitments, religious ceremonies, etc."[21] A series of court rulings have upheld the notion that marriage is intended to be heterosexual, although until recently it was not necessary to specify that marriage was between a man and a woman because heterosexual marriage was universally assumed. DOMA was conceived to address the absence of legal language explicitly mentioning heterosexuality. In the case of *Jones v. Hallahan*, where Tracy Knight and Marjorie Jones attempted to have Kentucky recognize their marriage, the court ruled that states do not have the authority to change the historical definition of marriage.[22] Such legal declarations are considered by some to be authoritative and logical. Robert H. Knight exemplifies this approach to the issue: "To place domestic partner relationships on a par with marriage denigrates the [meaning of marriage]. But to describe such relationships as 'marriage' destroys the definition of marriage altogether. When the meaning of a word becomes more inclusive, the exclusivity that it previously defined is lost."[23]

Of course, such semantic arguments can be countered by the principle that definitions can and do evolve. Witness, ironically, the transformation of the word *gay* over the past century. The historian Nancy Cott points out that "marriage has been a constantly evolving institution, and same-sex marriage is part of that evolution."[24] At the heart of semantic arguments against same-sex marriage is an attempt to use a formulaic rationality to resolve the controversy. If M (marriage) implies S (straight) and only S, then M is inconsistent with G (gay). The argument is valid, but it is also an abstraction that attempts to resolve the issue without involving feelings or real people. Proponents of same-sex marriage can counter these arguments by questioning the premises (why must M imply only S?) or by supplying their own (such as M implies S or G), but the discussion remains a logical abstraction.

Another deontological approach to same-sex marriage is to frame the arguments in terms of rights. Is the denial of same-sex marriage a violation of a right, and if so, is the right being abrogated a legal or a human right? Most of the arguments address legal rights. For example, William Eskridge Jr. dedicates a chapter of his book *The Case for Same-Sex Marriage* to constitutional arguments for legalizing same-sex marriage, including applications of the right to privacy and equal rights. The moral discussion involves the hierarchy of rights: "In light of the Supreme Court's precedents, a state's refusal to recognize same-sex marriage would seem to be both the denial of fundamental liberty and discrimination in the allocation of a fundamental right."[25] Robert Goss suggests that everyone, whether heterosexual or homosexual, has the positive right "to create family forms that fits his or her needs to realize the human potential for love in nonoppressive relationships."[26]

Sometimes the arguments surrounding rights address the unequal application of these rights. For example, M. D. A. Freeman argues that criminals such as "murderers and rapists" are allowed to marry, so why exclude homosexuals? Furthermore, he points out that no one is asked to prove sexual orientation when marrying, undermining the presumption that men and women who marry are heterosexual.[27] Another legal strategy is to claim that homosexuals occupy a position similar to those of oppressed ethnic groups (or "suspect class," in legal terms) and therefore deserve similar protection under the law.[28] Kevin Moss argues that the discrimination and stereotypes directed at homosexuals is one indication that they deserve status as a separate class.[29] Nevertheless, there has been strong legal and popular opposition to such a classification. I mention the previously cited examples not to debate the merits of the claim but to show how the pro-homosexual-marriage position can be as rational and detached as its opposite. These are not unimportant discussions. The law is the codification of social morality with significant real and symbolic implications. Framing the discussion in logical legalistic terms, however, leaves out the affective, emotive dimension. Embodied care does not appear to be at the fore of this semantic approach. How can the law reflect care? If context and affective knowledge were more highly valued, the arguments would be less concerned with winning the debate and more concerned with maintaining interconnectedness within the social fabric.

Yet another principle-based approach seeks a more solid foundation: religion. The orthodox teachings of Christianity, Islam, and Judaism all condemn homosexuality. Such religious claims are viewed as authoritative because they invoke the will of a deity. For example, although the Bible never specifically addresses same-sex marriage, it consistently condemns homosexuality.[30] Christianity does embrace pluralism to some extent,[31] but many conservative theologians find same-sex marriage to run counter to a core value of their faith. In 1999 Gordon B. Hinckley, then president of the Church of Jesus Christ of Latter-day Saints, addressed their annual general conference: "This issue has nothing to do with civil rights. For men to marry men or women to marry women, is a moral wrong."[32] Surprisingly, there is some ambivalence in the history of Christianity's regard for marriage. The historical denigration of sexual activity of any sort led to some suspicion about the actual motivation for marriage even among heterosexuals.[33] Nevertheless, even at its lowest theological status, marriage was upheld for its essential function of procreation. The *Catechism of the Catholic Church* states that the purpose of marriage largely revolves around the birthing and raising of children: "By its very nature the institution of marriage and married love is ordered to the procreation and education of the offspring and it is in them that it finds its crowning glory."[34] Of course, same-sex marriage precludes the possibility of procreation but not the raising of children. The *Catechism* does not provide an entry for same-sex marriage, but it does state that homosexual acts are "intrinsically disordered . . . [;] under no circumstances can they be approved."[35] The Roman Catholic Church's current teaching about sex is consistent in that any extramarital sex is illicit, and homosexual acts are by definition extramarital.

Still another religious approach to gay marriage does not invoke the Bible: natural law. As expounded by Thomas Aquinas, natural law consists of God-given moral principles that are discernible through reason. One of its tenets is that everything has a true nature and purpose. On this account, genitals are for procreation and so is marriage. This makes gay marriage unnatural and hence counter to natural law. According to the *Encyclopedia of Catholicism*, "The reason homosexuality is objectively immoral is that it lacks the finality that is proper to human sexuality."[36] For Aquinas, violations of natural law are extremely serious, because they run counter to God's law. In his analysis, homosexuality is comparable to homicide in its disregard for the natural order of human life.[37]

Legal, semantic, and religious arguments demonstrate how the discussion surrounding same-sex marriage can be framed around principle-based approaches to morality. They seek an authoritative rule or principle that supports a position. Accordingly, as in legal arguments, the opposition can attempt to find a counterprinciple to trump the original one. Principles play an important role in morality, and as I have suggested, embodied care is not antithetical to rule-based morality. Embodied care nevertheless recognizes that an abstract, formulaic approach to ethics does not capture the whole of human morality. Valuing embodied care involves asking questions that recenter the debate on the individuals involved, including their affections, relationships, and contexts. What are the emotions involved, and why are they so strong? How do various positions affect ongoing relationships? How do various positions affect social interconnectedness?

Not all the arguments surrounding gay marriage hinge on principles. There are numerous consequentialist arguments on both sides. One such approach is the claim that the state has a vested interest in a growing population, so it cannot legitimize same-sex marriage, for which procreation is not possible. Procreative consequences are ambiguous, however, since no intent to have children is required for heterosexual marriages.[38] Others, such as John M. Finnis, argue that same-sex marriage poses "an active threat to the stability of existing and future marriages."[39] Similarly, Robert George argues that the institution of marriage will be undermined if same-sex marriages are legitimized. George describes marriage as providing moral reasons for men and women to pledge exclusivity, fidelity, and permanence. He contends that allowing same-sex marriage transforms the institution into "a purely private matter designed solely to satisfy the desires of married parties."[40] Such a circumstance "would strike a blow against the institution more fundamental and definitive than the disastrous policy of 'no-fault' divorce."[41] According to George, the consequence of allowing same-sex marriages will be the end of marriage as we know it. Andrew Sullivan disputes this conclusion because same-sex marriage is not an alternative to heterosexual marriage: "There's precious little evidence that straights could be persuaded by any law to have sex with—let alone marry—someone of their own sex."[42] Still others argue that gay marriage harms children raised in such an environment. For example, Robert H. Knight states that gay marriage would "deny the procreative imperative that underlies society's traditional protection of marriage and family as the best environment in which to raise children" and that it poses a threat to "children's development of healthy sexual identities."[43] Knight claims that one outcome of gay marriage will be children who are confused about their sexuality, which is presumably a bad condition.

One sticky entanglement with abstract calculations of good is that they can be devised to support any number of positions depending on the slice of reality employed. For example, social conservatives equate marriage with a social good. The stability of society depends on these committed relationships. Taken at face value, more marriage must then equate with greater overall good. Therefore, allowing homosexuals to marry would result in more marriages and thus more good. Of course, there is a great deal of reservation in universally equating marriage with the good, but once again, the limitation of consequentialist logic is apparent.

Whereas the deontological arguments are abstract, often using textual evidence for support, the consequentialist arguments tend to cite empirical data and experience to point to possible outcomes. For example, Craig Benson, a pastor in the Cambridge United Church, claims that legalizing same-sex marriage is akin to supporting the idea that "motherless and fatherless families will not have an adverse effect on children. . . . that, from a developmental-psychology point of view, is a lie."[44] Benson claims that scientific data support his concern for the consequences to children. Of course, children readily elicit sympathy because of their vulnerability, so that people arguing about social issues often mention them when trying to justify their positions. Nevertheless, supporters of same-sex marriage can cite recent research that reveals children in homosexual families to suffer no significant disadvantage compared to children raised in heterosexual families.[45] Both sides of the issue have evidence to support their consequentialist perspectives. Those who favor same-sex marriage might even grant that there may be some negative results from legitimizing gay marriage; however, the good effects outweigh the bad. Sullivan proclaims that same-sex marriage is simply "good for gays. It provides role models for young gay people . . . [and] help[s] bridge the gulf often found between gays and their parents. . . . It could do much to heal the gay-straight rift."[46] The debate in this area thus centers on determining who has the most compelling evidence for their outcomes and which outcomes provide the greatest good for the most people.

Applying Embodied Care to the Issue of Same-Sex Marriage

As we have seen in the last three chapters, embodied care offers a different way of being moral. The term *being moral* is appropriate because the ethics associated with embodied care is not limited to the adjudication of particular acts. In many ways embodied care is a human comportment exhibited through habits. Habits of listening, touching, acting on behalf of others, and being present to others are all ways of being in the world. In this section I will discuss how an embodied-care approach would differ from justice-based approaches concerning same-sex marriage. In particular, I will discuss embodiment, imagination, and habits of listening as representative of the theoretical conclusions established in the previous three chapters. First I will focus on aspects of gay marriage that embodied care brings to the forefront, not formulas for making specific decisions. I will then discuss the process of developing social policy. Finally, I will indicate the conclusions that embodied care can yield concerning same-sex marriage.

The starting point for care is not an abstract theory of right and wrong but the concrete reality of interrelated human embodiment: *same-sex marriage is a controversial issue that involves members of the same species.* This seems like an absurdly obvious statement to begin the discussion, but as Merleau-Ponty has explained, human embodiment elaborates a great deal. Recall that Merleau-Ponty describes humans as "intercorporeal beings" whose embodied experiences—touch, sight, and so on—undergo a "propagation of these exchanges to all the bodies of the same type" resulting in a "transitivity from one body to another."[47] Earlier I employed Merleau-Ponty's phenomenology of the body to argue that knowledge is necessary but not sufficient for caring. This knowledge should be understood to include what the body implicitly knows and exhibits through its habits. The body's ability to perceive and focus, as well as its continuity with the flesh of the world, allows it to capture movements in habits. These habits not only give us the means for being in the world but also provide a basis for understanding and caring for others. The body is built for care. As I discussed earlier, however, the body is confronted with obstacles of time, space, and socially constructed differences that make caring difficult. These obstacles can be overcome by a caring imagination.

Sexual orientation has become just such an obstacle for caring. Labels such as *gay* and *straight* are so politically charged that it appears as if two completely different species are being addressed. For example, Richard D. Mohr describes one persistent stereotype of gay men as "child molester, and more generally as a sex-crazed maniac."[48] The persistence of such stereotypes allows homosexuals to be treated as dangerous others and perhaps as less-than-human predators. Collectively those fighting for gay rights have been marginalized through persistent labels. Goldberg-Hiller describes popular "stories about extensive gay and lesbian political agendas, outrageous queer direct action, poor hygiene and AIDS, pedophilia and the threat of youth 'recruitment'" as causing a reactionary retrenchment to romanticized notions of family and marriage.[49] Beginning with the obvious but commonly ignored idea that all the agents involved in the same-sex-marriage debate are humans who share an embodied nature produces a baseline of understanding.[50] Homosexual persons and heterosexual persons share much more than they do not in terms of physical movement, feelings, touch, sight, and so on. Although psychosocial forces have helped leverage differences in sexual orientation into central aspects of identity, the continuity of embodied experience provides tremendous potential resources for understanding across such differences.

Embodied care attends to the idea that at its core, the same-sex-marriage debate is about human beings and their relations. Fierstein recognizes the human continuity when he has Arnold Beckoff confront the social barriers that say, "Queers don't feel nothin'" and "Queers don't love." Fierstein is not presenting rational arguments or empirical evidence. In terms of traditional justice-based approaches, his play is morally ambiguous. Nevertheless, the affective knowledge disruptively forces audience members to confront the obvious, which they see and feel with the characters: of course homosexuals have the full range of human feelings. The resulting empathetic connection is more than a rational argument. This affective knowledge does not resolve the issue, but it does provide an important epistemological starting point and clarity about a basic human continuity.

Again, our bodies' affective knowledge provides a foundation for imaginative flights. You may not know what it is to be in love with someone of the same sex or to desire to demonstrate commitment through marriage, but you probably know what it is to be in love. Imagination plays a crucial role in embodied care. As Debra Shogun points out, "If I am to identify with another's situation I must . . . be able to imagine subjectively what this person's world is like."[51] If I allow my caring imagination to take flight, I can recall the feelings and affections of falling in love, having that relationship grow, and perhaps wanting to reify that feeling by getting married. I can also recall how important marriage was for me, or for family and friends, and how emotions run high at such events. For many the marriage ceremony and subsequent celebration are the highlights of their lives, marked by overwhelming joy, crying, hugs, kisses, and so on.[52] Perhaps the biggest imaginative leap is to extrapolate the feelings I have had, or observed in relationships, to a man who loves another man or a woman who loves another woman. What makes this a leap is that homosexuality has been made into such a tremendous social taboo and a powerful counternarrative to social norms. Adrienne Rich and others describe the prevalence of "compulsory heterosexuality" in our society, which has made heterosexuality not a choice but a social mandate.[53] For some, heterosexuality is such an ingrained normative construct that the imagination hits a roadblock. Personal identification becomes difficult because many heterosexuals view homosexuals as social outcasts. If the focus is placed on human continuity, however, then sexual expression is only one part of our existence. All the aforementioned emotions that arise in a mutual experience of love should be available to embodied beings for projecting onto others, even if they have a different sexual orientation.

In overcoming socially constructed roadblocks, Addams's injunction to experience one another widely is reinforced as an important habit of care that expands our knowledge base. The more experiences we have with people considered "others," the more the continuity of embodied existence is apparent. In their discussion of methods for building a caring society, Pearl M. Oliner and Samuel P. Oliner express a sentiment reminiscent of Addams's: "Physical proximity encourages the potential for contact and mutual understanding."[54] In the case of sexual orientation, the more acquaintances, friends, co-workers, family members, or even fictional characters that we come to know who are gay (and more than just caricatures or stereotypes), the greater the chance that such knowledge will break down the mystery and distrust of an unknown other. But we must make the effort to experience a variety of other people. The explicit or implicit discovery will be "In many ways, *they* are just like me."[55] This interpersonal understanding does not guarantee that minds will be changed, but it reminds us that morality is more than just winning an argument, being right, or celebrating moral superiority. Moral deliberation involves real people who are very much like us.

One example of an interpersonal connection emerged when the Vermont State legislature passed the aforementioned civil-union bill. One of the legislators who voted in favor of the bill (it passed by only eleven votes) was eighty-four-year-old William Fry, a Republican from a conservative working-class town. Given his background, one would not expect Fry to be a social liberal who would favor same-sex marriage. When asked why he voted for the bill, Fry answered, "There were two ladies who were my next door neighbors. . . . (sobbing) They were treated terrible. I'm just glad I could do something to help."[56] In this case Fry exhibited connected leadership. He made the connection between the treatment of fellow human beings (beginning with his neighbors) and the impact of policies that over which he had an influence. One can read principles or consequences into Fry's actions, but he acted on more than propositional knowledge. Fry acted out of care based on his ability to empathize imaginatively with a lesbian couple he knew.

The caring imagination can be thought of as a social habit that requires exercise and use to develop. If knowledge is valued, then making it a practice to empathize with and understand the opponents in a controversy such as that over same-sex marriage will make for a more informed discussion and decision on the issue. Part of the task of experiencing others widely is developing habits of active listening: to hear what others have to say without prejudging their words. Jane Addams reflected this nonjudgmental commitment to listening in her description of the settlement movement, saying of the settlement house residents that they "must be emptied of all conceit of opinion and all self-assertion, and ready to arouse and interpret the public opinion of their neighborhood."[57] Were Mrs. Beckoff to truly listen to her son, she would see the deep pain behind his words and perhaps better understand his grief. Unfortunately, she has already made up her mind about the lack of depth in homosexual relations. Of course, her position is exacerbated by her son's callous approach to her pain—another example of not really listening. Listening may be an important process issue, but a moral decision may not be far behind, because risk accompanies every act of authentic listening. The risk is that we may come to understand the speaker, and we may feel compelled to act on his or her behalf. The habit of listening, which is so crucial to embodied care, is demanding because it requires the listener to allow someone to encroach on his or her life and possibly change it forever. Avoidance is an understandable defense mechanism. If conversations are kept superficial to avoid affective information, then listeners' lives need not be disrupted. The most powerfully influential and disruptive active listening takes place face to face. When, for example, one is confronted with Frederick Douglass talking about his experiences of slavery—when the expressions on his face

can be seen and the inflection in his voice heard—it is difficult not to identify with the speaker, at least somewhat.

The media are also capable of invoking emotions if the message is allowed
to seep into the consciousnesses of the viewers, readers, or listeners. A *Time*
magazine cover had a close-up of the faces of two Africans, presumably a
mother and son, with the caption: "This is a story about AIDS in Africa. Look
at the pictures. Read the words. And then try not to care."[58] The challenge is
to listen actively. Let the words sink in. Allow the pictures into your life. The
journalists believe that readers' lives will be disrupted, care will result, and
actions will follow. This same challenge can be offered for the issue of same-
sex marriage. Taking embodied care seriously means attending to the narratives of people's lives rather than simply judging them. In an article that
appeared in the *National Catholic Reporter,* Donna Swartwout recounts her
lifelong love of Roman Catholicism and the challenges she faced when she
came out as a lesbian after years of hiding her sexuality. Swartwout is asking
to be listened to rather than labeled: "You might be wondering why I am
telling you all this. I want you to understand who I am. I want you to know
a little about the person that you call intrinsically evil."[59] Swartwout appears
to believe that anyone who hears her story will understand that she is not
wholly other. She indicates that she would "jump at the chance" to get married if given the opportunity. Swartwout's narrative provides the potential
for affective, disruptive knowledge. It disrupts stereotypes of homosexuals
as antireligious and averse to committed relationships. When we listen to
Donna Swartwout and others like her, we gain affective information with
which our caring imaginations can work.

What about the rules, standards, and norms of my society? Do I just ignore them? Empathy may be a crucial aspect of the caring imagination, but
we do not exist in a vacuum, and the rules, norms, and values of our society
inevitably come into play. Oliner and Oliner express this recognition: "A
caring society, as we conceive it, is one in which care penetrates all major
social institutions, including the family, schools, the workplace and religious
institutions. Penetrating means to be present in some important degree, but
it does not mean expunging or replacing all other modes of social relationships or goals."[60] Given embodied care as I have described it, such social standards are recognized but do not trump our capacity to care. For example, if
I identify with the Roman Catholic Church and yet, through my social habits of care—listening to and engaging with a variety of people—am compelled to empathize with those who wish to legitimize same-sex marriage, it
does not mean that I immediately reject my religious tradition (although
some may choose to do so). The caring imagination should also empathize

with those who oppose gay marriage and seek to genuinely understand their position. Such an understanding may motivate a variety of responses. One response may be to research the origins and arguments concerning injunctions against gay marriage, but always within the context of care that recognizes the individuals and emotions involved. The goal is not to find further evidence to "win" the debate but to understand those who have the opposing position because they are human beings who share an embodied existence with me as well.

To summarize, embodied care shifts the analysis of same-sex marriage from making arguments strictly from rules or consequences to attending to the voices, passions, relationships, and context of the people involved in the debate. What resources does embodied knowledge give me so that I can use habits of caring imagination to understand the relational, affective dimension of the issue? When habits of active listening are practiced, what can be learned from the people of each side of the issue? These activities exhibit care in a manner grounded in the body. They do not provide an easy or formulaic response. Sarah Hoagland describes rules and principles as attractive because they are "certain and secure."⁶¹ Embodied care does not offer the security of declaring same-sex marriage right or wrong in some absolute sense. Nevertheless, valuing embodied care brings into view disruptive affective knowledge that may contribute to a more holistic understanding of a moral dilemma.

Applying Embodied Care to Social Policy Regarding Same-Sex Marriage

> We are learning that a standard of social ethics is not attained by travelling a sequestered byway, but by mixing on the thronged and common road where all must turn out for one another, and at least see the size of one another's burdens.
>
> —Jane Addams, *Democracy and Social Ethics*

The same aspects of same-sex marriage relevant to developing a personal understanding can be applied to the development of social policy. There is a difference, however: justice-based approaches to morality are more prevalent in the public realm than in the private. Legal discourse and political rhetoric greatly favor the language of justice over that of care. Recall chapter 4, where I sought to overcome the persistent notion that care is less effective as a social ethic than as a personal morality. Using Jane Addams's approach as a model, I will again address embodiment, imagination, and listening as if I were in a position to influence social policy—just as an elected official might be.

Understanding the other is crucial to caring. If I wish to make public policy on same-sex marriage, the initial step would be to understand the agents involved in the controversy. When Addams began her work at Hull-House, she did not start with preconceived responses to the plights of her poor, working-class neighbors. First, she got to know many of them on an individual basis. Her epistemological method was embodied: she was physically present to them. Addams's physical presence was significant in many ways. It allowed her to gain tacit knowledge not available in any other way, observing facial expressions, comforting the distraught, and watching the lively, expressive dance of the human body in her neighbors. This presence also made Addams an "insider." She was accepted and trusted by the neighborhood and thus learned more than an outsider could have.

Can a policy maker have an embodied presence? Given the variety of issues lawmakers must address and the constant pressure to raise funds, there are constraints, yet elected officials still have tools that can leverage physical presence into important knowledge. In the case of same-sex marriage, actually meeting with those who argue for and against such unions is a start. A direct consultation with representatives of all sides of the issue provides an opportunity for remembering the basic human continuity underlying the controversy. How the lives and relationships of heterosexuals and homosexuals would be affected—their growth and flourishing—would have to be considered. As mentioned before, same-sex marriage occurs between human beings, and their embodied existence means that all humans share much more than they do not, even if some are gay and some are straight. Given that no one involved in the debate represents some wholly other, evil entity, a recognition of our shared humanity at the level of public discourse can establish a tone of civility.

Physical presence also enriches listening. It provides an opportunity for listening that goes beyond the words of the argument to the emotions and motivations. Oliner and Oliner argue that listening skills can contribute to creating a caring society. They define active listeners as those who "seek information beyond what they hear. They ask appropriate questions and seek clarification when messages are ambiguous."[62] For a policy maker, active listening creates an opportunity for interactive dialogue. Asking questions is an important means to clarity and understanding. Listening can be very difficult when those talking are considered morally despicable, such as Ku Klux Klan members, but even then listening, preferably face to face, is still important for understanding the people behind the ideas. We may never come to agree with their positions, but habits of care may create the possibility of understanding their motivations and their emotions, allowing us and society at large to operate with a more holistic knowledge base and a better opportunity for lateral progress. Policy makers have a number of means for active listening, including town hall meetings, focus groups, hearings, or simply meeting constituents. Addams's model of connected leadership exhibits social habits of nonjudgmental listening that can be applied in this case.

Finally, it will benefit the policy maker to develop an active caring imagination. Physical presence and active listening can permit a lawmaker to take the imaginative flights that are crucial for understanding and empathizing with members of society. What is it like to be an active member of a Christian denomination that portrays homosexuality as a sin and an affront to God? What is it like to be in love with someone but not have a means to legitimate your commitment in the eyes of society? If embodied care is valued, the elected official who must set policy has an obligation to imaginatively inhabit these and other positions. This is an attempt not to colonize the experiences of others and claim ownership of them but to leverage the tremendous continuity of the flesh to empathize and understand.

A policy maker who takes embodied care seriously and makes habits of social care part of his or her practices will vastly improve the affective knowledge and resources available for making a policy decision. Addams's social imperative for mutual understanding through experience is relevant here. Because the issue is controversial, a decision on same-sex marriage will not be easy for someone who answers to multiple constituencies. It may well be that circumstances will lead to intermediary steps, as when the Vermont legislature decided to allow civil unions rather than same-sex marriage, a move that many on both sides will find unsatisfactory. Ultimately policy makers must ask themselves whether they have earnestly attempted to resolve the issue in a caring manner. Addams expressed this sentiment in her approach to prostitution: "Sympathetic knowledge is the only way of approach to any human problem, and the line of least resistance into the jungle of human wretchedness must always be through that region which is most thoroughly explored, not only by the information of the statistician, but by sympathetic understanding."[63] Embodied knowledge does not negate history or social norms, but neither should they limit our capacity to care.

Making a Decision about Same-Sex Marriage

A certain dissatisfaction abounds in addressing a particular case through embodied care. On the one hand, as a paradigmatically different way of viewing morality, embodied care leaves those who seek a quick or formulaic response feeling unsatisfied. As the process considerations in the last two sections indicate, habits of caring such as attending to the body, widespread participation, and active listening are complex and time-consuming undertakings that do not lend themselves to quick decision making. On the other hand, any discussion of a particular case will be dissatisfying for those who adopt a care orientation because the full affect of the relations involved cannot be known or wholly expressed in words. The complexity of a lived context and the knowledge gained from it are important in a care orientation. Particular cases are always reductionist echoes of life's real complexity. Nevertheless, embodied care is not relativism. Although the ethical response may not be clear at the level of abstract theoretical discussion, learning the variables and relations of a given situation and employing social practices that emphasize human continuity make them clearer.

The reader has probably already foreseen what I believe habits of embodied care entail for the issue of same-sex marriage. The collapse of the normative and the descriptive makes this foresight possible. Embodied care consists of attending to and developing certain habits of the body. As these habits are emphasized, the normative response becomes clearer. As I contemplate my affective knowledge of committed relationships' importance to human beings, denying such an opportunity appears uncaring. Human relationships are challenging enough without prejudice from society. The promotion of growth and flourishing seems to warrant a removal of unnecessary social constraints. Given the practices, values, and commitments discussed, an approach consistent with embodied care appears to support same-sex marriage. What my body knows about feelings for loved ones and what I have learned through listening to others tells me that same-sex marriage will allow many relationships to flourish. There are outcomes and rules that can be cited to support this conclusion, but this endorsement is principally an expression of care for fellow human beings' well-being. It is difficult to care for a class of people such as "homosexuals" (although perhaps I can care *about* them, as Noddings describes), but I can care for concrete, individual gay people I have known. As I think about them and their humanity—they are always presented to me as faces and bodies with joys and sorrows like my own—how can I deny them a ritual commitment that is so important in our society? My human connection wants to give them this opportunity to marry if they desire it, just as I have this opportunity. The arguments against same-sex marriage are ultimately too steeped in justice-based approaches that are external to the human condition. Put in terms of Tronto and Fischer's definition of care, same-sex marriage will allow homosexuals to "live well" in our society.

What of the concern expressed toward the beginning of this chapter, that same-sex marriage is a veritable line drawn in the sand and that those on both sides of the issue view it as a watershed for the future of our society? So be it. Care ethics is not easy. It cannot rest on principles or consequences but must continually respond to context and relationships. If caring is indeed important, then legitimizing same-sex marriage as a form of caring needs to advance. When Jane Addams fought for the civil rights of women in the form of suffrage, it too was viewed as a watershed. She was also decried as attempting to alter society as it was known, and institutions with a vested interest in the status quo denounced her. At the beginning of this millennium same-sex marriage is a disruptive civil rights issue in the United States, but if caring is to take its rightful place at the heart of morality, then the socially constructed barriers to gay marriage—religious, legal, and political—must be traversed by our fundamental connection to one another.

What about those who oppose same-sex marriage? Does a decision to support same-sex marriage mean that care is unidirectional in this case? Just because embodied care appears to support gay marriage as licit does not mean that those who oppose gay marriage should be stigmatized as evil. The feelings that underlie the oppositions to same-sex marriage are just as legitimate as any feelings and cannot be summarily discounted. Mrs. Beckoff's feelings deserve as much attention as her son's do. One expression of care should not create another barrier to care. Without compromising the belief that same-sex couples should be allowed to express themselves through marriage, we should continue to listen to and care for those who oppose same-sex marriage. Part of the role of connected leadership is to maintain dialogue in an attempt to provoke the caring imagination, creating the best opportunity for all to live well.

Conclusion: Experiencing One Another, Deconstructing Otherness, Joyfully Moving Ahead

Jane Addams's simple yet powerful mandate that we boldly experience one another to create sympathetic knowledge and a more cohesive society is a roadmap for overcoming the boundaries that prevent caring in society today. There is a moral challenge in the tension between the push of individuation and the pull of community—the problem of the one and the many. In response to this challenge, we have sometimes artificially imposed claims about one another that have created "otherness." Here I am not addressing the simple alterity necessary for considering creatures separate from ourselves. Rather, I am concerned with a potentially harmful essentializing of the other that robs the named others of their subject positions and agency by relegating them to superficial categories, whether "woman," "black," "Jew," "gay," or "white male." Society interrupts the embodied connection of humanity by erecting barriers of understanding and attaching political meaning to otherness. Simone de Beauvoir claims that "only the intervention of someone else can establish an individual as an *other*."[1] Many other feminists, however, such as Sandra Harding, have called for "reinventing ourselves as other."[2] Such imaginative border crossings are not ethically neutral epistemological exercises but rather morally significant attempts at reinforcing a relational ethics. Caring knowledge, habits, and imagination that radiate from our shared embodied existence can facilitate deconstructing disempowering otherness.

Every chapter of this book begins with a fictional or historical character who has to overcome a socially constructed barrier to give or receive care. In each case the narrative creates an other: a marginalized person. And in each case the body plays an important role in transgressing the socially constructed boundary. Frederick Douglass, the denigrated and yet feared former slave other, used his body and words to allow his auditors to realize that their fundamental human continuity went beyond race. The master-slave narrative is powerful, but the connections Douglass elicited were able to transcend racist claims and create the potential for care. Through Shylock, Shakespeare uses body imagery to help others see past anti-Semitism, which creates a cultural-religious other. Religiously inspired convictions are some of our most powerful narratives, capable of uniting or dividing peoples. Shared embodied existence is even more basic to the human condition than are religious claims, however, and this connection makes Shylock's appeal effective. Hannah Arendt opened her imagination to the idea that Adolf Eichmann was not an unintelligible creature but a highly flawed human being. Many had cast Eichmann as an evil other: a shrewd, powerful mastermind. Arendt found the man she confronted on the witness stand to be quite ordinary and perhaps therefore scarier, because he committed an evil of which we are all capable if we are unthinking and unimaginative. Perley Kelso is able to overcome class prejudice to find common humanity with the poor through her relationship with Sip Garth. Garth is the poverty-stricken other: unclean, uneducated, and best kept hidden from society. Class differences are socially constructed around power and access and represent one of the oldest divisions in human history. Nevertheless, even people from different classes have bodies that provide resources for caring for one another, as Addams advocates in the philosophy behind Hull-House. Arnold Beckoff cries out for compassion from his own mother, who has been blinded by social prejudices regarding sexual orientation. The current constructs of sexual orientation are particularly divisive. Various social interests and insecurities have coalesced to place grave importance on what counts for legitimate sexual activity. Homosexuals are marginalized as moral outlaws: predatory others who subvert young people and undermine traditional values. Once again, even these barriers can be crossed if our fundamental embodied continuity is recalled.

In each story a more basic, common aspect of human existence—the body—confronts a powerful social construct. In summing up her analysis of the possibility of applying care to international relations, Fiona Robinson reflects the potent possibilities of care: "The ability to care about others involves not only learning how to be attentive and patient, how to listen and respond, but also how to rethink our own attitudes about difference and exclusion by locating that difference within relationships, thus dispelling the claim that any one person or group of persons is naturally and objectively 'different.'"[3] To "locate difference within relationships" one must have a relationship. As Addams has demonstrated, we must come to know one another, preferably in direct ways, to appreciate difference and create common cause.

Ultimately there is a joy to care and its embodied dimension. Embodied care represents a positive human ontology—that we are all capable of caring for one another, of being moral in our daily interactions. As with other behaviors, however, to become proficient at caring we must develop and exercise our habits of care. This is perhaps the greatest gift of Gilligan, Noddings, and the feminist philosophers who have developed care ethics: a positive, even joyful morality. There is an underlying belief in the human spirit, our connectedness, and our ability to understand and help one another, which has the potential to create the first unifying positive social morality since World War I and the subsequent rise of realism dashed many people's belief in society's ability to act toward a collective morality. Caring is associated with love, friendship, community, and democracy and can give hope in a way often unavailable to deontological or teleological approaches. In the face of the challenges of pluralism, bell hooks speaks of love: "Embedded in the commitment to feminist revolution is the challenge to love. Love can be and is an important source of empowerment when we struggle to confront issues of sex, race, and class. Working together to identify and face our differences—to face the ways we dominate and are dominated—to change our actions, we need a mediating force that can sustain us so that we are not broken in this process, so that we do not despair."[4] While love and care are not the same, they share many of the same resources. (Can true love be uncaring?) hooks eloquently recognizes the potential integrity of theory and experience in the manner that we treat one another even as we confront challenging obstacles. Embodied care takes that integrity to the level of corporeal existence.

Noddings claims that care should be posed as an attractive moral approach: "It must be emphasized that a life of care is not necessarily a life of 'care and burdens' but, rather, one of joy and fulfillment. It may require occasional sacrifices (what ethic does not?), but it does not require self-abnegation. The education and socialization of all children should include deeply satisfying lives in caring relationships."[5] One gets the sense that the residents of Hull-House were buoyed by the common cause of caring. Alice Hamilton recalls, "The life [at Hull-House] satisfied every longing for companionship, the excitement of new experience, for constant intellectual stimulation, and for the sense of being caught-up in a big movement which enlisted my enthusiastic loyalty."[6] Part of the joy of care is hope in humanity. This hope is not a romanticized belief in the certainty of social evolution, as the social settlement and Social Gospel movements were sometimes accused of being. This hope is grounded in the knowledge that countless acts of caring are occurring all the time. Caring is something that virtually everyone understands at some level, so the effort toward a more caring society has vast, if untapped, resources. In this sense, embodied care constitutes a kind of foundation. Noddings refers to caring as a "foundation without prescribed dimensions, open to the use of a wide variety of materials, subject to correction in the exchange characteristic of interdependence, and necessarily enhanced by a superstructure of intellectual, emotional, and spiritual qualities."[7] I would add embodied knowledge and habit to Noddings's list of superstructures. If the root of morality is caring, then there is something promising and accessible about ethics. This promise is particularly true for social ethics. If our fundamental way of being is interdependent and interconnected, and we do not forget that connection, then the potential for improving society increases.

In *Beyond Poverty and Affluence: Toward an Economy of Care* Bob Goudzwaard and Harry de Lange describe what they call the care paradox: "In the midst of more wealth, we have fewer opportunities to practice care than before."[8] Although this is a common lament, I respectfully disagree. There may be powerful barriers to caring—homophobia, racism, sexism—and perhaps technology creates more opportunities to avoid caring than ever before. As long as we have bodies built as they are, however, and as long as we live on a planet populated with other embodied beings, there will be plenty of opportunities to exercise and develop our imagination and habits of embodied care.

Notes

Introduction

1. *Webster's Encyclopedic Unabridged Dictionary* lists fourteen definitions of care, and *Webster's New World Thesaurus* lists over one hundred synonyms for the various forms of the word *care*.

2. *The Oxford Dictionary of Philosophy* fails to make any reference to care ethics (Blackburn, *Oxford Dictionary of Philosophy*).

3. Reich, *Encyclopedia of Bioethics*, 328.

4. Noddings, *Starting at Home*, 11.

5. Koehn, *Rethinking Feminist Ethics*, 23.

6. Clement, *Care, Autonomy, and Justice*, 11.

7. Koehn, *Rethinking Feminist Ethics*, 26.

8. Fisher and Tronto, "Toward a Feminist Theory," 40.

9. Tronto, *Moral Boundaries*, 127.

10. Bowden, *Caring*, 183.

Chapter 1: The Landscape of Current Care Discourse

1. Douglass, *My Bondage*, 160.

2. Ibid., 150.

3. Cynthia Willet explicitly argues that care ethics fosters subjugation, using the writings of Frederick Douglass as an example. Willet contends that sentimentality, a forerunner of modern ideas about care, employs a rhetoric that facilitates unequal power dynamics, a "slave morality" (*Maternal Ethics and Other Slave Moralities*, 135). Similarly, Bernard Boxill supports Willet's thesis by arguing that Douglass believed slave violence, which aroused the slaveholders' fear of personal danger, and not empathy or care, was potent moral suasion in favor of abolition; see Boxill, "Fear and Shame," 721.

4. Douglass, *Narrative*, 23.

5. Foner, *Life and Writings*, 47–50.

6. Sundquist, *Frederick Douglass,* 5.

7. Ibid.

8. Tronto, *Moral Boundaries,* 177.

9. Garrison, Preface, 5.

10. Meyer, Introduction, xv.

11. There is some indication that as Douglass matured as a writer, he recognized the importance of garnering care from his readers. Harold K. Bush Jr. argues that in Douglass's subsequent revisions of his autobiographies he employs language such as "my dear readers" in an attempt to frame himself as "a voice seeking consensus and communion" (*American Declarations,* 46).

12. Kant, *Critique of Practical Reason,* 58.

13. The theoretical arc of chapters 2 through 4 will develop the notion of habit more fully, but note here that I am defining habit broadly to include the dynamic practices of the body that have epistemological and ethical significance.

14. Feminists are all too familiar with the marginalizing impact of reductionist characterizations. Those interested in care should be considered no differently than are consequentialists or those with deontological allegiances whose views differ widely from those of their colleagues.

15. In his later work Kohlberg identifies a "soft" stage 7 that reflects religious and "cosmic" thinking but is not strictly ethical (Levine, Kohlberg, and Hewer, "Current Formulation," 95–96).

16. Gilligan, *In a Different Voice,* 19.

17. Blum, "Gilligan and Kohlberg," 50–53.

18. In response to Gilligan, Kohlberg ("Synopses and Detailed Replies," 341) originally attempted to demonstrate how care fits within his model, describing care as a duty that arises out of special obligations to family, friends, and group members. Kohlberg's later work avoided the consideration of care altogether: "[Critics] have failed to appreciate that Kohlberg's primary concern has been with the study of justice reasoning per se, and not with all those factors which, in addition to justice, comprise the moral domain. (Levine, Kohlberg, and Hewer, "Current Formulation," 99).

19. This dilemma was devised by Kohlberg, whom I quote here ("Stage and Sequence," 379), and later administered by Gilligan (*In a Different Voice,* 25–32).

20. Colby, Kohlberg, Gibbs, Candee, *Assessing Moral Stages,* 82.

21. Qtd. in Gilligan, *In a Different Voice,* 29.

22. Ibid., 32.

23. Those who are critical of Gilligan's work on care can be placed in three broad categories. The first consists of those who interpret Gilligan as offering a gendered system of morality where women favor care and men favor justice. These critics dispute Gilligan's empirical evidence and methodology; see, for example, Larrabee, "Checking the Data," 143–99; Pollitt, "Are Women Morally Superior?" 799–808; and Walker, "Sex Differences," 667–91. The second category of criticism finds the notion of care to be less than empowering for women; see, for example, Holmes, "Call to Heal Medicine," 1–6; Moody-Adams, "Gender," 195–212; O'Neill, "Justice, Gender, and International Boundaries," 55; and Sherwin, *No Longer Patient.* The third category includes those who have difficulty finding a compelling social theory in care; see, for example, Barry, *Justice as Impartiality.*

Because I am interested in a general empathetic response, I will ignore the first category. I discuss issues of empowerment in chapter 3, however, and social theory in chapter 4.

24. For example, in a 1988 article Gilligan wrote with Jane Attanucci, the authors conclude from a study of responses to moral dilemmas that everyone generally employs both care and justice perspectives, but some have a care focus and others have a justice focus. They further found that men have a propensity toward a justice focus and women have a propensity toward a care focus, but they are not interested in making universal statements: "The promise of our approach to moral development in terms of moral orientation lies in its potential to transform debate over cultural and sex differences in moral reasoning into serious questions about moral perspectives that are open to empirical study" (Gilligan and Attanucci, "Two Moral Orientations," 84). Gilligan's claim about the connection between gender and ethics, albeit tenuous, nevertheless overshadowed her broader conclusions for many readers.

25. Gilligan, Lyons, and Hanmer, *Making Connections,* 321.

26. Heyes, "Anti-Essentialism in Practice," 142.

27. Noddings, *Caring,* 8.

28. Ibid., 36.

29. From a relational standpoint, this story raises many difficult questions. What kind of parents would offer to kill their son to prove their faith? What kind of god would make such a request? Even if the death is ultimately not required, how will such a test affect the ongoing father-son relationship?

30. Noddings, *Caring,* 144.

31. Ibid., 130.

32. Ibid., 123.

33. Ruddick, *Maternal Thinking,* 186.

34. Ruddick, "Care as Labor," 14.

35. Bubeck, *Care, Gender, and Justice,* 159–70.

36. Ibid., 163.

37. I am concerned about the negative political consequences of identifying care as a "feminine" ethics. There is the dangerous potential to marginalize care as a "woman's ethics"—for example, by limiting it to interpersonal relationships—which leaves other ethical structures untouched. This approach artificially limits care, as chapter 4 will demonstrate. After all, as embodied creatures men and women share much more than they do not.

38. Although almost every author qualifies the association of care with virtue ethics, the following texts explicitly characterize care as a virtue: Baier, "Hume"; Groenhoot, "Care Theory"; Knowlden, "The Virtue of Caring"; Slote, "The Justice of Caring"; Tong, "The Ethics of Care."

39. MacIntyre, *After Virtue,* 191.

40. Hume, *Enquiry,* 176.

41. Hume, *Treatise,* 575.

42. Ibid., 317.

43. Ibid., 481.

44. Baier, "Hume," 46.

45. Hume, *Enquiry,* 215.

46. Baier, "Hume," 44.

47. Manning, *Speaking from the Heart*, 82–83.

48. Ibid., 69.

49. Ibid., 83.

50. Noddings, *Caring*, 79.

51. Tong, "The Ethics of Care," 145.

52. Ibid., 150.

53. Held, *Feminist Morality*, 79.

54. Tong, "The Ethics of Care," 132.

55. Groenhout, "Care Theory," 172–73.

56. Slote, "The Justice of Caring," 173.

57. Groenhout, "Care Theory," 174.

58. Veatch, "The Place of Care," 215.

59. Noddings, *Women and Evil*, 237.

60. Card, *Feminist Ethics*, 25.

61. Bennett, *The Book of Virtues*.

62. Hekman, *Moral Voices, Moral Selves*, 58.

63. Shrage, *Moral Dilemmas of Feminism*, 30.

64. Sher, "Other Voices, Other Rooms?"

65. Pollitt, "Are Women Morally Superior?" 800.

66. Gilligan, *In a Different Voice*, 27.

67. Ibid., 18, 30, 73, 174.

68. Gilligan, "Hearing the Difference," 127.

69. Clement, *Care, Autonomy, and Justice*, 11.

70. Seyla Benhabib argues that relational theories of morality such as care ethics have an advantage over traditional moral theories because they are not "substitutionist" in their consideration of the participants in a moral dilemma. A care approach valorizes the particularities of a situation, thus concretizing the other ("The Generalized and the Concrete Other").

71. Lango, "Does Kant's Ethics Ignore Relations?" 251.

72. Clement, *Care, Autonomy, and Justice*, 15.

73. Friedman, "Feminism, Autonomy, and Emotion," 37.

74. Mayeroff, *On Caring*, 79.

75. Noddings, *Caring*, 5.

76. Ibid.

77. Ibid., 201. I will return to Noddings's idea of meeting the other when I discuss alterity in chapter 3.

78. Noddings, "A Response," 120.

79. Noddings, *Starting at Home*, 22.

80. Tronto offers another care phenomenology in her description of the four phases of caring (*Moral Boundaries*, 105–8).

81. Walker, "Moral Understandings," 18.

82. Held, "Liberalism," 302.

83. Mayeroff, *On Caring*, 87.

84. Hekman, *Moral Voices, Moral Selves*, 32.

85. Ibid., 65.

86. Walker, "Moral Understandings," 20.

87. Moore, *Principia Ethica*, 10.

88. Ibid., 26.

89. Robinson, *Globalizing Care*, 12.

90. Fisher and Tronto, "Toward a Feminist Theory," 56.

91. Held, "Liberalism," 302.

92. Held, *Feminist Morality*, 43.

93. Sevenhuijsen, *Citizenship*, 39.

94. Ruddick, *Maternal Thinking*, 46. Similarly, Joan Tronto (*Moral Boundaries*, 112) describes care as work not so much as a metaphor for better understanding but as a tool for addressing her political concerns about class structure and caring labor.

95. Held, "Liberalism," 302.

96. Fisher and Tronto, "Toward a Feminist Theory," 56.

97. Veatch, "The Place of Care," 220.

98. Koehn, *Rethinking Feminist Ethics*, 30–31.

99. Ibid.

100. Bowden, *Caring*, 3–4.

101. Kuhn, *Structure of Scientific Revolutions*, 149.

Chapter 2: Merleau-Ponty and Embodied Epistemology

1. Shakespeare, *The Merchant of Venice*, act 3, sc. 1, ll. 55–62.

2. Kenneth Myrick notes that "one key to the meaning of a Shakespeare play is the way he directs our sympathies" (in ibid., xxx). This is particularly true of Shylock, who in each of his appearances in *The Merchant of Venice* manages to pull at the sympathies of the audience.

3. The animal rights activist and educator Steven M. Wise (*Rattling the Cage*, 187–88) uses Shylock's plea as an eloquent justification for the concern for animals that share an embodied existence including pleasure and pain.

4. Ihde, *Experimental Phenomenology*, 13.

5. Merleau-Ponty, *Phenomenology of Perception*, viii.

6. Many consider Franz Brentano (1838–1917) to be the "father of phenomenology," but G. W. F. Hegel (1770–1831) was the first to use the term *phenomenology* in a technical sense. Hegel viewed phenomenology as the science of describing the progression from natural phenomenological consciousness toward absolute knowledge of the Absolute.

7. Husserl, *Crisis of European Sciences*, 9.

8. Husserl, *Cartesian Meditations*, 13.

9. Husserl, "Thesis of the Natural Standpoint," 76–77.

10. Merleau-Ponty, *Phenomenology of Perception*, xxi.

11. Merleau-Ponty argues that phenomenology offers epistemic significance unrealized in a Cartesian approach: "The recognition of phenomena then implies a theory of reflection and a new 'cogito'" (ibid., 50).

12. Kwant, "Merleau-Ponty and Phenomenology," 391.

13. Lingis, "Segmented Organisms," 172.

14. Grosz, "Merleau-Ponty and Irigaray," 150.

15. Sullivan, *Living across and through Skins,* 65.

16. Mayeroff, *On Caring,* 13.

17. Benhabib, *Situating the Self,* 163.

18. Walker, "Moral Understandings," 169.

19. Walker, "Moral Epistemology," 364.

20. One may justifiably ask about all the abstract categories of embodied creatures about which we care. For example, what if I am a member of a fraternal organization and I exhibit care for one of my "brothers" without knowing him as an individual? In this case the caring imagination will fill in the gaps. One might also observe that the care may appear to be motivated by a form of macho loyalty rather than genuine concern. Caring is not a binary condition. Many different forces can motivate what appears to be care, but the activities still radiate from some concrete experience. Even disingenuous caring draws on caring habits to create the façade. The caring imagination is the subject of the next chapter.

21. Kolbe, "Pen Pals."

22. Hoagland, *Lesbian Ethics,* 283.

23. Hekman, *Moral Voices, Moral Selves,* 30.

24. Wilshire, "The Uses of Myth," 93.

25. Johnson, "Embodied Reason," 83.

26. Merleau-Ponty, *The Visible and the Invisible,* 150.

27. Merleau-Ponty, *Primacy of Perception,* 7.

28. Merleau-Ponty, *The Visible and the Invisible,* 114.

29. Merleau-Ponty, *Phenomenology of Perception,* 142.

30. Merleau-Ponty, *Primacy of Perception,* 3–4.

31. Abram, *Spell of the Sensuous,* 52.

32. Blackburn, *Oxford Dictionary of Philosophy,* 280–81.

33. Merleau-Ponty, *Phenomenology of Perception,* x–xi.

34. Merleau-Ponty, *Signs,* 15.

35. Merleau-Ponty, *Phenomenology of Perception,,* 206.

36. Merleau-Ponty, *The Visible and the Invisible,* 22.

37. Noddings, *Caring,* 4.

38. Gilligan, *In a Different Voice,* 173.

39. Merleau-Ponty, *Phenomenology of Perception,* 169.

40. Merleau-Ponty, *The Visible and the Invisible,* 9.

41. Merleau-Ponty, *Phenomenology of Perception,* 13.

42. Ibid., 92.

43. Ibid.

44. Noddings, *Caring,* 30.

45. Ibid., 17.

46. Drawing on the writing of Merleau-Ponty, Drew Leder describes the conscious focus on the activity rather than the involved body parts as the disappearance or recession of the sense organ from the perceptual field it discloses (*The Absent Body,* 14). Given Leder's notion of disappearance, engrossment appears to be an extension of the manner in which our bodies thematize the world.

47. Weiss, *Body Images,* 160.

48. Merleau-Ponty, *The Visible and the Invisible,* 139.

49. Ibid., 143.

50. Ibid., 146.

51. Ibid., 139.

52. Ibid., 144.

53. Ibid., 148.

54. Johnson, "Inside and Outside," 30–31.

55. Merleau-Ponty, *The Visible and the Invisible,* 248.

56. Ibid., 143.

57. Merleau-Ponty, *The Prose of the World,* 138.

58. Abram, *Spell of the Sensuous,* ix.

59. Ibid.

60. Sometimes our bodily reaction requires imaginative moderation (see the next chapter). I may wince at the sight of a surgeon performing an operation although I know that the intent of such a bodily violation is beneficial.

61. Merleau-Ponty, *Signs,* 15.

62. Merleau-Ponty, *Phenomenology of Perception,* 356.

63. Ibid., 143.

64. Ibid., 144.

65. Noddings, *Caring,* 122–23.

66. In this case I am using a tactile example, but habits of care need not involve touch. For example, I can care for people by listening attentively to what they have to say. My body has habits surrounding listening that can demonstrate care without ever touching the speaker. Eye contact, posture, facial expressions, and stillness participate in care-centered listening. These bodily behaviors can communicate a real interest, or engrossment, in what the speaker has to say. As I will explore in chapter 4, listening is an important component of a caring relationship.

67. Because of its commitment to context, embodied care cannot adjudicate an activity such as spanking with a universal principle such as "all spanking is wrong." Nevertheless, embodied care can ask in particular cases whether the practice was motivated by care or something else. How does spanking affect the relationship between the parent and the child? What does spanking contribute to the embodied knowledge of the spanker and the one spanked?

68. Polanyi, *The Tacit Dimension,* 4.

69. Michael Polanyi contends that there is so much that we cannot verbalize that "the transmission of knowledge from one generation to the other must be predominately tacit." In describing the phenomenal structure of tacit knowing, Polanyi refers to attending from a proximal term, or object, to a distal term. We invest meaning in the distal term through bodily "subception," or the tacit acquisition of knowledge through transposition of bodily experiences into perception (ibid., 61). Following a trajectory consistent with Merleau-Ponty's work, Polanyi claims that the tacit knowledge of the body comes about through active participation, or what he calls "indwelling" (ibid., 17). Care, empathy, and compassion can be described at length, but there remains an element of understanding that is available only through direct embodied experience. Rita Manning claims that praxis is

an essential part of care ethics: "We cannot develop and sustain the ability to care unless we do some active caring" (*Speaking from the Heart*, 69).

70. Weiss, *Body Images*, 161.

71. Merleau-Ponty, *Visible and Invisible*, 149.

Chapter 3: Caring Imagination

1. For a discussion of the political and philosophical controversy surrounding Arendt's reporting of the Eichmann trial, see Benhabib, *Reluctant Modernism*, 172–85.

2. Arendt, *Eichmann in Jerusalem*, 19.

3. Ibid., 54.

4. Merleau-Ponty, *The Phenomenology of Perception*, 214.

5. Ibid., 227.

6. Ibid., 230.

7. In chapter 2 I argued that knowledge is a prerequisite for care, but the Eichmann example points out why this cannot be a linear understanding. Care and the openness that comes with it may be important precursors for understanding. Had Arendt confronted Eichmann by never letting down her guard—had she steadfastly stuck to the idea that he was a wholly other monster and ignored her bodily perceptions of the mere man she witnessed—she would never have come to the empathetic insights and understanding that she did come to.

8. Arendt, *Life of the Mind*, 4.

9. The implication of our embodied, human continuity with those, such as Eichmann, who have wrought horrific acts has enormous potential for moral discussion. There is a negative dimension to this understanding in that we are not that far removed from great acts of evil, because one who was in many ways like us did them. There is also a promising dimension because evil is not understood as an entity unto itself, separate from human existence. Therefore we can understand and guard against it. When confronted with the Nazi attempts at the Final Solution, the massive amount of death and suffering is incomprehensible. When the events are broken down to the individuals involved, however, as in the Eichmann case, there is greater potential for understanding how a person could become so utterly misguided.

10. Arendt, *Eichmann in Jerusalem*, 49.

11. Ibid., 287.

12. Merleau-Ponty, *The Visible and the Invisible*, 147.

13. The rational and empathetic approaches to moral imagination are not the only approaches, but they are representative of two important schools of thought in Western philosophy.

14. Arendt, *Eichmann in Jerusalem*, 49.

15. Although Adam Smith is best known for writing the foundational text of modern capitalism, *The Wealth of Nations*, he was a professor of moral philosophy at the University of Glasgow and wrote extensively on ethics.

16. Hume, *Treatise*, 427.

17. Engell, *The Creative Imagination*, 56.

18. Hume was also somewhat ambivalent about sympathy because he believed that the

passions are too powerful and unpredictable. This led him to develop the balancing notion of the general point of view, which I address later in this chapter.

19. Smith, *Theory of Moral Sentiments,* 9.

20. Ibid., 3.

21. Kant, *Foundations of a Metaphysics of Morals,* 411.

22. Kant, *Critique of Practical Reason,* 72.

23. Our knowledge of others should be characterized in shades of understanding rather than in a binary distinction between known and unknown others. What we really mean when we identify unknown others is that we know very little about them, and in particular, we lack direct personal experience of any extended length of time. To address even the most superficial understanding of other people, however, is to have some knowledge of them. For example, aboriginal Australians are unknown others for me because I have never traveled to Australia, let alone met any of the continent's indigenous peoples. Yet even to utter the category "aboriginal Australians" is to lay claim to some knowledge. Further reflection reveals that I know more than is initially apparent. While my knowledge of their inscribed social reality and values is nil, I do know that they are human beings who share embodied experience of a certain kind. In this sense, no human being is entirely unknown to me.

24. I am not attempting, as some philosophers have done, to distinguish empathy from sympathy. This is an intentional move to blur the dichotomy between feeling with another and having some knowledge of their feelings. Given my emphasis on the embodied aspect of care, my account leaves open the question of when knowledge of someone's plight becomes shared feeling.

25. Merleau-Ponty, *The Visible and the Invisible,* 77.

26. Shogan, *Care and Moral Motivation,* 68–69.

27. Ibid., 69.

28. Hume, *Treatise,* 579.

29. Ibid., 586.

30. Ibid., 581.

31. Tronto, *Moral Boundaries,* 44.

32. Hume, *Treatise,* 580.

33. Stein, *The Problem of Empathy,* 6–7.

34. Ibid., 10.

35. Ibid., 59–60.

36. Ibid., 41.

37. Ibid., 49.

38. Ibid., 52.

39. See the discussion in Haney, *Intersubjectivity Revisited,* 60.

40. Johnson, *The Body in the Mind,* xiv.

41. Ibid.

42. Johnson, *Moral Imagination,* 51.

43. See, for example, Weigel, Caiola, and Pittman-Foy, "4-H Animal Care."

44. Johnson, *Moral Imagination,* 190.

45. Ibid., 192.

46. Merleau-Ponty, *The Visible and the Invisible,* 149.

47. Abram, "Merleau-Ponty," 103.

48. Merleau-Ponty, *The Visible and Invisible*, 22.

49. Recall the case used by Kohlberg and Gilligan, where a man (Heinz) needs to obtain a drug to save his wife, who is dying from an illness. The local druggist has the only stock of the drug, but Heinz cannot afford it.

50. Manning, *Speaking from the Heart*, 62.

51. Held, "Liberalism," 302.

52. Although I am highlighting the differences between empathy and critical reflection to clarify their roles, they work together in and through the body.

53. Hume, *Treatise*, 385.

54. Ibid., 580.

55. Balmer, "Why I Stopped," B9.

56. What Balmer fails to do, and Jane Addams's social morality will challenge us to do, is consider factors beyond the exchange of money. Actively listening to the panhandler may reveal the stranger's plight in a richer sense. Caring may involve more interaction than simply giving money. It may also involve viewing the homeless and unemployed as part of a larger social problem that requires policy-level solutions or social habits of care.

57. Hoagland, "Some Thoughts about 'Caring,'" 255.

58. Ibid., 253.

59. Moody-Adams, "Gender," 203.

60. Sullivan, *Living across and through Skins*, 132.

61. Stein, *The Problem of Empathy*, 105.

62. Hoagland, *Lesbian Ethics*, 88.

63. Gilligan, "Moral Orientations," 24.

64. Mead, *On Social Psychology*, 217.

65. Moore Campbell, *Brothers and Sisters*.

66. Mead, *On Social Psychology*, 218.

67. Hanson, *The Self Imagined*, 84.

68. Manning, *Speaking from the Heart*, 105.

69. Moore, *Roger and Me*.

70. Adams, *The Sexual Politics of Meat*, 64.

71. Held, "Liberalism," 289.

72. Manning, *Speaking from the Heart*, 20.

73. Nussbaum, *Poetic Justice*, 5.

74. Ibid., 12.

75. Ibid., 18.

Chapter 4: Jane Addams and the Social Habits of Care

1. Phelps, *The Silent Partner*, 22.

2. Ibid., 23.

3. Ibid., 44.

4. Ibid., 49.

5. Ibid., 95.

6. Ibid., 18.

7. Ibid., 49.

8. Ibid.

9. Ibid., 74.

10. Sharer, "Going into Society," 178.

11. Buhle and Howe, Afterword, 382.

12. Cudd, "Review"

13. Shrage, *Moral Dilemmas of Feminism*, 20.

14. See, for example, Sullivan, *Living across and through Skins*.

15. Pratt, *Native Pragmatism*, xiv.

16. For a detailed delineation of the characteristics of American philosophy, see Stuhr, *Classical American Philosophy*, 4–11, and Smith, *The Spirit of American Philosophy*.

17. James, *The Will to Believe*, 10.

18. Diggins, *The Promise of Pragmatism*, 2.

19. Peirce, *Collected Papers*, 50.

20. James, *Pragmatism and Other Essays*, 25.

21. Dewey, *Reconstruction in Philosophy*, 86.

22. Pratt, *Native Pragmatism*, 22.

23. Addams, *Democracy and Social Ethics*, 6.

24. The pragmatist commitment to growth is consistent with the fundamental value of care as "living well" expressed by Tronto and Fisher. To live well is generally not regarded as a static existence but one that is marked by growth. To care for others is not to hope that they stay as they are but to foster their growth.

25. Addams, *Democracy and Social Ethics*, 23.

26. Ibid., 22.

27. Dewey, *Logic*, 46.

28. James, *The Will to Believe*, 216.

29. Dewey, *Ethics*, 170–71.

30. Sullivan, "Reconfiguring Gender," 26.

31. Dewey, *Human Nature and Conduct*, 32.

32. Ibid., 190.

33. Phelps, *The Silent Partner*, 18.

34. Stebner, *The Women of Hull House*, 13.

35. Kellog, "Twice Twenty Years at Hull-House," 191.

36. Addams, *Twenty Years at Hull-House*, 109.

37. Ibid., 111–12.

38. Seigfried, *Pragmatism and Feminism*, 58.

39. Consistent with the reciprocity of care discussed in chapter 2, the Hull-House experience had many interpersonal benefits for those who lived and worked there, as well as the community members. Addams describes one of the motivations for Hull-House as meeting the needs of people to help others in a spirit of community. "Our young people feel nervously the need of putting theory into action, and respond quickly to the Settlement form of activity" ("Subjective Necessity," 22).

40. Dewey, "The School as Social Center," 107.

41. According to Merle Curti ("Jane Addams on Human Nature," 240), Theodore Roosevelt referred to Addams as "poor bleeding Jane."

42. James qtd. in Lasch, *Social Thought of Jane Addams*, 62.

43. Ibid., 176.

44. Mary B. Mahowald offers three reasons for the neglect of Jane Addams as a serious philosopher. First, Addams was an activist, and there has been a bias against the ability of activists to do credible theoretical work. Second, Addams was not an academician. Addams did not hold an advanced degree, and she was largely self-taught on issues of contemporary philosophy. Third, many claimed that Addams's work, like that of other pragmatists, was not "philosophical" in nature (Mahowald, "What Classical American Philosophers Missed," 39–54). Similar criticisms have been leveled at Mead, Dewey, and James, although their defenders have been more numerous. An obvious fourth reason is Addams's gender.

45. Fischer, "Jane Addams' Feminist Ethics," 51.

46. Addams, *A New Conscience*, 7.

47. Seigfried, Introduction, xxi.

48. Noddings, *Starting at Home*, 301.

49. Addams extols literature's ability to add to our experience indirectly: "While the business of literature is revelation and not reformation, it may yet perform for the men and women now living that purification of the imagination and intellect which the Greeks believed to come through pity and terror" (*A New Conscience*, 8).

50. Addams, *Twenty Years at Hull-House*, 391.

51. M. Regina Leffers ("Pragmatists Jane Addams and John Dewey," 70) argues that Addams assumes a "universalized caring standpoint" in extrapolating neighborhood experiences found in personal relationships to others in need.

52. Addams, *Democracy and Social Ethics*, 17.

53. Ibid., 37.

54. Ibid., 46–47.

55. Ibid., 92.

56. Seyla Benhabib explains this notion in her distinction between the generalized and the concrete other. Traditional notions of morality rely on an abstracted, generalized other to create universal principles. Care ethics calls on real encounters, or extrapolations from real encounters, as motivating empathy and action. The more the plight of another is made "real" for someone, the easier it is to care and act on that person's behalf. For care ethics, the people, places, and events under consideration are a significant component of moral deliberation and cannot be easily abstracted into formulaic cases. Care ethicists are not categorically against rules, but they do not view rules to be the entire content of morality. "A universalistic [justice-based] moral theory restricted to the standpoint of the 'generalized other' falls into epistemic incoherencies that jeopardize its claim to adequately fulfill reversibility and universizability" (Benhabib, *Situating the Self*, 152).

57. Addams's evolutionary sense of morality does not preclude the possibility of dialogue with the religious tradition, as the numerous biblical allusions in her writing show.

58. Addams, *Democracy and Social Ethics*, 5.

59. Ibid., 13.

60. Christopher Lasch describes one of the great contributions of *Democracy and Social Ethics* as its ability to "make it clear, perhaps for the first time, that the working class represented not merely a class but a culture" (*Social Thought of Jane Addams*, 62).

61. Addams does state, "The demand [a sense of the common weal] should be universalized; in this process it would also become clarified, and the basis of our political organization become perforce social and ethical" (*Democracy and Social Ethics*, 117). Here Addams employs a "weak" notion of universalization. She is not advocating a universal imperative for discerning moral dilemmas in a fixed manner; instead, she is calling for a wider acceptance of our social responsibility to one another: a social acceptance of care.

62. Addams, *Democracy and Social Ethics*, 98.

63. Addams, *Newer Ideals of Peace*, 11.

64. Noddings, *Caring*, 47.

65. Addams, *Democracy and Social Ethics*, 8.

66. In *Moral Boundaries* Joan Tronto attempts to challenge the traditional lines of demarcation that society has placed on issues of morality and politics. Tronto cites Jane Addams as an example of a woman whose views on morality were quite popular until the social context shifted with the onset of World War I. Tronto argues that in the face of war, it was easy to marginalize Addams as espousing a bleeding-heart "women's morality." Tronto's primary lens of analysis on the politics of Addams's social ethics is gender, and she contends that Addams, like many women, lost moral authority when her ethical claims were extended into a broader social arena, in this case geopolitical conflict (*Moral Boundaries*, 5 and 8). Tronto's observation places an interesting twist on the relationship between care and politics. Has care ethics simply not been effectively adapted or applied to social-political concerns, or is there a resistance to allowing a care orientation into these spheres?

67. Addams, *Democracy and Social Ethics*, 17.

68. Noddings, *Caring*, 47.

69. Addams, *Democracy and Social Ethics*, 6.

70. Fischer, "Jane Addams' Feminist Ethics," 53.

71. Elshtain, *Jane Addams*, 219.

72. Addams recognized the perplexity in issues of partiality: the leap from caring about known individuals to caring for strangers. This tension is the linchpin in much of the discussion surrounding the political efficacy of care. Addams declares, "Just when our affection becomes large enough to care for the unworthy among the poor as we would care for the unworthy among our own kin, is certainly a perplexing question" (*Democracy and Social Ethics*, 31).

73. Addams, *Twenty Years at Hull-House*, 116.

74. Addams, *Democracy and Social Ethics*, 9.

75. Note that the language employed here is that of "understanding" and "respect" rather than a more passive notion of tolerance for diversity and pluralism.

76. Addams, *Democracy and Social Ethics*, 6.

77. Ibid., 7.

78. Addams, "The Subjective Necessity," 17.

79. Elshtain, *Jane Addams*, 154.

80. Fischer, "Jane Addams' Feminist Ethics," 52.

81. Addams, *Peace and Bread*, 68–71.

82. Lugones and Spelman, "Have We Got a Theory for You!" 501.

83. Addams, *Twenty Years at Hull-House*, 136.

84. Lugones and Spelman, "Have We Got a Theory for You!" 506.

85. McCree Bryan and Davis, *100 Years at Hull-House*, 171. The Russian-born Rachelle Yarros and her husband lived at Hull-House from 1907 to 1927. She was a pioneer physician and teacher in obstetrics, human sexuality, contraception, and social hygiene. Alice Hamilton moved to Hull-House in 1907 and stayed for twenty-two years. She was the first woman on the faculty at Harvard Medical School and was a pioneer in industrial medicine (Haslett, "Hull House," 261–78).

86. Stebner, *The Women of Hull House*, 179.

87. Friedman, *What Are Friends For?* 192–93.

88. Addams, *Twenty Years at Hull-House*, 366.

89. Ibid., 145.

90. Fischer, "Jane Addams' Feminist Ethics," 55.

91. Addams, *Democracy and Social Ethics*, 97.

92. Ibid., 64.

93. Ibid., 66.

94. Addams, *A New Conscience*, 27–30.

95. Addams, *Democracy and Social Ethics*, 69.

96. Knight ("Biography's Window, 112) finds that Addams transcended the prevalent ethics of benevolence that those of wealth and power imposed on others.

97. Addams, "A Modern Lear," 174.

98. Here Addams provides one response to Hoagland's trepidation about care set forth in the previous chapter. Taking embodied care seriously means attending to the kinds of relationships formed in social institutions. Social habits of care such as widespread participation mitigate the possibility of exploitative structures and practices about which Hoagland is rightly concerned.

99. Addams, *Democracy and Social Ethics*, 7.

100. Ibid., 8.

101. Ibid., 7.

102. Ibid., 99.

103. The following demonstrates Niebuhr's "realism" concerning the relation of individuals and groups: "As individuals, men believe that they ought to love and serve each other and establish justice between each other. As racial, economic and national groups they take for themselves, whatever their power can command" (*Moral Man and Immoral Society*, 9).

104. Addams, *Democracy and Social Ethics*, 99.

105. Ibid.

106. Ibid.

107. Ibid., 101.

108. Ibid., 102.

109. In "A Modern Lear" Addams criticizes George Pullman for exhibiting this lack of contact and understanding.

110. Addams, *Democracy and Social Ethics*, 119–20.

111. Addams became quite self-reflective about her leadership of Hull-House after an encounter with Leo Tolstoy but concluded that leadership is indeed necessary. Her pragmatism balanced her moral ideals. See Addams, *Twenty Years at Hull-House*, 186–99.

112. Addams, *Democracy and Social Ethics*, 119.

113. In *The Long Road of Women's Memory* Addams addresses the interaction of personal moral codes and political moral codes that stand "in constant need of revision" (40).

114. Addams, *Democracy and Social Ethics*, 33.

115. Addams, *Newer Ideals of Peace*, 21.

116. Addams, *Democracy and Social Ethics*, 119.

117. Addams, "A Modern Lear," 175.

118. Fischer, "Jane Addams' Feminist Ethics," 54.

119. Noddings, *The Challenge to Care*, xiv.

Chapter 5: What Difference Does Embodied Care Make?

1. Fierstein, *Widows and Children First*, 144–45.

2. Ibid., 146.

3. "There is no human . . . whose happiness does not affect us, when brought near to us, and represented in lively colors" (Hume, *Treatise*, 481). See chapter 1 for a discussion of Hume's notion of fellow feelings.

4. Noddings, "Feminist Morality and Social Policy," 63.

5. Addams, *Democracy and Social Ethics*, 119.

6. Recall that for Nussbaum, experiencing fiction is not a luxury but an integral part of developing the public imagination. Nussbaum claims that the reader's experience of fiction "develops moral capacities without which citizens will not succeed in making reality out of the normative conclusions of any moral or political theory, however excellent" (*Poetic Justice*, 12).

7. Jane Addams was not afraid to take unpopular stances. For example, her pacifism in the face of the popular World War I effort brought her widespread criticism, including biting condemnation from the president.

8. Walker, *Moral Understandings*, 18.

9. Ibid., 13.

10. Gilligan, *In a Different Voice*, 47–48.

11. Countries recognizing "registered partnerships" include Denmark (1989), Greenland (1994), Sweden (1995), Iceland (1996), the Netherlands (1998), and France (1999) (Goodman, "A More Civil Union," 53). Events in Ontario in 2003 make it appear that Canada may soon legalize same-sex marriage or registered domestic partnerships.

12. Over 1,000 responsibilities and privileges accrue to married couples under federal law (ibid).

13. Purcell, "Current Trends," 31–32. A poll of Hawai'ians in 1998 had similar results, with only 6 percent of respondents agreeing that same-sex marriage should be allowed (Goldberg-Hiller, *The Limits to Union*, 190).

14. Goldberg-Hiller, *The Limits to Union*, 8.

15. Sullivan, *Virtually Normal*, 185.

16. Blunt, "Defining Marriage," 16; George, "The 28th Amendment."

17. See Eskridge Jr., *The Case for Same-Sex Marriage*, ch. 3; Ettelbrick, "Since When Is Marriage a Path to Liberation?"; Polikoff, "We Will Get What We Ask For."

18. Weeks, Heaphy, and Donovan, *Same Sex Intimacies*, 47.

19. Schwartz and Rutter, *The Gender of Sexuality*, 128.

20. Primoratz, *Ethics and Sex*, 129.

21. *Webster's Encyclopedic Unabridged Dictionary of the English Language*, s.v. *marriage*.

22. *Jones v. Hallahan*, 588, 589.

23. Knight, "Domestic Partnerships," 114.

24. Cott, qtd. in Goodman, "A More Civil Union," 50.

25. Eskridge, *The Case for Same-Sex Marriage*, 130.

26. Quoted in Weeks, Heaphy, and Donovan, *Same Sex Intimacies*, 9.

27. Goldberg-Hiller, *The Limits to Union*, 6–7.

28. Gamson, "Must Identity Movements Self-Destruct?" 396.

29. Moss, "Legitimizing Same-Sex Marriage."

30. Condemnations of homosexuality occur throughout the Bible: Genesis 19:1–29, Leviticus 18:22 and 20:13, 1 Corinthians 6:9, and Romans 1:27. The original texts did not have a word with precisely the same meaning as the modern *homosexuality*. Nevertheless, the most common popular belief about the Old Testament is that it condemns homosexuality. Although Jesus is depicted as alluding to Sodom on several occasions, there is no canonical account of him condemning homosexuality. See Boswell, *Christianity, Social Tolerance, and Homosexuality*, 92.

31. See Haldeman, "Ceremonies and Religion," 141–64.

32. Qtd. in Goldberg-Hiller, *The Limits to Union*, 6.

33. Augustine would go so far as to state that children are a product of their parents' lustful sin (McBrien, *Catholicism*, 854). See Hamington, *Hail Mary?* for the role of the iconography and myth of Mary in Catholic sexual ethics.

34. *Catechism of the Catholic Church*, 460.

35. Ibid., 625.

36. McBrien, *The HarperCollins Encyclopedia of Catholicism*, 638.

37. "After the sin of homicide whereby a human nature already in existence is destroyed, this type of sin [sperm wasted on nonprocreative activities] appears to take next place, for by it the generation of human nature is precluded" (Aquinas, *Summa Contra Gentiles*, 146).

38. Moss, "Legitimizing Same-Sex Marriage," 105.

39. Finnis, "Law Morality and Sexual Orientation," 1070.

40. George, "The 28th Amendment," 33.

41. Ibid.

42. Sullivan, "A Conservative Case," 471.

43. Knight, "Domestic Partnerships," 108.

44. Goodman, "A More Civil Union," 78.

45. See Green, "Lesbian Mothers," 188–98; Golombok and Taster, "Do Parents Influence Sexual Orientation?" 3–11; Patterson, "Children of Lesbian and Gay Parents," 1025–42; Patterson, "Children of the Lesbian Baby Boom"; Patterson, "Families of the Lesbian Baby Boom," 115–25; Townsend, "Mental Health Issues," 93–95.

46. Sullivan, "A Conservative Case," 471.

47. Merleau-Ponty, *The Visible and the Invisible*, 143.

48. Mohr, *A More Perfect Union*, 2.

49. Goldberg-Hiller, *The Limits to Union*, 45.

50. To focus on human continuity through embodiment is not to negate the difference in experience created by society.

51. Shogun, *Care and Moral Motivation,* 69.

52. I recognize that fully half of all marriages end in divorce, and many people get married under circumstances that preclude celebration, but marriage remains a joyfully evocative event in the public imagination.

53. Rich, "Compulsory Heterosexuality."

54. Oliner and Oliner, *Toward a Caring Society,* 103.

55. For example, there is no evidence that homosexuals have a higher rate of sexual predation than heterosexuals, but scientific studies will not overcome stereotypes to the same degree that the confirmation of interpersonal experience will (Mohr, *A More Perfect Union,* 2).

56. Goodman, "A More Civil Union," 56.

57. Addams, *Twenty Years at Hull-House,* 126.

58. *Time,* February 12, 2001, cover.

59. Swartwout, "No Room for Our Gift?" 17.

60. Oliner and Oliner, *Toward a Caring Society,* 2.

61. Hoagland, *Lesbian Ethics,* 11.

62. Oliner and Oliner, *Toward a Caring Society,* 81.

63. Addams, *A New Conscience,* 11.

Conclusion

1. Beauvoir, *The Second Sex,* 9.

2. Harding, "Subjectivity, Experience, and Knowledge," 105.

3. Robinson, *Globalizing Care,* 164–65.

4. hooks, "Feminism," 192.

5. Noddings, *Starting at Home,* 46.

6. Hamilton, *Exploring the Dangerous Trades,* 69.

7. Noddings, *Starting at Home,* 223.

8. Goudzwaard and Lange, *Beyond Poverty and Affluence,* 4.

Bibliography

Abram, David. "Merleau-Ponty and the Voice of the Earth." *Environmental Ethics* 10 (Summer 1988): 101–20.

———. *The Spell of the Sensuous: Perception and Language in a More-Than-Human World.* New York: Vintage Books, 1996.

Adams, Carol. *The Sexual Politics of Meat: A Feminist-Vegetarian Critical Theory.* New York: Continuum, 1990.

Addams, Jane. *Democracy and Social Ethics.* Urbana: University of Illinois Press, 2002.

———. *The Long Road of Women's Memory.* Urbana: University of Illinois Press, 2002.

———. "A Modern Lear." In *The Jane Addams Reader.* Ed. Jean Bethke Elshtain. 163–76. New York: Basic Books, 2002.

———. *A New Conscience and an Ancient Evil.* Urbana: University of Illinois Press, 2002.

———. *Newer Ideals of Peace.* New York: Macmillan, 1907.

———. *Peace and Bread in Time of War.* Urbana: University of Illinois Press, 2002.

———. "The Subjective Necessity for Social Settlements." In *The Jane Addams Reader.* Ed. Jean Bethke Elshtain. 14–28. New York: Basic Books, 2002.

———. *Twenty Years at Hull-House.* New York: Macmillan, 1910.

Aquinas, Thomas. *Summa Contra Gentiles.* Trans. V. J. Bourke. South Bend, Ind.: Notre Dame University Press, 1997.

Arendt, Hannah. *Eichmann in Jerusalem: A Report on the Banality of Evil.* New York: Penguin Books, 1964.

———. *The Life of the Mind: Thinking.* New York: Harcourt Brace Jovanovich, 1977.

Baier, Annette. "Hume, the Women's Moral Theorist?" In *Women and Moral Theory.* Eds. Eva Feder Kittay and Diana T. Meyers. 37–55. Lanham, Md.: Rowman and Littlefield, 1987.

Balmer, Robert. "Why I Stopped Giving Money to Panhandlers." *Oregonian,* March 24, 2001, p. B9.

Barry, Brian. *Justice as Impartiality.* Oxford: Oxford University Press, 1995.

Beauvoir, Simone de. *The Second Sex.* London: New English Library, 1970.

Benhabib, Seyla. "The Generalized and the Concrete Other: The Kohlberg-Gilligan Controversy and Moral Theory." In *Women and Moral Theory*. Ed. Eva Feder Kittay and Diana T. Meyers. 154–78. Savage, Md.: Rowman and Littlefield, 1987.

———. *The Reluctant Modernism of Hannah Arendt*. Thousand Oaks, Calif.: Sage, 1996.

Bennett, William. *The Book of Virtues: A Treasury of Great Moral Stories*. New York: Simon and Schuster, 1992.

Blackburn, Simon, ed. *The Oxford Dictionary of Philosophy*. Oxford: Oxford University Press, 1994.

Blum, Lawrence. "Gilligan and Kohlberg: Implications for Moral Theory." In *An Ethic of Care: Feminist and Interdisciplinary Perspectives*. Ed. Mary Jeanne Larrabee. 49–68. New York: Routledge, 1993.

Blunt, Sheryl Henderson. "Defining Marriage." *Christianity Today* 45 (Oct. 1, 2001): 225–52.

Boswell, John. *Christianity, Social Tolerance, and Homosexuality: Gay People in Western Europe from the Beginning of the Christian Era to the Fourteenth Century*. Chicago: University of Chicago Press, 1980.

Bowden, Peta. *Caring: Gender Sensitive Ethics*. New York: Routledge, 1997.

Boxill, Bernard R. "Fear and Shame as Forms of Moral Suasion in the Thought of Frederick Douglass." *Transactions of the Charles S. Peirce Society* 31 (Fall 1995): 713–44.

Bubeck, Diemut Elisabet. *Care, Gender, and Justice*. Oxford: Clarendon, 1995.

Buhle, Mari Jo, and Florence Howe. Afterword. In *The Silent Partner*, by Elizabeth Stuart Phelps. 355–86. New York: Feminist, 1983.

Bush, Harold K., Jr. *American Declarations: Rebellion and Repentance in American Cultural History*. Urbana: University of Illinois Press, 1999.

Card, Claudia, ed. *Feminist Ethics*. Lawrence: University Press of Kansas, 1991.

Carson, Mina. *Settlement Folk: Social Thought and the American Settlement Movement, 1885–1930*. Chicago: University of Chicago Press, 1990.

Catechism of the Catholic Church. New York: Doubleday, 1995.

Chute, Marchette. *Shakespeare of London*. New York: Dutton, 1949.

Clement, Grace. *Care, Autonomy, and Justice: Feminism and the Ethic of Care*. Boulder, Colo.: Westview, 1996.

Colby, A., L. Kohlberg, J. Gibbs, D. Candee. *Assessing Moral Stages: A Manual*. New York: Cambridge University Press, 1983.

Cudd, Ann. "Review of Virginia Held, *Feminist Morality*." *Philosophical Review* 104:611–13.

Curti, Merle. "Jane Addams on Human Nature." *Journal of the History of Ideas* 23 (Jan.–Mar., 1961): 240–53.

Dewey, John. *Ethics*. Vol. 7 of *John Dewey: The Later Works, 1925–1953*. Ed. Jo Ann Boydston. Carbondale: Southern Illinois University Press, 1989.

———. *Human Nature and Conduct*. New York: Henry Holt, 1922.

———. *Logic: The Theory of Inquiry*. Carbondale: Southern Illinois University, 1991.

———. *Reconstruction in Philosophy*. Boston: Beacon, 1948.

———. "The School as Social Center." In *100 Years at Hull House*. Ed. Mary Lynn McCree Bryan and Allen F. Davis. 103–8. Bloomington: Indiana University Press, 1990.

Diggins, John Patrick. *The Promise of Pragmatism: Modernism and the Crisis of Knowledge and Authority.* Chicago: University of Chicago Press, 1994.

Douglass, Frederick. *My Bondage and My Freedom.* In *Frederick Douglass: The Narrative and Selected Writings.* Ed. Michael Meyer. 129–74. New York: Random House, 1984.

———. *Narrative of the Life of Frederick Douglass an American Slave.* In *Frederick Douglass: The Narrative and Selected Writings.* Ed. Michael Meyer. 3–127. New York: Random House, 1984.

Engell, James. *The Creative Imagination: Enlightenment to Romanticism.* Cambridge, Mass.: Harvard University Press, 1981.

Elshtain, Jean Bethke. *Jane Addams and the Dream of American Democracy.* New York: Basic Books, 2002.

Eskridge, William N., Jr. *The Case for Same-Sex Marriage: From Sexualized Liberty to Civilized Commitment.* New York: Free Press, 1996.

Ettelbrick, Paula L. "Since When Is Marriage a Path to Liberation?" In *Lesbian and Gay Marriage: Private Commitments, Public Ceremonies.* Ed. Suzanne Sherman. 20–26. Philadelphia: Temple University Press, 1992.

Fierstein, Harvey. *Widows and Children First. Torch Song Trilogy.* New York: Villard Books, 1983.

Finnis, John M. "Law, Morality, and Sexual Orientation." *Notre Dame Law Review* 69 (1993/4): 1049–76.

Fischer, Marilyn. "Jane Addams' Feminist Ethics." In *Presenting Women Philosophers.* Ed. Cecile T. Tougas and Sara Ebenreck. 51–58. Philadelphia: Temple University Press, 2000.

Fisher, Bernice, and Joan Tronto. "Toward a Feminist Theory of Caring." In *Circles of Care: Work and Identity in Women's Lives.* Ed. Emily K. Abel and Margaret K. Nelson. 35–62. Albany, N.Y.: State University of New York Press, 1990.

Foner, Philip S., ed. *The Life and Writings of Frederick Douglass.* Vol. 1. New York: International, 1950.

Friedman, Marilyn. "Feminism, Autonomy, and Emotion." In *Norms and Values: Essays on the Work of Virginia Held.* Ed. Joram C. Haber and Mark S. Halfon. 61–72. Lanham, Md.: Rowman and Littlefield, 1998.

———. *What Are Friends For?* New York: Cornell University Press, 1993.

Gamson, Joshua. "Must Identity Movements Self-Destruct? A Queer Dilemma." *Social Problems* 42:390–407.

Garrison, William Lloyd. Preface. In *Frederick Douglass: The Narrative and Selected Writings.* Ed. Michael Meyer. 4–13. New York: Random House, 1984.

George, Robert P. "The 28th Amendment." *National Review* 53 (July 23, 2001): 32–34.

Gilligan, Carol. "Hearing the Difference: Theorizing Connection." *Hypatia* 10 (1995): 120–27.

———. *In a Different Voice: Psychological Theory and Women's Development.* Cambridge, Mass.: Harvard University Press, 1982.

———. "Moral Orientations and Moral Development." In *Women and Moral Theory.* Ed. Eva Feder Kittay and Diana T. Meyers. 19–33. Lanham, Md.: Rowman and Littlefield, 1987.

Gilligan, Carol, and Jane Attanucci. "Two Moral Orientations." In *Mapping the Moral*

Domain. Ed. Carol Gilligan, Jane Victoria Ward, and Jill McLean Taylor. 73–86. Cambridge, Mass.: Harvard University Press, 1988.

Gilligan, Carol, Nona P. Lyons, and Trudy J. Hanmer, eds. *Making Connections: The Relational Worlds of Adolescent Girls at Emma Willard School.* Cambridge, Mass.: Harvard University Press, 1990.

Golombok, Susan, and Fiona Taster. "Do Parents Influence the Sexual Orientation of Their Children? Findings from a Longitudinal Study of Lesbian Families." *Developmental Psychology* 32 (1996): 3–12.

Goodman, David. "A More Civil Union." *Mother Jones* 25 (July–August 2000): 48–53, 78–79.

Goudzwaard, Bob, and Harry de Lange. *Beyond Poverty and Affluence: Toward an Economy of Care.* Grand Rapids, Mich.: Eerdmans, 1995.

Groenhoot, Ruth. "Care Theory and the Ideal of Neutrality in Public Moral Discourse." *Journal of Medicine and Philosophy* 23 (1998): 179–89.

Green, G. Dorsey. "Lesbian Mothers: Mental Health Considerations." In *Gay and Lesbian Parents.* Ed. Frederick Bozett. 188–98. New York: Praeger, 1987.

Grosz, Elizabeth. "Merleau-Ponty and Irigaray in the Flesh." In *Merleau-Ponty: Interiority and Exteriority, Psychic Life and the World.* Ed. Dorothea Olkowski and James Morley. 145–66. Albany, N.Y.: State University of New York Press, 1999.

Haldeman, Douglas C. "Ceremonies and Religion in Same-Sex Marriage." In *On the Road to Same-Sex Marriage.* Ed. Robert P. Cabaj and David W. Purcell. San Francisco: Josey-Bass, 1997.

Hamilton, Alice. *Exploring the Dangerous Trades: The Autobiography of Alice Hamilton, M.D.* Boston: Little, Brown, 1943.

Hamington, Maurice. *Hail Mary? The Struggle for Ultimate Womanhood in Catholicism.* New York: Routledge, 1995.

Haney, Kathleen M. *Intersubjectivity Revisited: Phenomenology and the Other.* Athens: Ohio University Press, 1994.

Hanson, Karen. *The Self Imagined: Philosophical Reflections on the Social Character of Psyche.* New York: Routledge and Kegan Paul, 1986.

Haslett, Diane C., "Hull House and the Birth Control Movement: An Untold Story." *Journal of Women and Social Work* 12 (Fall 1997): 261–78.

Hekman, Susan J. *Moral Voices, Moral Selves: Carol Gilligan and Feminist Moral Theory.* University Park: Pennsylvania State University Press, 1995.

Held, Virginia. *Feminist Morality: Transforming Culture, Society, and Politics.* Chicago: University of Chicago Press, 1993.

———. "Liberalism and the Ethics of Care." In *On Feminist Ethics and Politics.* Ed. Claudia Card. 288–309. Lawrence: University Press of Kansas, 1999.

Heyes, Cressida J. "Anti-Essentialism in Practice: Carol Gilligan and Feminist Philosophy." *Hypatia* 12 (Summer 1997): 142–63.

Hoagland, Sarah. *Lesbian Ethics: Toward New Value.* Palo Alto, Calif.: Institute of Lesbian Studies, 1988.

———. "Some Thoughts about 'Caring.'" In *Feminist Ethics.* Ed. Claudia Card. 246–63. Lawrence: University Press of Kansas, 1991.

Holmes, Helen. "A Call to Heal Medicine." *Hypatia* 4 (Summer 1989): 1–6.

hooks, bell. "Feminism: A Transformational Politic." In *Theoretical Perspectives on Sexual Difference.* Ed. Deborah Rhode. 185–93. New Haven, Conn.: Yale University Press, 1990.

Hume, David. *An Enquiry Concerning the Principles of Morals.* Ed. L. A. Selby-Bigge. 3d ed. Oxford: Clarendon, 1975.

———. *A Treatise of Human Nature.* Ed. L. A. Selby-Bigge. 2d ed. Oxford: Clarendon, 1978.

Husserl, Edmund. *Cartesian Meditations: An Introduction to Phenomenology.* Trans. Dorion Cairns. Dordrecht, the Netherlands: Kluwer, 1995.

———. *The Crisis of European Sciences and Transcendental Phenomenology.* Trans. David Carr. Evanston, Ill.: Northwestern University Press, 1970.

———. "The Thesis of the Natural Standpoint and Its Suspension." In *Phenomenology: The Philosophy of Edmund Husserl and Its Interpretation.* Ed. Joseph J. Kockelmans. 68–79. New York: Doubleday, 1967.

Ihde, Don. *Experimental Phenomenology: An Introduction.* New York: Putnam's, 1977.

James, William. *Pragmatism and Other Essays.* New York: Washington Square, 1963.

———. *The Will to Believe.* New York: Dover, 1956.

Johnson, Galen. "Inside and Outside: Ontological Considerations." In *Merleau-Ponty: Interiority and Exteriority, Psychic Life and the World.* Ed. Dorothea Olkowski and James Morley. 25–34. Albany, N.Y.: State University of New York Press, 1999.

Johnson, Mark. *The Body in the Mind: The Bodily Basis of Meaning, Imagination, and Reason.* Chicago: University of Chicago Press, 1987.

———. "Embodied Reason." In *Perspectives on Embodiment: The Intersections of Nature and Culture.* Ed. Gail Weiss and Honi Fern Haber. 81–102. New York: Routledge, 1999.

———. *Moral Imagination: Implications of Cognitive Science for Ethics.* Chicago: University of Chicago Press, 1993.

Jones v. Hallahan. 501 S.W.2d 588, 589. Kentucky Court of Appeals, 1973.

Kant, Immanuel. *Critique of Practical Reason and Other Writings in Moral Philosophy.* Trans. Lewis White Beck. Englewood Cliffs, N.J.: Prentice-Hall, 1993.

———. *The Foundations of a Metaphysics of Morals.* Trans. Lewis White Beck. New York: Bobbs-Merrill, 1959.

Kellog, Paul. "Twice Twenty Years at Hull-House." In *100 Years at Hull House.* Ed. Mary Lynn McCree Bryan and Allen F. Davis. 189–94. Bloomington: Indiana University Press, 1990.

Knight, Louise W. "Biography's Window on Social Change: Benevolence and Justice in Jane Addams' 'A Modern Lear.'" *Journal of Women's History* 9 (Spring 1997): 111–38.

Knight, Robert H. "Domestic Partnerships and 'Gay Marriage' Threaten Family." In *Same-Sex Marriage: The Moral and Legal Debate.* Ed. Robert M. Baird and Stuart E. Rosenbaum. 108–21. New York: Prometheus Books, 1997.

Knowlden, Virginia. "The Virtue of Caring in Nursing." In *The Ethical and Moral Dimensions of Care.* Ed. Madeleine M. Leininger. 89–94. Detroit, Mich.: Wayne State University Press, 1990.

Koehn, Daryl. *Rethinking Feminist Ethics: Care, Trust, and Empathy.* New York: Routledge, 1998.

Kohlberg, Lawrence. "Stage and Sequence: The Cognitive Developmental Approach to Socialization." In *Handbook of Socialization Theory and Research.* Ed. D. A. Goslin. Chicago: Rand McNally, 1969.

Kohlberg, Lawrence, with Charles Levine and Alexandra Hewer. "Synopses and Detailed Replies to Critics." In *The Psychology of Moral Development,* vol. 2 of *Essays on Moral Development.* Ed. Lawrence Kohlberg. San Francisco: Harper and Row, 1984.

Kolbe, Winrich, director; Melinda M. Snodgrass, writer. "Pen Pals." *Star Trek: The Next Generation.* Television broadcast. Paramount Productions (aired May 1, 1989).

Kuhn, Thomas. *The Structure of Scientific Revolutions.* 3d ed. Chicago: University of Chicago Press, 1996.

Kwant, Remy C. "Merleau-Ponty and Phenomenology." In *Phenomenology: The Philosophy of Edmund Husserl and Its Interpretation.* Ed. Joseph J. Kockelmans. 375–92. New York: Doubleday, 1967.

Lango, John W. "Does Kant's Ethics Ignore Relations between Persons?" In *Norms and Values: Essays on the Work of Virginia Held.* Ed. Joram C. Haber and Mark S. Halfon. 251–66. Lanham, Md.: Rowman and Littlefield, 1998.

Larrabee, Mary Jeanne, ed. *An Ethic of Care: Feminist Interdisciplinary Perspectives.* New York: Routledge, 1993.

Lasch, Christopher. *The Social Thought of Jane Addams.* Indianapolis: Bobbs-Merrill, 1965.

Leder, Drew. *The Absent Body.* Chicago: University of Chicago Press, 1990.

Leffers, M. Regina. "Pragmatists Jane Addams and John Dewey Inform the Ethic of Care." *Hypatia* 8 (Spring 1993): 64–77.

Levine, Charles, Lawrence Kohlberg, and Alexandra Hewer. "The Current Formulation of Kohlberg's Theory and a Response to Critics." *Human Development* 28 (1985): 94–100.

Lingis, Alphonso. "Segmented Organisms." In *Merleau-Ponty: Interiority and Exteriority, Psychic Life and the World.* Ed. Dorothea Olkowski and James Morley. 167–82. Albany, N.Y.: State University of New York Press, 1999.

Lugones, Maria C., and Elizabeth V. Spelman. "Have We Got a Theory for You! Feminist Theory, Cultural Imperialism, and the Demand for 'Woman's Voice.'" In *Feminism and Philosophy: Essential Readings in Theory, Reinterpretation, and Application.* Ed. Nancy Tuana and Rosemarie Tong. 494–507. Boulder, Colo.: Westview, 1995.

MacIntyre, Alasdair. *After Virtue: A Study in Moral Theory.* Notre Dame, Ind.: University of Notre Dame Press, 1984.

Mahowald, Mary B. "What Classical American Philosophers Missed: Jane Addams, Critical Pragmatism, and Cultural Feminism." *Journal of Value Inquiry* 31 (1997): 39–54.

Manning, Rita. *Speaking from the Heart: A Feminist Perspective on Ethics.* Lanham, Md.: Rowman and Littlefield, 1992.

Mayeroff, Milton. *On Caring.* New York: Harper and Rowe, 1971.

McBrien, Richard P. *Catholicism.* San Francisco: HarperSanFrancisco, 1994.

———, ed. *The HarperCollins Encyclopedia of Catholicism.* New York: HarperCollins, 1995.

McCree Bryan, Mary Lynn, and Allen F. Davis, eds. *100 Years at Hull-House.* Bloomington: Indiana University Press, 1990.

Mead, George Herbert. *On Social Psychology.* Chicago: University of Chicago Press, 1956.

Merleau-Ponty, Maurice. *Phenomenology of Perception.* Trans. Colin Smith. London: Routledge, 1994.

———. *The Primacy of Perception.* Trans. James M. Edie. Evanston, Ill.: Northwestern University Press, 1964.

———. *The Prose of the World.* Ed. Claude Lefort. Trans. John O'Neill. Evanston, Ill.: Northwestern University Press, 1973.

————. *Signs.* Trans. Richard C. McCleary. Evanston, Ill.: Northwestern University Press, 1964.

————. *The Visible and the Invisible.* Evanston, Ill.: Northwestern University Press, 1968.

Meyer, Michael. Introduction. In *Frederick Douglass: The Narrative and Selected Writings.* Ed. Michael Meyer. ix–xxx. New York: Random House, 1984.

Mohr, Richard D. *A More Perfect Union: Why Straight America Must Stand Up for Gay Rights.* Boston: Beacon, 1994.

Moody-Adams, Michelle M. "Gender and the Complexity of Moral Voices." In *Feminist Ethics.* Ed. Claudia Card. 195–212. Lawrence: University Press of Kansas, 1991.

Moore Campbell, Bebe. *Brothers and Sisters.* New York: Putnam, 1994.

Moore, G. E. *Principia Ethica.* Cambridge: Cambridge University Press, 1988.

Moore, Michael, director. *Roger and Me.* Film. 1989.

Moss, Kevin. "Legitimizing Same-Sex Marriage." *Peace Review* 14 (2002): 101–7.

Niebuhr, Reinhold. *Moral Man and Immoral Society: A Study in Ethics and Politics.* New York: Scribner's, 1932.

Noddings, Nel. *Caring: A Feminine Approach to Ethics and Moral Education.* Berkeley: University of California Press, 1984.

————. *The Challenge to Care in Schools: An Alternative Approach to Education.* New York: Teachers College Press, 1992.

————. "Feminist Morality and Social Policy." In *Norms and Values: Essays on the Work of Virginia Held.* Ed. Joram Haber and Mark Halfon. 61–72. New York: Rowman and Littlefield, 1998.

————. "A Response." *Hypatia* 5 (Spring 1990): 120–26.

————. *Starting at Home: Caring and Social Policy.* Berkeley: University of California Press, 2002.

————. *Women and Evil.* Berkeley: University of California Press, 1989.

Nussbaum, Martha. *Poetic Justice: The Literary Imagination and Public Life.* Boston: Beacon, 1995.

Oliner, Pearl M., and Samuel P. Oliner. *Toward a Caring Society: Ideas into Action.* Westport, Conn.: Praeger, 1995.

O'Neill, Onora. "Justice, Gender, and International Boundaries." In *International Justice and the Third World.* Ed. Robin Attfield and Barry Wilkins. London: Routledge, 1992.

Patterson, Charlotte J. "Children of Lesbian and Gay Parents." *Child Development* 63 (1992): 1025–42.

————. "Children of the Lesbian Baby Boom: Behavioral Adjustment, Self-Concepts and Sex-Role Identity." In *Lesbian and Gay Psychology: Theory, Research and Clinical Applications.* Ed. Beverly Green and Gregory Herek. 156–75. Beverly Hills, Calif.: Sage, 1994.

————. "Families of the Lesbian Baby Boom: Parents, Division of Labor, and Children's Adjustment." *Developmental Psychology* 31 (1995): 115–23.

Peirce, Charles Sanders. *Principles of Philosophy.* Vol. 1 of *Collected Papers.* Ed. Charles Hartshorne and Paul Weiss. Cambridge, Mass.: Harvard University Press, 1931.

Phelps, Elizabeth Stuart. *The Silent Partner.* New York: Feminist, 1983.

Polanyi, Michael. *The Tacit Dimension.* New York: Anchor Books, 1967.

Pollitt, Katha. "Are Women Morally Superior to Men?" *The Nation* 255 (Dec. 28, 1992): 799–808.

Polikoff, Nancy. "We Will Get What We Ask For: Why Legalizing Gay and Lesbian Marriage Will Not 'Dismantle the Legal Structure of Gender in Every Marriage.'" *Virginia Law Review* 79 (1993): 1535–50.

Pratt, Scott. *Native Pragmatism.* Bloomington: Indiana University Press, 2002.

Primoratz, Igor. *Ethics and Sex.* London: Routledge, 1999.

Purcell, David W. "Current Trends in Same-Sex Marriage." In *On the Road to Same-Sex Marriage.* Ed. Robert P. Cabaj and David W. Purcell. San Francisco: Josey-Bass, 1997.

Reich, Warren T. *Encyclopedia of Bioethics.* New York: Macmillan, 1995.

Rich, Adrienne. "Compulsory Heterosexuality and Lesbian Existence." In *Powers of Desire.* New York: Monthly Review Press, 1973.

Robinson, Fiona. *Globalizing Care: Ethics, Feminist Theory, and International Relations.* Boulder, Colo.: Westview, 1999.

Ruddick, Sara. "Care as Labor and Relationship." In *Norms and Values: Essays on the Work of Virginia Held.* Ed. Joram C. Haber and Mark S. Halfon. 3–26. Lanham, Md.: Rowman and Littlefield, 1998.

———. *Maternal Thinking: Toward a Politics of Peace.* Boston: Beacon, 1995.

Schwartz, Pepper, and Virginia Rutter. *The Gender of Sexuality.* Thousand Oaks, Calif.: Pine Forge, 1998.

Seigfried, Charlene Haddock. Introduction. In *Democracy and Social Ethics,* by Jane Addams. ix–xxxviii. Urbana: University of Illinois Press, 2002.

———. *Pragmatism and Feminism: Reweaving the Social Fabric.* Chicago: University of Chicago Press, 1996.

Sevenhuijsen, Selma. *Citizenship and the Ethics of Care: Feminist Considerations on Justice, Morality, and Politics.* London: Routledge, 1998.

Shakespeare, William. *The Merchant of Venice.* Ed. Kenneth Myrick. New York: Signet Classics, 1965.

Sharer, Wendy B. "'Going into Society' or 'Bringing Society In'?: Rhetoric and Problematic Philanthropy in *The Silent Partner.*" *ATQ (The American Transcendental Quarterly)* 11 (Sept. 1997): 171–90.

Sher, George. "Other Voices, Other Rooms? Women's Psychology and Moral Theory." In *Women and Moral Theory.* Ed. Eva Feder Kittay and Diana T. Meyers. 178–89. Lanham, Md.: Rowman and Littlefield, 1987.

Sherwin, Susan. *No Longer Patient: Feminist Ethics and Health Care.* Philadelphia: Temple University Press, 1992.

Shogan, Debra. *Care and Moral Motivation.* Toronto: Ontario Institute for Studies in Education, 1988.

Shrage, Laurie. *Moral Dilemmas of Feminism: Prostitution, Adultery, and Abortion.* New York: Routledge, 1994.

Slote, Michael. "The Justice of Caring." *Social Philosophy and Policy* 15 (Winter 1998): 171–95.

Smith, Adam. *The Theory of Moral Sentiments.* Ed. D. D. Raphael and A. L. Macfie. London: Oxford University Press, 1976.

Smith, John. *The Spirit of American Philosophy.* London: Oxford University Press, 1963.

Stebner, Eleanor J. *The Women of Hull House: A Study in Spirituality, Vocation, and Friendship.* Albany, N.Y.: State University of New York Press, 1997.

Stein, Edith. *On the Problem of Empathy.* Trans. Waltraut Stein. Washington, D.C.: ICS, 1989.

Stuhr, John, ed. *Classical American Philosophy.* New York: Oxford University Press, 1987.

Sullivan, Shannon. *Living across and through Skins: Transactional Bodies, Pragmatism, and Feminism.* Bloomington: Indiana University Press, 2001.

———. "Reconfiguring Gender with John Dewey: Habit, Bodies, and Cultural Change." *Hypatia* 15 (Winter 2000): 23–42.

Sundquist, Eric. *Frederick Douglass: New Literacy and Historical Essays.* New York: Cambridge University Press, 1990.

Swartwout, Donna. "No Room for Our Gift, No Room for Our Faith?" *National Catholic Reporter* 37 (Jan. 26, 2001): 17.

Tong, Rosemarie. "The Ethics of Care: A Feminist Virtue Ethics of Care for Healthcare Practitioners." *Journal of Medicine and Philosophy* 23 (1998): 131–52.

Townsend, Mark. "Mental Health Issues and Same-Sex Marriage." In *On the Road to Same-Sex Marriage.* Ed. Robert P. Cabaj and David W. Purcell. 93–95. San Francisco: Josey-Bass, 1997.

Tronto, Joan. *Moral Boundaries: A Political Argument for an Ethic of Care.* New York: Routledge, 1993.

Veatch, Robert. "The Place of Care in Ethical Theory." *Journal of Medicine and Philosophy* 23 (1998): 210–24.

Walker, Lawrence J. "Sex Differences in the Development of Moral Reasoning: A Critical Review." *Child Development* 55 (1984): 667–91.

Walker, Margaret Urban. "Moral Epistemology." In *A Companion to Feminist Philosophy.* Ed. Alison M. Jaggar and Iris Marion Young. 363–71. Oxford: Blackwell, 1998.

———. *Moral Understandings: A Feminist Study in Ethics.* New York: Routledge, 1998.

———. "Moral Understandings, Alternative 'Epistemology' for a Feminist Ethics." *Hypatia* 4 (Summer 1989): 15–28.

Webster's Encyclopedia Unabridged Dictionary. New York: Portland House, 1989.

Weeks, Jeffrey, Brian Heaphy, and Catherine Donovan. *Same Sex Intimacies: Families of Choice and Other Experiments.* London: Routledge, 2001.

Weigel, Randy R., Brenda Caiola, and Lise Pittman-Foy. "4-H Animal Care as Therapy for At-Risk Youth." *Journal of Extension* 40 (Oct. 2002); available at www.joe.org.

Weiss, Gail. *Body Images: Embodiment as Intercorporeality.* New York: Routledge, 1999.

West, Cornel. *The American Evasion of Philosophy: A Genealogy of Pragmatism.* Madison: University of Wisconsin Press, 1989.

Willet, Cynthia. *Maternal Ethics and Other Slave Moralities.* New York: Routledge, 1995.

Wilshire, Donna. "The Uses of Myth, Image, and the Female Body in Re-Visioning Knowledge." In *Gender, Body, Knowledge: Feminist Reconstructions of Being and Knowing.* Ed. Alison M. Jaggar and Susan R. Bordo. 92–114. New Brunswick, N.J.: Rutgers University Press, 1992.

Wise, Steven M. *Rattling the Cage: Toward Legal Rights for Animals.* Cambridge, Mass.: Perseus Books, 2000.

Index

Abraham, sacrifice of son by, 18, 151n29
Abram, David, 47, 53, 74
acaring habits, 57
Adams, Carol, 84
Addams, Jane: as an American philosopher, 93–97; background of, 97; on connected leadership, 115–17, 162n109, 162n111; contribution of, to care ethics, 104–8, 136; criticisms of, 159n41, 161n66; critique of capitalism by, 112–13; on democracy, 6, 34, 113–15; embodied epistemology of, 99–100, 140; ethics of, 97–108, 162n98; in a genealogy of care, 120–21; on lateral progress, 119–20; on listening, 109–12, 137; neglected as a philosopher, 160n44; and relational approach to morality, 102–3; religious allusions by, 160n57; on social action, 118–19, 125; on social habits of embodied care, 6, 108–19, 158n56, 162n98; on suffrage, 143; on sympathetic knowledge, 100, 141; on war, 18, 163n7; works: *Democracy and Social Ethics*, 95, 99, 101–4, 112, 115–16, 118–19, 139, 160n60, 161n61, 161n72; *The Long Road of Women's Memory*, 109; "A Modern Lear," 99, 113–14, 162n109; *A New Conscience and an Ancient Evil*, 110, 113, 160n49; *Newer Ideals of Peace*, 104, 118; *Peace and Bread in Time of War*, 109; "The Subjective Necessity of Social Settlements," 159n39; *Twenty Years at Hull-House*, 100, 110. *See also under* Hull-House

affective knowledge, 56, 87, 125, 135, 141–42
After Virtue (MacIntyre), 20
ambiguity of human existence, 49
American philosophy: commitment to community in, 94–95, 107; commitment to growth in, 95, 107; commitment to interaction in, 94, 97; commitment to pluralism in, 94, 107; and fallibalism, 95–96; origins of, 93–94
Anthony, Susan B., 98
Aquinas, Thomas, 132, 164n37
Arendt, Hannah: on Adolf Eichmann, 61–64, 66, 69, 146, 156n1, 156n7; on banality of evil, 63–64
Attanucci, Jane, 151n24
Augustine, 164n33

Baier, Annette, 20–21
Balmer, Robert, 77, 158n56
Beauvoir, Simone de, 145
Beloved (Morrison), 87
Ben-Gurion, David, 61
Benhabib, Seyla, 42, 152n70, 156n1, 160n56
Bennett, William, 25
Benson, Craig, 133
Beyond Poverty and Affluence (Goudzwaard and de Lange), 148
body: as basis for morality, 46; as marginalized, 44; as recessive, 50; as a resource for care, 45–46, 60; and tacit knowledge, 48
Book of Virtues, The (Bennett), 25
Bowden, Peta, 3, 36

MAURICE HAMINGTON, an assistant professor of philosophy at the University of Southern Indiana, received a Ph.D. in religion and ethics and a Graduate Certificate in the Study of Men and Women in Society from the University of Southern California, as well as a Ph.D. in philosophy at the University of Oregon. He served as a research scholar in the study of women at the University of California, Los Angeles, and founded the Women's Studies Program at Mount St. Mary's College in Los Angeles. He is the author of *Hail Mary? The Struggle for Ultimate Womanhood in Catholicism* (1995) and coeditor of *Revealing Male Bodies* (2002), which includes his article "A Father's Touch: Caring Embodiment and a Moral Revolution." He has written several articles on Jane Addams and continues to be inspired by feminist pragmatism and care ethics.

The University of Illinois Press
is a founding member of the
Association of American University Presses.

Composed in 10.5/13 Adobe Minion
at the University of Illinois Press
Manufactured by Thomson-Shore, Inc.

University of Illinois Press
1325 South Oak Street
Champaign, IL 61820-6903
www.press.uillinois.edu